Inclusive Pedagogies for Early Childhood Education

This essential textbook explores inclusive pedagogies by presenting theoretical viewpoints and research on everyday practices in early childhood education that affirm diversity in relation to learning, disability and culture.

The authors consider the pedagogical practices involved in supporting educational inclusion for young children. The book focuses on key issues in relation to inclusive pedagogy including young children's learning subjectivities, socio-material realities of learning in early childhood contexts and perspective-taking of children and adults in relation to learning and difference.

The book draws together findings from experts who are employing innovative methods for research in early childhood education, including conversation analysis, phenomenological enquiry and participant ethnography, in order to create new knowledge and understanding about how young children are and feel themselves to be included.

This textbook will be essential reading for students and practitioners alike. The book is particularly pertinent for undergraduate and postgraduate students studying early years as well as courses which focus on education or teaching or inclusion.

Carmel Conn is Associate Professor in Inclusive Pedagogy and Course Leader for the MA in Autism in the School of Education, Early Years and Youth Work at the University of South Wales in the UK.

Alison Murphy is a Lecturer in Primary Education Studies in the Institute of Education, Childhood and Youth at University of Wales Trinity St David in the UK.

Inclusive Pedagogies for Early Childhood Education
Respecting and Responding to Differences in Learning

Edited by
Carmel Conn and Alison Murphy

LONDON AND NEW YORK

Cover image: © Getty Images

First published 2022
by Routledge
4 Park Square, Milton Park, Abingdon, Oxon OX14 4RN

and by Routledge
605 Third Avenue, New York, NY 10158

Routledge is an imprint of the Taylor & Francis Group, an informa business

© 2022 selection and editorial matter, Carmel Conn and Alison Murphy; individual chapters, the contributors

The right of Carmel Conn and Alison Murphy to be identified as the authors of the editorial material, and of the authors for their individual chapters, has been asserted in accordance with sections 77 and 78 of the Copyright, Designs and Patents Act 1988.

All rights reserved. No part of this book may be reprinted or reproduced or utilised in any form or by any electronic, mechanical, or other means, now known or hereafter invented, including photocopying and recording, or in any information storage or retrieval system, without permission in writing from the publishers.

Trademark notice: Product or corporate names may be trademarks or registered trademarks, and are used only for identification and explanation without intent to infringe.

British Library Cataloguing-in-Publication Data
A catalogue record for this book is available from the British Library

Library of Congress Cataloging-in-Publication Data
A catalog record has been requested for this book

ISBN: 978-0-367-75612-3 (hbk)
ISBN: 978-0-367-75613-0 (pbk)
ISBN: 978-1-003-16320-6 (ebk)

DOI: 10.4324/9781003163206

Typeset in Bembo
by Taylor & Francis Books

Contents

List of figures vii
Contributing authors viii

Introduction: Inclusive pedagogy as an ethics of responsibility and care 1
CARMEL CONN AND ALISON MURPHY

PART I
Theoretical perspectives on inclusive pedagogy 11

1 The children's rights approach to early childhood education: Policy and context in Wales 13
ALISON MURPHY AND JANE WATERS-DAVIES

2 Placing inclusion at the heart of things: The 'tricky challenge' for educational leadership 29
MATT HUTT

3 Seeing children's learning subjectivities for inclusive pedagogy in early childhood education 43
CARMEL CONN

4 Children's agency and negotiation of space for enabling environments: The use of Tuff spots for practitioner education 59
CLAIRE PESCOTT

PART II
Using research to develop inclusive pedagogies 77

5 Socialising a pedagogy of care in a New Zealand early childhood refugee centre 79
AMANDA BATEMAN AND LINDA MITCHELL

6 Social embodiment in early childhood education for children with PMLD 94
   BEN SIMMONS

7 Foundation Phase teachers' understandings and enactment of participation in school settings in Wales 111
   ALISON MURPHY, JACKY TYRIE, JANE WATERS-DAVIES, SARAH CHICKEN AND JENNIFER CLEMENT

8 Using an environmental affordance perspective to consider children's 'challenging behaviour' in the classroom and at Forest School 135
   ANGELA REKERS

9 Inclusion, participation and interaction: Challenging the discourse of in-class ability groupings in early childhood education 148
   ELERI JOHN

10 The capable child as a threshold concept for inclusive early childhood education and care 164
   JANE WATERS-DAVIES AND NATALIE MACDONALD

Index 182

Figures

4.1	Example of a minibeast Tuff spot. (Photograph taken by the author)	68
4.2	Example of a potion-making Tuff spot. (Photograph taken by the author)	69
4.3	A Tuff spot with a mathematical focus. (Photograph taken by the author)	70
8.1	A model of environmental affordance perspective. (Rekers-Power 2020)	138

Contributing authors

Amanda Bateman is Associate Professor in Early Childhood Education at the University of Waikato, New Zealand. She began her career in early childhood education as an early childhood practitioner, before moving into research. Her doctoral degree used conversation analysis and membership categorisation analysis to investigate the resources used by four-year-old children in the co-construction of social organisation. Amanda has led several funded projects focused on early childhood education and published widely from these, including the books *Early Childhood Education: The Co-Production of Knowledge and Relationships*, as a single author, and *Children's Knowledge-in-Interaction: Studies in Conversation Analysis*, which she co-edited.

Sarah Chicken is Senior Lecturer in Childhood and Education at the University of the West of England, Bristol. She has extensive experience of working as an educator at all age phases, from nursery to higher education in both national and international settings. Sarah's recent research interests include curricula which prioritise levels of child voice and agency, and teacher understandings of creativity within primary settings. As an adult with dyspraxia, Sarah is also interested in issues related to creating inclusive curricula models and assessment practices.

Jennifer Clement is Lecturer in the School of Education and Social Policy at Cardiff Metropolitan University. Interested in early childhood education and pedagogical space, she has been a teacher in both national and international settings, an early childhood education researcher, and is currently exploring early childhood through play, participation and learning with Initial Teacher Education and Early Childhood Studies students.

Carmel Conn is Associate Professor in the School of Education, Early Years and Youth Work at the University of South Wales, UK. Her expertise is in inclusive education and disability having worked for over 20 years as an educational practitioner across pre-school, primary and secondary school settings. As a researcher, Carmel is interested in a participatory approach to investigating inclusive pedagogies and children's experiences of learning. Recent research includes small-scale projects focused on the learning interactions of autistic children within education as well as large-scale evaluations of the special educational needs system and of teachers' professional standards in Wales. Carmel has published numerous articles as well as books, the most recent of which is *Autism, Pedagogy and Education: Critical Issues for Value-based Teaching*.

Matt Hutt is Head of Professional Learning in the School of Education, Early Years and Youth Work at the University of South Wales, UK. Having spent over 20 years as a teacher and senior leader in schools in England and Wales, Matt now leads the MA course in Leadership and Management (Education) at University of South Wales. His doctorate explored narratives of trust, accountability and professional autonomy at different levels in the education system, and his research interests are focused on examining the discourses of educational policy, effective leadership and school improvement.

Eleri John is currently Senior Lecturer in Early Years and Course Leader for Working with Children and Families at the University of South Wales, UK. She began her career as a primary school teacher working across the key stages in both England and Wales. Eleri is currently in the dissertation stage of her professional doctorate and her research interests lie in the areas of ability groupings in the early years, academic self-concept and efficacy, agency and altruism in early childhood, and practitioner perceptions of classroom organisation and interaction.

Natalie Macdonald is Programme Director at the University of Wales Trinity Saint David, UK, specialising in provision for early childhood education, policy and pedagogy. Natalie has significant experience in early childhood education, including Flying Start and working in the Foundation Phase. She has extensive experience of working with children and families in areas of disadvantage and has keen research interest in the impact of early intervention strategies, policy implementation, pedagogy and quality of provision. Natalie has a background in Law and is currently undertaking a Doctorate in Education. Natalie currently sits on the Welsh Government Foundation Phase Expert Group and is a member of the Early Years Network.

Linda Mitchell is Professor of Early Childhood Education and Director of the Early Years Research Centre at the University of Waikato, New Zealand. She has built a national and international reputation through her research and publications in early childhood education policy, and has been a strong critic of the marketisation and commercialisation of education and their impact on children, families and early childhood services. Other current areas of her research are assessment, culturally responsive pedagogy, and connections with parents, families and community. A main interest is in democratic policies and practices in early childhood education.

Alison Murphy is Lecturer in the Athrofa: Institute of Education at the University of Wales Trinity Saint David, UK. Alison originally trained as a primary school teacher and taught in a variety of educational settings, often working with children experiencing disadvantage. She held the role of Head of Early Years at University of South Wales and has worked in a range of higher education settings. Alison's research interests are focused on children's perceptions of national identity and what it means to be Welsh. She is also interested in inclusion and children's rights and participatory research methods. Alison has published in a number of books and journals including *Education 3–13* and *Children and Society*.

Claire Pescott is Senior Lecturer across two courses in Early Years and Working with Children and Families at the University of South Wales, UK. She has considerable experience as an early childhood educator. In her move to higher education, sharing these experiences with students has enabled links between theory and practice to be made. She is currently engaged in doctoral study and is carrying out a project focused on young children's experiences of social media. This explores how children understand their digital identities and uses creative and participatory research methods with children.

Angela Rekers completed her PhD at the University of Wales Trinity Saint David, UK, in 2020. Her research explored marginalised children's participation, both indoors and outdoors, as the enactment of entangled relationships within social, material and pedagogical space(s). Angela's research interests include motive-demand dynamics, inclusion, literacy and education for ecological/social well-being and justice. She is co-editor of *Outdoor Learning and Play: Pedagogical Practices and Children's Cultural Formation* (2021) in the Springer book series 'International Perspectives on Early Childhood Education and Development'. Angela has taught for 30 years in the fields of language arts and environmental education for all ages and abilities. She is a Lecturer in Early Childhood Education in the Educator Preparation Program at St. Ambrose University in Davenport, Iowa.

Ben Simmons is Senior Lecturer at the Institute for Education and co-directs the Centre for Research in Equity, Inclusion and Community (CREIC) at Bath Spa University, UK. His area of expertise lies in special and inclusive education, with particular reference to children with profound and multiple learning disabilities (PMLD). His research examines the social and educational inclusion of children with PMLD and he was a British Academy Postdoctoral Fellow between 2014 and 2017, leading a three-year project examining the social interaction of children with PMLD who attended mainstream school. This work significantly built upon Ben's ESRC-funded doctoral research and book, co-authored with Debbie Watson, titled *The PMLD Ambiguity: Articulating the Life-Worlds of Children with Profound and Multiple Learning Disabilities*.

Jacky Tyrie is Lecturer in Early Childhood Studies at Swansea University School of Education, UK. Jacky's research explores early childhood from sociological and geographical perspectives with a focus on children's participation rights within early childhood care and education settings. Jacky is a national leader in children's rights and co-ordinates the Children's Rights in Early Years Network (CREYN).

Jane Waters-Davies is Associate Professor and the Applied Research Lead (Education) in the Athrofa: Institute of Education at the University of Wales Trinity Saint David, UK. Having worked previously as a classroom teacher, then lecturer in undergraduate Early Childhood Studies and postgraduate Initial Teacher Education, she now works most closely with postgraduate research students. She is passionate about the potential in Wales for innovative, engaging early childhood education and sits on the Welsh Government advisory panel for curriculum reform. Jane's research interests lie in early childhood education, adult-child interaction, the affordance of different educative spaces, young children's agency and voice, and young children's experiences of outdoor spaces.

Introduction

Inclusive pedagogy as an ethics of responsibility and care

Carmel Conn and Alison Murphy

Inclusive education, as it is currently conceived, is focused on providing for all children within communities of practice that seek to reduce the marginalisation of some (Nilholm 2020). The emphasis is less on the use of discriminatory practices that reproduce inequalities in our society, and more on practitioners finding ways of extending existing practices which are socially just and meet the needs of all children in their care. As Florian (2019) argues, educational practitioners need to pay more attention to the centre ground of teaching itself, not seeing this as a 'norm' outside of which some children naturally exist in terms of their learning. Practitioners must enlarge their understanding of what is considered natural in learning and be more accepting of differences that children bring. Rather than the notion of the 'average child', diversity should be seen as more accurately reflecting a natural order for human beings (Florian 2013).

It is notable, of course, that the agenda of inclusion has been hard to achieve in the two decades since its inception. Exclusionary practices continue to exist widely and even proliferate in some places. Here in the UK, it is possible to see that the incidence of educational exclusion has been on a worryingly sharp upward turn in recent years (DfE 2019). A good deal of confusion exists about what constitutes inclusion in an educational setting, moreover, with disagreement about this apparent amongst practitioners, but also amongst educational leaders and policy makers. For some, inclusive practice may simply take the form of differentiated teaching, whilst for others, the level of perceived challenge presented by a child's participation in learning may determine whether they can be included (Conn and Hutt 2020).

Some academics have questioned, indeed, whether a fully inclusive education system is a realistic goal since inclusion is a process and a mind-set that will always require ongoing work. The language of certainty, Allan (2008) writes, is not the language of inclusion, and striving to be inclusive means constantly having questions posed that challenge what we think we know about children and their learning. As Nutbrown and Clough (2013) point out, there can be no such thing as a fully inclusive institution since being inclusive means always being in a state of 'becoming'.

But it is apparent that some educational practices are more inclusive than others, and that children feel more of a sense of belonging in some settings compared to others. It seems that the system that currently operates in education can support the ongoing work of inclusion given certain conditions. We can be employed in, visit and read about inclusive early childhood education settings, for example, and we can ask children whether they are happy and feel they are included. Increasingly, the difference between settings in terms of their inclusivity is located in the values and beliefs that operate there, most specifically, whether practitioners are prepared to take responsibility for all children within a setting and to find ways of valuing them as they are. Where practitioners own children in this way and see themselves as capable of supporting their learning, then greater progress towards inclusion will be made (Slee 2019).

Values and beliefs are at the heart of inclusion today and this is why we want to give our book a title that reflects this. Respecting and responding to differences in learning are values more than specific practices, though it is inclusive practices that we want to illustrate here. Inclusion is about changing practice and firm belief gives an individual energy to assume the burden of responsibility for change and pursue related goals. Having a certain value system can mean someone feels more invested in questioning the existing order and more confident in thinking 'outside the box'.

Thinking outside the box is an important process for inclusion, which is, above all, a coming to terms with difference. It is not the case that a child is included into a system that remains unchanged since inclusion will challenge basic understandings of the system itself. Inclusion is the result of people coming to know each other, accepting the other as they are and adjusting to people's different ways of being in the world. In order to be inclusive, we need to consider what we understand about children and how they learn and interact, and perhaps rethink our fundamental beliefs about this. This requires complex thinking about all aspects of practice, including learning relationships, pedagogy and the learning environment. The term inclusive pedagogy is important here since it focuses specifically on educational practices, but also the ideas, values and knowledge that shape and justify these (Alexander 2015). It is possible to see, therefore, that the *how* of inclusion is far from straightforward, and, perhaps for this reason, it is an overlooked area in terms of how theory translates into practice. Educational theorists have drawn attention to the fact that, though theory in relation to inclusive education is well versed, how it occurs on a day-to-day practical level is much less clear (Florian and Camedda 2020).

Certainly, what does not help the progress towards inclusion is the existence of two competing discourses about children and their learning that operate in early childhood education today. One discourse focuses on the individual child within a normative culture of documentation and assessment (Karlsrudd 2021). This is a discourse of learning as deficit that validates the marginalisation of some children. Within this discourse, some children are constructed as underdeveloped, incapable and in need of being brought into a world of knowledge, understanding and competency. They are constructed as a 'problem' to be addressed and the focus of any support. Set against this discourse of learning as deficit, however, is a second educational discourse that is focused on enabling environments and the removal of barriers to learning and participation (Hodgman 2015). This discourse locates any problem of learning, not in the individual child, but in the conditions of learning, including the understandings and expectations of other people.

Lenz Taguchi (2010) has described this second discourse as belonging to a *complexity/diversity increase* movement within early childhood education since it embraces difference and seeks to grapple with issues of complexity. She contrasts this with a *complexity/diversity reduction* movement that also operates and tries to essentialise children by flattening out their differences and decontextualising their individual experiences of learning. Learning as deficit is aligned with *complexity/diversity reduction* since it seeks to promote a simple cause and effect narrative for teaching and learning: children's learning is assessed against a set of standards and then supported individually using certain practices that produce easily measurable outcomes. The standards, practices and processes of measurement are not problematised in any way, but rather are presented as common sensical and inherently good. By contrast, inclusive education is associated with *complexity/diversity increase* since it seeks to acknowledge children's diverse learning subjectivities and the complex array of influences on learning and development that exist. The burden of change is not on the individual child but on the system and, in this model, inclusion is not something we do to someone, but something that starts with ourselves (Allan 2008).

It is apparent that practitioners in early childhood education are pulled in two different directions, each end of the *complexity/diversity* polarity promoting strong, but mutually exclusive narratives of learning and support. Despite now longstanding arguments about inclusion, social justice and fairness in education, the discourse of learning as deficit continues to be a prominent one. The simplicity of the narrative has an appeal and perhaps speaks to fundamental beliefs about a natural hierarchical order (Francis et al. 2017). Whatever the reason, a belief in learning as deficit continues to operate at all levels of our education system, undoubtedly contributing to the confusion that exists around inclusive education.

This was an important issue for us in developing our ideas for a book about inclusion in early childhood education. Many of us are based in Wales in the UK where major educational reform is taking place in relation to the curriculum, teacher education, professional standards and the system for learners with additional learning needs. We are aware that, in this time of change, policy and guidance has not always been clear and is often not consistent. In respect of inclusion and diversity, for example, policy and guidance promote *complexity/diversity reduction* principles, but also at times endorse *complexity/diversity increase* as well (Knight and Crick 2021). It is unclear to us, in fact, whether real change is taking place and we have a concern that competing discourses will, in effect, reproduce or create tensions as they have in other recent reform programmes in the UK (Allan 2008, Allan and Youdell 2017).

We are compiling this book at a time of global pandemic too, which has served to reinforce existing disadvantages within our societies. This creates added urgency for us to address educational inequalities by presenting information about the complex ways in which inclusion and equity is achieved at the everyday level of practice. In doing this, we are aware of researchers working in or near the south Wales area who are fully focused on the issue of *complexity/diversity increase* in early childhood education and applying research methods suited to the type of in-depth analysis that supports inclusive thinking. Inclusion sets us the challenge of how to make sense of another person who we experience as different to ourselves. Finding ways of *seeing* children is a central issue. We are aware that, through application of important theoretical perspectives and innovative research practices, these researchers are seeking to do just that. They are trying to find ways of understanding children, not as members of diagnostic or statistical categories, but as fully formed subjects whose lives are rich with experience. They are drawing on ontologies and epistemologies that allow them to really connect with children's experience as it is lived in the moment, as a way of better understanding their learning subjectivities. Trying to really connect with a child and understand how they are making sense of the world allows them to become 'thicker' to us as individuals. Weaving together the rich detail of their ongoing, embodied and intersubjective day-to-day experiences gives rise to the possibility of seeing that experience as fully meaningful, relating to its context and worthy of consideration. For children who we experience as different from ourselves, we need to pay particularly close attention to them and resist the urge of making hasty judgements. Research practices which are focused on the intricate details of learning relationships and individual decision making within interaction are more likely to allow us to do that and it is these that we want to present here.

It is apparent to us that research, in the form of methodology, and early childhood practice, in the form of pedagogy, are closely aligned and have much to offer each other (Kuby 2018). Research methodologies presented here have the aim of focusing on social phenomena in such a way as to see it with fresh eyes that generates new knowledge. Similarly, effective pedagogy for early childhood education engages in processes of tuning into children through close observation and reflective practice that allows deeper understanding of their perspective in learning. We believe the need for this book rests in the detailed information it provides for early childhood practitioners and researchers about educational practices, especially as they relate to certain groups of marginalised children.

Above all, we see this as ethical work since we believe that knowing more about someone and having a better understanding of their lifeworld leads to greater respect for them as individuals and a greater sense of responsibility (Dahlberg and Moss 2005). The aim of this book is to illustrate inclusion by describing how it is enacted in everyday actions and interactions and as the result of certain beliefs and sets of values, but, we should emphasise, this is in order to address the key challenge of inclusion, that is, valuing and owning all children in our care. We hope that by seeing inclusion in practice, in the ways it is described 'thickly' in this book, we are more able to see ourselves as responsible for all children and capable of supporting them.

The book is structured into two parts. Part I has a theoretical focus and explores inclusive pedagogies via different theoretical viewpoints and educational policy, beginning with an exploration of the Welsh context and use of a rights-based approach to inclusion. Other chapters in this section consider the links between theoretical principles which support inclusive pedagogies and how this translates into the early years learning environment from leader, practitioner and, perhaps most importantly, child perspectives. Part II of the book presents research in order to illustrate inclusive pedagogies in action as well as reflective thinking on relevant policy and practices in early childhood education.

In Chapter 1, Alison Murphy and Jane Waters-Davies introduce the notion of inclusion as a key element of the 1989 United Nations Convention on the Rights of the Child (UNCRC). Non-discrimination, optimal development, the best interests and the voice of the child, all of which are central to UNCRC, underpin inclusive pedagogies. The chapter introduces the children's rights-based agenda in Wales, illustrating how the 'child first' approach has shaped legislation policy and practice in the early years. It also considers other initiatives designed to promote children's rights in educational contexts, such as *The Right Way: A Children's Rights Approach for Education in Wales* (Children's Commissioner for Wales 2017) and *Rights Respecting Schools Award* (UNICEF 2021). The chapter argues that children's rights must become a central tenet of policy agenda in order to support pedagogies which allow the voices, needs and interests of young children to be properly acknowledged.

In Chapter 2, Matt Hutt further considers inclusion, this time from a leadership perspective, contending that, to support inclusive pedagogies, leaders must welcome learner and employee diversity. The concepts of inclusive leadership and shared leadership are deliberated on and their role in early childhood education is explored. In terms of applying these principles in practice, Hutt discusses the application of leadership for inclusion and how it can impact on both the organisation in question and the local community. Lastly, crucial aspects of leadership activity are questioned in order to establish whether they are essentially compatible with an inclusive pedagogy viewpoint.

Following on from the examination of the leadership for inclusion, Chapter 3 focuses on practice and the role of the practitioner in inclusive pedagogy for early childhood education. It is centred on relational and attentional practices used with children whose learning subjectivities are not well understood by practitioners. In this chapter, Carmel Conn argues that children who are considered as 'complex' are often described in terms of diagnostic categories, but should be viewed more three-dimensionally. She argues that it is important to see children as singular subjects who connect with the world in particular ways by attending to their body-world experiences and to the presence of relationships with human but also more-than-human aspects of the learning environment. The hypothetical experience of a young autistic boy in relation to the interactive whiteboard in his early years classroom is presented as a recurring motif to explore the ways in which the world offers itself to children in educational spaces and what possibilities for learning exist.

The practical aspects of planning and implementing inclusive pedagogies through enhanced provision is the focus of Chapter 4. Claire Pescott uses Foucauldian theory to stress the need for critical reflection in early childhood education and a deconstructed pedagogy that confronts inequalities within the early years environment. Case studies from initial teacher education are presented to show how inclusive pedagogy can be integrated into the early years learning environment. These learning environments are viewed from a post-structuralist standpoint in this chapter: as landscapes where an interaction of power and complex relationships occurs.

In Part II of the book, the first of our chapters based on empirical research showcases a single case study of a collaborative play interaction between two toddler refugee children in a family centre in New Zealand. Amanda Bateman and Linda Mitchell employ conversation analysis to investigate how early socialisation practices are co-constructed by teacher–toddler interactions in early childhood education. They suggest that empathic socialisation practices within diverse linguistic and cultural early years settings are essential to support collective and inclusive belonging. Practices which foster a sense of belonging and inclusion are considered, providing guidance to teachers on making use of opportunities of space, resource and learning for children to practise social organisation activities with each other.

Ben Simmons' chapter contributes to the continuing debate around mainstream educational provision for children with profound and multiple learning difficulties (PMLD). There is a paucity of research on this topic, particularly research focused on early childhood education. In Chapter 6, Simmons presents the findings from a project that examined how mainstream and specialist early childhood settings supported the social interaction of children with PMLD. The results of the study indicate that mainstream and specialist settings can employ similar practices in terms of how staff support children with PMLD, but that peer interactions may produce unexpected outcomes. He uses an enactivist theoretical framework to clarify who leads social interaction and how this affects the social identity of children with PMLD.

In Chapter 7, Jacky Tyrie and colleagues report on a collaborative study undertaken by a group of researchers from four different universities. It explores early years practitioners' perceptions of child participation within the classroom and school. The chapter focuses on teachers' perceptions of children's participation rights within Foundation Phase settings in Wales. It examines how these rights translate into practice and records the tensions and opportunities identified in the responses. The results indicate that practitioners' perception of participation is varied and concept specific. The rights-based terminology utilised in this study caused practitioners to reflect on their understanding and enactment of participation, with some being unaware of where participation was part of their pedagogy and others being acutely aware and reflective about the role of participation in their daily pedagogical decision making. However, perceptions of participation both in terms of knowledge and practices were bounded in some instances by notions about the competency and agency of young children. For some respondents, participation is enacted within specific activities rather than being an overarching inclusive, participatory pedagogy.

The enactment of participation in early childhood education is further investigated in Angela Rekers' chapter, Chapter 8. She considers children's engagement with each other, the teacher, the space and the resources available in relation to participation in institutional practices from the child's perspective. Rekers utilises environmental affordance theory and cultural-historical activity theory in an analysis of the different ways in which children are allowed to be themselves in a space. Findings are used to reflect on how 'challenging behaviour' may be reframed as an opportunity for recognising all children's developing competencies and capabilities as learners.

Eleri John contemplates the ongoing discourse around the concept of ability and in-class ability groupings in Chapter 9, identifying concerns about the way ability is measured, perceived and implemented in early years classrooms. She maintains that these groupings conflict with the dominant social message of inclusion, opportunity and participation. Drawing on a qualitative study, this chapter explores the voices of 5–6-year-olds in the Welsh Foundation Phase and their 'experience-derived' understandings of ability groupings in the classroom. She analyses both the internal and external stimuli that are present during the pedagogic interaction. Using the results of the study, the chapter further debates the impact these in-class groupings have on children's inclusion, participation and interaction in order to highlight children's agency, voice and achievement of greater mutuality of adult and child subjectivities.

In the final chapter, Jane Waters-Davies and Natalie Macdonald explore the barriers to inclusive working in the early childhood education and care sector. They report on the findings from a study that explored the process and outcomes of professional learning for a group of pre-school staff working in this sector in a socio-economically deprived area. The professional learning was aimed at developing the pedagogical practice of the staff in order to support children's conceptual and higher order thinking. This chapter reports on the deficit views about the capability of the children in their care to think conceptually held by a minority of staff who took part in the professional learning programme. Waters-Davies and Macdonald use the notion of the *threshold concept* (Meyer and Land 2003) to look at the conceptual construction of the capable child and maintain that the concept of the dependent, deficit child as opposed to the capable, agential child may be in evidence across many early childhood education and care contexts. Conclusions support the need for the practitioner to construct *every* child as capable to support inclusive practice.

We hope these chapters will contribute to the ongoing conversation about best practices suitable for all children in early childhood education and serve to highlight the importance of close attention to the ways in which we think about and engage with them as learners. In presenting our research, the hope is to make the connection clearer between educational theory and everyday practice as a way of creating new understandings about how young children are and feel themselves to be included.

References

Alexander, R. (2015) Teaching and learning for all? The quality imperative revisited, *International Journal of Educational Development*, 40(C): 250–258.

Allan, J. (2008) *Rethinking Inclusive Education: The Philosophers of Difference in Practice*. Dordrecht: Springer.

Allan, J. and Youdell, D. (2017) Ghostings, materialisations and flows in Britain's special educational needs and disability assemblage, *Discourse Studies in the Cultural Politics of Education*, 38(1): 70–82.

Children's Commissioner for Wales (2017) *The Right Way: A Children's Rights Approach in Wales*. Available: https://www.childcomwales.org.uk/resources/childrens-rights-approach/right-way-childrens-rights-approach-wales/ [accessed 25 February 2021].

Conn, C. and Hutt, M. (2020) Successful futures for all? Additional learning needs in Wales in the light of curriculum reform, *British Journal of Special Education*, 47(2): 152–169.

Dahlberg, G. and Moss, P. (2005) *Ethics and Politics in Early Childhood Education*. London: Routledge.

Department for Education (2019) *Timpson Review of School Exclusion DfE-00090–2019*. Available: www.gov.uk/government/publications [accessed 27 April 2021].

Florian, L. (2013) Reimagining special education: why new approaches are needed. In: Florian, L. (Ed.), *The Sage Handbook of Special Education*, pp. 9–22. Los Angeles, London, New Delhi, Singapore, Washington DC: Sage.

Florian, L. (2019) On the necessary co-existence of special and inclusive education, *International Journal of Inclusive Education*, 23(7–8): 691–704.

Florian, L. and Camedda, D. (2020) Enhancing teacher education for inclusion, *European Journal of Teacher Education*, 431: 4–8.

Francis, B., Archer, L., Hodgen, J., Pepper, D., Taylor, B. and Travers, M-C. (2017) Exploring the relative lack of impact of research on 'ability grouping' in England: a discourse analytic account, *Cambridge Journal of Education*, 47(1): 1–17.

Hodgman, L. (2015) *Enabling Environments in the Early Years: Making Provision for High Quality and Challenging Experiences in Early Years Settings*. Second edition. Salisbury: Practical Pre-School Books.

Karlsrudd, P. (2021) When differences are made into likenesses: the normative documentation and assessment culture of the preschool, *International Journal of Inclusive Education*. doi:10.1080/13603116.2021.1879951.

Knight, C. and Crick, T. (2021) Inclusive education in Wales: interpreting discourses of values and practice using critical policy analysis, *ECNU Review of Education*. doi:10.1177/20965311211039858.

Kuby, C. R. (2018) Rhizomes and intra-activity with materials. In: Iorio, J. M. and Parnell, W. (Eds), *Meaning Making in Early Childhood Research: Pedagogies and the Personal*, pp. 146–165. New York and London: Routledge.

Lenz Taguchi, H. (2010) Rethinking pedagogical practices in early childhood education: a multidimensional approach to learning and inclusion. In: Yelland, N. (Ed.), *Contemporary Perspectives on Early Childhood Education*, pp. 14–32. Berkshire: Open University Press.

Meyer, J. H. F. and Land, R. (2003) Threshold concepts and troublesome knowledge 1–Linkages to ways of thinking and practising. In: Rust, C. (Ed.), *Improving Student Learning–Ten Years On*, pp. 412–424. Oxford: Oxford Brookes University, Oxford Centre for Staff and Learning Development.

Nilholm, C. (2020) Research about inclusive education in 2020–how can we improve our theories in order to change practice? *European Journal of Special Needs Education*. doi:10.1080/08856257.2020.1754547.

Nutbrown, C. and Clough, P. (2013) *Inclusion in the Early Years*. Second edition. Los Angeles, London, New Delhi, Singapore, Washington DC: Sage.

Slee, R. (2019) Belonging in an age of exclusion, *International Journal of Inclusive Education*, 23(9): 909–922.

UNICEF (2021) *Rights Respecting Schools Award*. Available: https://www.unicef.org.uk/rights-respecting-schools/ [accessed 25 February 2021].

Part I
Theoretical perspectives on inclusive pedagogy

1 The children's rights approach to early childhood education

Policy and context in Wales

Alison Murphy and Jane Waters-Davies

Introduction and background

It is important to remember that inclusion and human rights are inextricably linked. In 1945, when the United Nations adopted the Universal Declaration of Human Rights, this was the first time that a set of fundamental human rights had been set out. These rights were deemed as applicable to everyone (universal), interlinked, inalienable, meaning that they cannot be sold or given away, and are unconditional, that is, they are not subject to the behaviour of the individual. The European Convention on Human Rights (ECHR) was drawn up by the Council of Europe in Strasbourg in 1949. Over 100 members of parliament from across Europe (including the UK) gathered to compose the charter. The UK was the first nation to ratify the convention in March 1951. However, it took until 1998 for the UK to enshrine these rights into domestic law. Prior to this time the UK was signed up to other human rights treaties, even though human rights were not protected by legislation. In the UK, the Human Rights Act (HRA 1998) became law in the UK and has been operational since 2000. The devolved administrations in Scotland, Wales and Northern Ireland were required to adhere to the Act from their instigation in 1999. The UK government announced a review of the HRA in December 2020.

However, with the UK effectively leaving the European Union (EU) in 2021, there has been some debate around human rights and how this will be affected by 'Brexit': Britain's exit from the EU. According to Cowell (2021) the UK is still committed to the European Convention on Human Rights (ECHR) and subsequently the jurisdiction of the European Court on Human Rights as part of the EU-UK Trade and Cooperation Agreement. He goes on to discuss the challenges that exist regarding this 'locking in' to the ECHR and the possibilities of the introduction of UK law to limit the powers of the European Court of Human Rights in the UK. The European Court of Human Rights has been instrumental in advocating inclusion and supporting the rights of disabled people in the UK; therefore any erosion of their authority to act upon these rights would be potentially detrimental to inclusion and inclusive practice.

DOI: 10.4324/9781003163206-3

Alongside the HRA in the UK is the Equality Act of 2010; this was introduced to combine a number of existing pieces of legislation in order to strengthen the law which protects people from discrimination and disadvantage. This included the Sex Discrimination Act 1975, Race Relations Act 1976 and Disability Discrimination Act 1995. The Equality Act (2010) states that 'it is unlawful for any education provider, including a private or independent provider, to discriminate between pupils on grounds of disability, race, sex, gender reassignment, pregnancy and maternity, religion or belief, or sex' (Centre for Studies on Inclusive Education 2018). These 'protected characteristics' make it unlawful to discriminate on these grounds regarding the admission of new pupils, pupils currently at the school (including absent or temporarily excluded pupils) and former pupils. The Equality and Human Rights Commission was set up in 2007 incorporating the work of the Equal Opportunities Commission, the Commission for Racial Equality and the Disability Rights Commission. The Commission also took on other aspects of equality including age, sexual orientation, and religion or belief, as well as promoting an understanding of the HRA and the Equality Act. According to the Equality and Human Rights Commission (2020), they are a statutory non-departmental public body and their role is to safeguard and enforce laws to protect people's rights.

The inception of United Nations Convention on the Rights of the Child (UNCRC) in 1989 was a milestone in the awakening of interest around children's rights. The Convention, which incorporates 54 articles that cover all aspects of a child's life, was ratified by the UK government and enshrined in subsequent legislation such as the Children Act of 1989 and 2004. It outlines children's civil, political, economic, social and cultural rights supporting the view that children should be involved in decisions which affect them individually and collectively. In 2016, the UN examined the UK government on their compliance with the UNCRC. The UN concluded that the UK needed to further develop inclusive education and prioritise this, making sure that mainstream schools are fully accessible to children with disabilities (UN Committee on the Rights of the Child 2016). Concern was also expressed regarding how the opinions of children with disabilities were sought and how these views were incorporated into the decision-making process. Thus, the participation rights of children with disabilities was seen as lacking and needing to be strengthened in UK government policies and subsequent practice.

Historically Wales has led the way on children's rights in the UK and politicians have prioritised children's rights since devolution in 1998 with a 'child first' approach. Wales was the first nation in the UK to establish a Children's Commissioner; this was followed by the ground-breaking Rights of Children and Young Persons (Wales) Measure (2011). The latter reflected the Welsh Government's commitments to supporting children's rights through legislation and policy in Wales. The law requires all Welsh Ministers, whenever they exercise their functions, to have due regard to the UNCRC.

Since the Rights of Children and Young Persons (Wales) Measure in 2011, a number of policies have been developed to support children's rights in Wales.

In 2016, Young Wales developed the Children and Young People's National Participation Standards. These standards were designed to help organisations and individuals who work with children and young people to make sure that participation is central to the work that they do. The Standards are underpinned by the UN Convention on the Rights of the Child, and the Well-being of Future Generations (Wales) Act 2015, which puts the involvement of children at the centre of improving well-being (Children in Wales 2016).

The Additional Learning Needs and Education Tribunal (Wales) Bill was passed by the National Assembly for Wales in 2017 and became law in January 2018 after receiving Royal Assent. The new Act aims to create a new unified statutory framework for children and young people with additional learning needs (ALN) aged 0–25. It will replace the current system which involves the statementing of children with special educational needs (SEN), which has been in place for over 30 years. Some of the key features of the Bill include the change in terminology (from SEN to ALN) and the extension of support for young people up to the age of 25. Statements and Individual Education Plans (IEP) and Learning Support Plans will be replaced by the new support plan called an Individual Development Plan (IDP). In terms of inclusion, the Act commits to actively including learners in person-centred planning approaches. The Welsh Government (WG 2020a, 3) states that 'It is imperative that children and young people see the planning process as something which is done with them rather than to them'. Learners and their parents/carers should be participants in all aspects of the process.

There has been a significant delay in the implementation of the Act due to the Covid pandemic and as such the phased implementation did not begin until September 2021. The ALN Code for Wales (WG 2021a), which replaces the previous code of practice, also came into force at this time. Initial feedback from the Children's Commissioner for Wales (CCW 2019) regarding the draft Code recognised the acknowledgement of the five principles of *The Right Way: A Children's Rights Approach for Education in Wales* (CCW 2017) within the ALN Code and the call for local education authorities to consider these as part of the Act. The Commissioner also expressed concerns about whether the Code is doing enough to promote and protect the rights of children and young people with additional learning needs on an everyday basis. The transition to the new system will involve major changes for local authorities, schools and further education colleges and the voice of pupils and parents needs to be central to the implementation process in order to allay stress and anxiety as well ensuring continuous provision of support for children and young people with ALN during the transitionary period.

This chapter will explore how participation rights have been enacted in Wales acknowledging the changing landscape of statutory guidance in Wales as well as the UN report of 2016 which expressed concerns regarding the participation rights of children with disabilities and the challenges that they face in terms of being able to express their views and have these views taken into account. We will examine participation rights in terms of the existing early years curriculum and the proposed new Curriculum for Wales as well as initiatives such as *The Right Way: A Children's Rights Approach for Education in Wales* (CCW 2017), a guide that was developed for education settings in Wales, and the Rights Respecting Schools Award (UNICEF 2021).

Early childhood education in Wales

Education policy for the first decade of Welsh devolution was informed by the vision document *The Learning Country* (NAfW 2001a, 2001b), which set out the intention to 'build stronger foundations for learning in primary schools with a radical improvement for early years provision' (NAfW 2001b, 12). The subsequent consultation document, *The Learning Country: Foundation Phase 3–7 Years* (NAfW 2003), set out the proposals for a Foundation Phase curriculum framework for children aged 3–7 years to 'create a rich curriculum under seven Areas of Learning for children in the Foundation Phase' (Welsh Assembly Government (WAG) 2008, 3). This radical overhaul of early childhood education and care in Wales signalled a shift away from UK central government education policy. It was also predicated upon a concern, supported by research literature, about the 'detrimental' (NAfW 2001a, 8) effect of an overly formal approach to early childhood education and care for children below 6 years of age.

Wales is in the midst of major reform of its education system as this chapter is in development (WG 2017a, 2021b). The Foundation Phase remains the statutory curriculum document for children aged 3–7 years until 2022, when it will be superseded by the new Curriculum for Wales (WG 2021b) which is designed for learners aged from 3–16 years.

The Foundation Phase Framework (WAG 2008) was introduced for school children aged 3–7 years (Nursery, Reception, Year 1 and Year 2 classes) and those children aged 3 and over in maintained and non-maintained settings in an annual roll-out over the period from 2008 to 2011. The statutory curriculum document was updated in 2015 and still advocates the adoption of a play-based, experiential approach to early childhood education within the context of a balance of adult-directed and child-directed activity. Educational settings are required to provide children with access to 'indoor and outdoor environments that are fun, exciting, stimulating and safe' and to 'promote children's development and natural curiosity to explore and learn through first-hand experiences' (WG 2015a, 3). In addition, children are to interact with adults with whom they should share episodes of sustained and shared thinking and adults are to 'build on what they [children] already know and can do, their interests and what they understand' (WG 2015a, 4). The Foundation Phase Framework requires, therefore, that practitioners, in part at least, engage flexibly and contingently with child-initiated activity in order to support learning indoors and outdoors. This requirement is situated within the broader context of the Welsh Government's overall vision for children and young people which is based around seven core aims developed from the UN Convention on the Rights of the Child (see WAG

2006, 2008). The Foundation Phase sits within this overarching and emancipatory vision for children with an emphasis on the personal development and well-being of the child:

> Children learn through first-hand experiential activities with the serious business of 'play' providing the vehicle. Through their play, children practise and consolidate their learning, play with ideas, experiment, take risks, solve problems, and make decisions individually, in small and in large groups. First-hand experiences allow children to develop an understanding of themselves and the world in which they live. The development of children's self-image and feelings of self-worth and self-esteem are at the core of this phase.
>
> (WG 2015a, 3)

Seven areas of learning are identified, the first of which is situated 'at the heart of the Foundation Phase' (WG 2015a, 8):

- Personal and social development, well-being and cultural diversity
- Language, literacy and communication skills
- Mathematical development
- Welsh-language development
- Knowledge and understanding of the world
- Physical development
- Creative development.

The implicit emphasis in the Foundation Phase documentation on 'proactive and intentional pedagogy' (Wood 2007b, 127) was recognised, at the time, as providing the potential for Welsh practitioners to 'develop the integrated approaches that are advocated in contemporary play research' (Wood 2007a, 313). However, two sets of disappointing Programme for International Student Assessment scores for Wales (OECD 2014) heralded an intense focus on pupils' development in literacy and numeracy throughout the Welsh education system. A national literacy and numeracy framework was made statutory in September 2012 and has been incorporated into the revised Foundation Phase orders for areas of learning for language, literacy and communication, and mathematical skills (WG 2015a). The associated imposition of national tests in literacy and numeracy for 7-year-olds have introduced some tensions in relation to the play-based, child-initiated aspects of the Foundation Phase initiative. However, as a part of the national education reform programme, detailed further below, assessment arrangements are under review.

Looking to the future

Since the introduction of the Foundation Phase, the Welsh Government has re-emphasised its education priorities; the 'National Mission' (WG 2017a,

2020b) sets out aims for the Welsh education sector, to 'raise standards, reduce the attainment gap and deliver an education system that is a source of national pride and confidence' (Ministerial foreword, WG 2017a). There have been two evaluations of the Foundation Phase curriculum initiative. The first to report was a review of progress or 'stocktake', undertaken by Siraj and Kingston (2014) at the request of the Welsh Government. The stocktake highlighted that where the Foundation Phase was working well the outcomes for children appeared to be good (Siraj and Kingston 2014, 18–19). However, the report emphasised that there was significant variation in the experiences of children in the Foundation Phase within and across the maintained and non-maintained sectors.

The Welsh Government also instigated a three-year evaluation of the Foundation Phase which reports in more detail, though with similar headline findings (WG 2015a). This evaluation highlights the warm support that the Foundation Phase received from stakeholders and that children experiencing Foundation Phase pedagogy are engaged and achieving well. The evaluation reported that:

> The Foundation Phase is associated with improved attainment for pupils eligible for free school meals, but the evaluation has found no evidence to suggest it has made any observable impact so far on reducing inequalities in attainment at the end of Key Stage 2.
>
> (WG 2015a, 3)

Therefore, the variation in provision across Wales remains a significant issue. Maynard et al. (2013) undertook a review of the curriculum documentation as a part of the three-year evaluation and highlighted possible tensions within the Foundation Phase Framework, for example, tension between the play-based pedagogy, underpinned by a developmental approach, and detailed statutory curriculum expectations, especially for Years 1 and 2. Such tensions have been recognised across the Welsh education system and were identified as part of the review of the curriculum and assessment arrangements in Wales (Donaldson 2015). The review preceded the introduction of the new Curriculum for Wales, a radical overhaul of mainstream education provision for 3–16-year-olds. The intention of the overhaul is that much of the prescriptive content in the old curriculum is removed and teachers are supported to create local curricular experiences that support the attainment of the four purposes of the curriculum: that is, that children are:

- Ambitious, capable learners, ready to learn throughout their lives.
- Enterprising, creative contributors, ready to play a full part in life and work.
- Ethical, informed citizens of Wales and the world.
- Healthy, confident individuals, ready to lead fulfilling lives as valued members of society.

(see WG 2021b, 2021c)

Within the Curriculum for Wales guidance material there will be designated resources addressing the pedagogy required for the early years section of the new curriculum. Practitioners, advisors, academics and policy makers who have a deep knowledge of Foundation Phase practice are developing this guidance. They have sought to maintain the essence of what has been termed effective foundation phase pedagogy while ensuring that practice reflects contemporary understandings of how young children learn (Donaldson 2015).

The Children's Commissioner for Wales has undertaken a mapping exercise across the proposed purposes of the Curriculum for Wales (CCW 2018a). This demonstrates that the articles of the UNCRC are well represented within the new curriculum purposes as are the three main elements of human rights education:

- Learning about human rights: The acquisition of knowledge and skills about human rights.
- Learning through human rights: The development of respectful values and attitudes and changed behaviour that reflects human rights values.
- Learning for human rights: The motivation of social action and empowerment of active citizenship to advance respect for the rights of all.

It is worth noting that the Children's Commissioner for Wales provided a paper imploring that the new curriculum is underpinned by a commitment to children's rights delivered by a workforce that is 'rights-informed, rights-aware and rights-based' (CCW 2018a, 9) and that all teachers should have professional learning in children's rights. Within the early years of the new curriculum there appears to be an ongoing commitment to a responsive and relational pedagogy in which children's experiential learning is prioritised. For the youngest children, such a pedagogical approach should support the enactment of Articles 12, 28, 29, 30 at the very least, though the extent of workforce commitment to the rights-based vision of such pedagogy from the start is likely to be limited to certain groups who have already undertaken specific professional learning in this regard, 'Rights respecting school' staff for example (see below).

Following the Well-being of Future Generations Act (Wales) 2015 (WG 2016), the Welsh Government launched 'Prosperity for All: The National Strategy' aimed at building 'a Wales that is prosperous and secure, healthy and active, ambitious and learning, and united and connected' (WG 2017c, 2). Early years provision (0–3) is identified as one of the five cross-cutting priority areas in Wales and this has instigated significant changes and targeted improvements to the workforce and availability of 0–3 early years provision. The Welsh Government published the Childcare, Play and Early Years Workforce Plan (WG 2017d) acknowledging the intention 'to develop a skilled childcare and play workforce, which is highly regarded as a profession and a career of choice and recognised for the vital role the sector plays in supporting our children's development' (WG 2017d, 5). This sits alongside continued investment in the Flying Start childcare element for 2–3-year-olds and the 30 hours funded childcare for 3–4-year-olds of working parents (WG 2014, 2019).

This demonstrates an apparent ongoing commitment to Welsh Government's seven core aims for children and young people which include:

> to ensure a flying start in life; to provide a comprehensive range of education and learning opportunities; to ensure a safe home and a community which supports physical and emotional wellbeing; and to ensure children ... are not disadvantaged by poverty.
>
> (WG 2015b, 4)

Embedding rights-based approaches in practice

As stated at the start of this chapter Wales has taken a proactive approach to embedding children's rights in legislation and policy. The role of the Children's Commissioner for Wales and her team has been central to this. In 2017, the Commissioner introduced *The Right Way: A Children's Rights Approach for Education in Wales* (CCW 2017) which was developed for education settings in Wales, both statutory and non-statutory provision. This framework is predicated by the UN Convention on the Rights of the Child (1989) and is consistent with the statutory duties of settings as expressed in legislation such as The Rights of Children and Young Persons (Wales) Measure (2011). This approach places the UNCRC centrally in children's educational experiences so that it is at the core of school planning, teaching, decision-making, policies and practice. The principles of a children's rights approach are:

- Embedding children's rights
- Equality and non-discrimination
- Empowering children
- Participation
- Accountability.

(CCW 2017, 7)

The model set out in the guide demonstrates how the principles of the children's rights approach can be embedded into policy and practice in educational settings from early years to post-16. Case studies illustrate how these policies translate into pedagogical practice. One of the case studies explores how participation can be reflected in practice in a school which has pupils with a range of additional needs. This is the only example provided which considers supporting disabled children to realise their rights.

Following on from this, in 2018, the Right Way Education Survey was carried out nationwide. The survey looked at how children were experiencing the five principles of a children's rights approach, as set out *The Right Way: A Children's Rights Approach for Education in Wales*. In total, 391 teachers and 6392 children and young people took part in the review from 108 schools (94 per cent of these schools were Children's Commissioner Ambassador Schools). The report specifies that 122 of these children were 'SEN pupils', which is 1.9 per cent of the total number of children surveyed.

Results of the survey indicate that 75 per cent of children had heard of children's rights, while 65 per cent thought that their parents had heard of children's rights. Seventy-six per cent of teachers said that they would like more training on children's rights. In terms of participation rights, around 70 per cent of primary school children felt that they could share their opinions about learning and their lessons, although for older pupils this was much lower, around 45 per cent. In terms of having choice about what they learn then percentages are much lower, notably 58 per cent of primary school pupils and 32 per cent of secondary pupils. Throughout the majority of the data there is evidence to show that children are experiencing some elements of a children's rights approach in their schools. However, this approach seems to be more prevalent in primary schools as acknowledged by the children participating, although the survey does not account for differentials in the understanding of what a rights-based approach means in practice. As this data was gathered predominantly in Children's Commissioner Ambassador Schools, it could also be argued that other children in other schools might not be experiencing their rights in the same way or to the same extent. It is also worth noting that there is no explicit indications of how children with disabilities are experiencing their rights.

UNICEF UK started the Rights Respecting Schools Award (RRSA) throughout England, Wales and Northern Ireland in 2004 (UNICEF 2021). The Award is centred around schools' commitment to embedding the UN Convention on the Rights of the Child in planning, policies, practice and ethos. In order for a school to achieve accreditation, the setting must evidence how it has placed the RRSA strands at the heart of all policies and processes, thus promoting children and young people's rights. Sebba and Robinson carried out an evaluation of the scheme across the UK in 2010. The aim of the evaluation was to assess the impact of the RRSA on the well-being and achievement of children and young people in the participating schools (12 schools where longitudinal data was gathered over three years and 19 schools which received one-off visits). Conclusions were positive and the authors reported that the scheme had a 'profound effect on the majority of the schools involved in the programme. For some school communities, there is strong evidence that it has been a life-changing experience' (Sebba and Robinson 2010, 3). Key findings noted the increased knowledge of the UN Convention on the Rights of the Child (1989), positive relationships with staff and pupils as well as increased levels of empowerment for pupils and the opportunity to make informed decisions within their schools. There were also improved levels of engagement resulting in raised attainment in two-thirds of the 31 schools. In terms of inclusive practice, 'positive attitudes to diversity were reported towards peers and staff with disabilities, and towards those with behavioural or emotional problems' (Sebba and Robinson 2010, 5). The study also reported that there were instances recorded in the interviews where disabled children challenged the externally imposed stereotypes placed upon them. However, there was concern expressed, particularly by special schools and those with resource units for pupils with special educational needs, that their pupils had experienced difficulties in accessing the RRSA language or in participating with the values of the scheme. The evaluation emphasised the need to publicise the scheme further in light of the generally positive outcomes; however the authors do recommend the need for greater guidance around addressing the complex notions expressed in the scheme, particularly for those practitioners that work with disabled children.

Since 2010, the scheme has developed further and there has been an increase in uptake, currently around 5,000 schools across the UK (UNICEF UK 2021). In its current format, there are three evidence-based strands of the RRSA. The strands cover the leadership of the school, knowledge and understanding of children's rights, ethos and relationships, and the empowerment of children and young people. According to UNICEF UK (2021) the strands are as follows:

- *Strand A: Teaching and learning about rights.* The UN Convention on the Rights of the Child is made known to children, young people and adults, who use this shared understanding to work for improved child well-being, school improvement, global justice and sustainable living.
- *Strand B: Teaching and learning through rights–ethos and relationships.* Actions and decisions affecting children are rooted in, reviewed and resolved through rights. Children, young people and adults collaborate to develop and maintain a school community based on equality, dignity, respect, non-discrimination and participation; this includes learning and teaching in a way that respects the rights of both educators and learners and promotes well-being.
- *Strand C: Teaching and learning for rights–participation, empowerment and action.* Children are empowered to enjoy and exercise their rights and to promote the rights of others locally and globally. Duty bearers are accountable for ensuring that children experience their rights.

Schools are awarded a particular level dependant on the evidence provided. The levels are:

- Bronze–Rights Committed
- Silver–Rights Aware
- Gold–Rights Respecting

Silver and gold accreditations are valid for three years and then the school must be re-accredited.

The 2018 impact survey was carried out by UNICEF and the resulting report represented the opinions of over 80,400 children and young people from over 700 schools across the UK. UNICEF (2018, 2) reported that:

> results found that Child Rights Education through RRSA often enhances and strengthens effective practice within a school. Rights have been described as a 'heartbeat' in school life; like a 'golden thread' or 'stick of rock' that underpins and informs their practice.

The effect of this approach is obviously more pronounced as schools move through the award process with gold schools achieving positive performance across a broad range of outcomes including children's knowledge of rights, children's happiness and safety as well as their engagement in school life. The adults surveyed also reported having positive relationships and enjoying their job.

In 2019/2020 there were 1480 maintained schools in Wales, 183 secondary schools, 1234 (nursery/primary schools), 41 special schools and 22 middle schools (StatsWales 2021). In Wales as of February 2021(UNICEF 2021), there were currently 44 schools with the silver award (3 per cent of schools in Wales) and 37 of these schools were primary schools, 4 special schools and 3 secondary schools. There were 33 schools with the gold award (2 per cent of schools in Wales), 27 of which are primary schools, 1 special school and 1 pupil referral unit as well as 4 secondary schools. The uptake of the RRSA is heavily weighted to the primary school sector (for example, out of the 77 gold/silver wards, 83 per cent were primary schools). In terms of special schools, 4 per cent of schools have achieved the gold and silver award. Therefore, the enactment of children's rights and children's participation in this is heavily skewed to the primary sector in Wales and there is a need to promote and develop children's rights and participation in special schools and secondary schools in order to achieve the positive outcomes noted by Sebba and Robinson (2010). This lack of uptake in special schools and secondary schools is also mirrored in the outcomes of the Right Way Education Survey (CCW 2018b) as discussed earlier, where the children's responses reflected a more positive view of children's rights approaches being enacted in primary schools compared to secondary schools.

The role of the teacher is central in driving rights-based approaches and implementing inclusive and participatory practice in the classroom. Research by Jerome et al. (2015) has acknowledged that there is a lack of emphasis on children's rights in initial teacher education. The researcher examined teacher education in the UK and concluded that within the devolved nations of the UK, there is no specific requirement that ensures that all teachers are trained in children's rights and are familiar with the UN Convention on the Rights of the Child. In Wales, the new Professional Standards for Teaching and Leadership were introduced in 2017 and these specify requirements for teachers to develop overarching values and dispositions where the 'needs and rights of learners will be central and take priority in the teacher's approach to their job' (WG 2017b). These values and dispositions should have been integrated into initial teacher training programmes in Wales as well as current practice for all those working with learners. Therefore, with the emphasis on learner rights implicit in driving professional practice for teachers in Wales, there may be a greater drive towards using rights-based approaches in the classroom in the future. The Welsh Government has commissioned an independent evaluation of the standards; the report is due in 2022 and may provide an insight into whether the inclusion of rights-based approaches is more evident in classroom practice.

In the meantime however, the final report of the Black, Asian and Minority Ethnic Communities, Contributions and Cynefin in the New Curriculum Working Group (WG 2021d) suggests that a rights-based, inclusive education environment in which all children thrive may be some distance away. The ministerial foreword indicated that there are 'hard truths' in the report, and that the recommendations offer 'serious challenges'. Professor Charlotte Williams OBE led the working group that was commissioned to undertake an independent review to advise on and improve the teaching of themes and experiences relating to Black, Asian and Minority Ethnic communities across all parts of the school curriculum. In the opening foreword by the chair, Professor Williams reports:

> The facts of racial inequality in the Welsh education system are now well evidenced and documented. The attainment of children and young people from some Minority communities is being hampered by a curriculum that has failed to represent their histories, and the contributions of their communities, past and present. They are hampered by the lack of positive role models in an education workforce that does not adequately reflect the ethnically diverse profile of Wales; and they are hampered by experiences of racism in their everyday school life.
>
> (WG 2021d, 4)

The recommendations made as a result of the independent review are wide ranging and related to five areas for action: resources used in school, workforce training and professional development, professional learning at all stages of the teacher career, school-level actions and actions for sustainability. The concluding sections of the report acknowledge that part of this development is about 'changing mindsets, ingrained practices and developing positive cultures of change'. This is associated with 'an interrogation of the attitudes and values that underpin competency, and the commitment and willingness to change' (WG 2021d, 68). We would argue that the findings of this report demonstrate in the strongest terms that, despite the positive policy backdrop with regard to children's rights in Wales, and despite the gains made in this area in education, much is yet to be done, and there is no room for complacency.

Conclusion

The Welsh Government's commitment to children's rights has been evidenced in legislation and policy since the Rights of Children and Young Persons (Wales) Measure in 2011. The Foundation Phase curriculum and pedagogy embraces an understanding of how children learn through first-hand experiences with child-initiated activity acknowledged as central. While the curriculum in Wales is currently in a state of flux, the new proposals evidenced in the Curriculum for Wales (WG 2021b) do go some way to addressing the need for children's rights to be at the heart of the curriculum but at the point of writing this chapter we do not know whether a child-first, play-based approach will be put into practice. In order to enact a pedagogy which has the rights of the child as a central tenet, we advocate that practitioners and teachers need to be trained in rights-based approaches as part of all early years care and education courses, initial teacher education and ongoing professional development. This would ensure that child-first approaches would be implemented across all parts of Wales with parity in the maintained and non-maintained sectors.

In 2016, the UN Committee on the Rights of the Child identified that the UK (including Wales) should further develop inclusive education and that the voice of children with additional learning needs should be considered in all aspects of educational provision and decision-making. With regard to changing policy, the ALN Act (2018) in Wales reflects a commitment to person-centred planning, taking into account the views of learners and their parents at all stages. These substantial changes in ALN provision in Wales will require a commitment from all practitioners and agencies involved to adopt this participatory approach if the voices of children with ALN are going to be strengthened. This commitment will again need to be supported by training for new and existing practitioners in order to support a view of the child as a participant in the process.

Although Wales has been seen as leading the way in terms of the UK context, in the discussion above we have illustrated that some of the drivers and initiatives seen in practice have been focussed on mainstream primary age pupils and beyond, rather than in the early years or indeed those children with additional learning needs. This raises questions about practitioner notions of maturity and competence of young children and children with ALN. Initiatives which support the rights-based approaches in schools need to be adapted to support implementation with younger children and children with additional needs, so that these children are able to express their views and become participants in the processes relating to their learning and provision. Legislation, policy and practice for all children in Wales must adopt a consensual approach to developing child-centred pedagogy where the voice, the needs and the interests of all children are dominant.

Key points

- The voices, needs and interests of young children and children with ALN must be heard and barriers removed to enable these children to participate and express their views.
- Children's rights must be at the heart of statutory curricula in both policy and practice, in order that pedagogic approaches enabling children to learn about and enact their rights.
- All practitioners working with children should be trained to embrace a rights-based pedagogy in daily practice; notions about lack of maturity and competency in young children and children with ALN must be challenged.

Further reading

Florian, L. (2015) Inclusive pedagogy: a transformative approach to individual differences but can it help reduce educational inequalities? *Scottish Educational Review* 47 (1), 5–14.

Lyle, S. (2014) Embracing the UNCRC in Wales (UK): policy, pedagogy and prejudices', *Educational Studies*, 40 (2), 215–232.

References

Centre for Studies on Inclusive Education (CSIE) (2018) *Equalities Act 2010.* Available: http://www.csie.org.uk/inclusion/equalities-act-2010.shtml [accessed 10 February 2021].

Children in Wales (2016) *Participation.* Available: https://www.childreninwales.org.uk/our-work/participation/ [accessed 3 February 2021].

Children's Commissioner for Wales (CCW) (2017) *The Right Way Approach: A Children's Rights Approach in Wales.* Available: https://www.childcomwales.org.uk/resources/childrens-rights-approach/right-way-childrens-rights-approach-wales/ [accessed 25 February 2021].

Children's Commissioner for Wales (CCW) (2018a) *Human Rights Education in the New Curriculum: Position Paper of the Children's Commissioner for Wales.* Available: https://www.childcomwales.org.uk/wp-content/uploads/2018/11/CCFW-Children-Rights-and-Curriculum-Reform-Position-Paper-2018.pdf [accessed 27 February 2021].

Children's Commissioner for Wales (CCW) (2018b) *The Right Way Education Survey.* Available: https://www.childcomwales.org.uk/wp-content/uploads/2018/10/Childrens-Rights-Survey.pdf [accessed 25 February 2021].

Children's Commissioner for Wales (CCW) (2019) *ALN Code of Practice Consultation Response.* Available: https://www.childcomwales.org.uk/our-work/policy-positions/aln-code-of-practice-consultation-response/ [accessed 5 May 2021].

Cowell, F. (2021) The Brexit deal locks the UK into continued Strasbourg Human Rights Court membership. Available: https://blogs.lse.ac.uk/brexit/2021/01/17/the-brexit-deal-locks-the-uk-into-continued-strasbourg-human-rights-court-membership [accessed 10 February 2021].

Donaldson, G. (2015) *Successful Futures Independent Review of Curriculum and Assessment Arrangements in Wales.* Cardiff: Welsh Government.

Equality and Human Rights Commission (2020) *Who We Are.* Available: https://www.equalityhumanrights.com/en [accessed 3 February 2021].

Jerome, L., Emerson, L., Lundy, L. and Orr, K. (2015). *Teaching and Learning about Children's Rights.* London: UNICEF. Available: https://www.unicef.org/media/63086/file/UNICEF-Teaching-and-learning-about-child-rights.pdf [accessed 25 February 2021].

Maynard, T., Taylor, C., Waldron, S., Rhys, M., Smith, R., Power, S. and Clement, J. (2013) *Evaluating the Foundation Phase: Policy Logic Model and Programme Theory*, Social Research No. 37/2012. Cardiff: Welsh Government.

NAfW (2001a) *Laying the Foundations: Early Years Provision for Three Year Olds.* Cardiff: NAfW.

NAfW (2001b) *The Learning Country: A Paving Document.* Cardiff: NAfW. Available: http://www.elwa.ac.uk/doc_bin/SkillsObservatory/learning_country_paving_document.pdf [accessed 23 June 2010].

NAfW (2003) *The Learning Country: The Foundation Phase - 3–7 years.* Cardiff: NAfW.

Organisation for Economic Cooperation and Development (OECD) (2014). *Improving Schools in Wales: An OECD Perspective*. Paris: Directorate for Education and Skills.
Sebba, J. and Robinson, C. (2010). *Evaluation of UNICEF UK's Rights Respecting Schools Awards (RRSA) Scheme. Final Report*. Brighton: Universities of Sussex and Brighton.
Siraj, I. and Kingston, D. (2014) *An Independent Stocktake of the Foundation Phase in Wales*. Cardiff: Welsh Government. Available: https://dera.ioe.ac.uk/20340/1/140519-independent-stocktake-of-the-foundation-phase-in-wales-en.pdf [accessed 1 August 2021].
StatsWales (2021) *Schools and teachers*. Available: https://statswales.gov.wales/Catalogue/Education-and-Skills/Schools-and-Teachers [accessed 21 February 2021].
UN Committee on the Rights of the Child (2016) Concluding observations on the fifth periodic report of the United Kingdom of Great Britain and Northern Ireland. Available: https://www.unicef.org.uk/babyfriendly/wp-content/uploads/sites/2/2016/08/UK-CRC-Concluding-observations-2016-2.pdf [accessed 25 February 2021].
UNICEF (2018) *Impact Report: Creating Active and Engaged Citizens*. Available: https://www.unicef.org.uk/rights-respecting-schools/wp-content/uploads/sites/4/2019/07/Impact-Report-2018_Final-170719.pdf [accessed 21 February 2021].
UNICEF (2021) *Rights Respecting Schools Award*. Available: https://www.unicef.org.uk/rights-respecting-schools/ [accessed 25 February 2021].
Welsh Assembly Government (WAG) (2006) *The Learning Country 2: Delivering the Promise*. Cardiff: Welsh Assembly Government.
Welsh Assembly Government (WAG) (2008) *Foundation Phase Framework for Children's Learning for 3–7 Year Olds in Wales*. Cardiff: Welsh Assembly Government.
Welsh Government (WG) (2014) *Flying Start Strategic Guidance*. Available: http://gov.wales/docs/dhss/publications/120913fsguidanceen.pdf [accessed 16 January 2017].
Welsh Government (WG) (2015a) *Foundation Phase Framework (Revised 2015)*. Cardiff: Welsh Government. Available: https://hwb.gov.wales/api/storage/d5d8e39c-b534-40cb-a3f5-7e2e126d8077/foundation-phase-framework.pdf [accessed 3 May 2021].
Welsh Government (WG) (2015b) *Programme for Children and Young People: Comprehensive Version–Core Aims 1 to 7*. Available: https://gov.wales/sites/default/files/publications/2019-06/seven-core-aims-for-children-and-young-people.pdf [accessed 16 January 2017].
Welsh Government (WG) (2016) *Shared Purpose: Shared Future: Statutory Guidance on the Well-being of Future Generations (Wales) Act 2015*. Available: https://gov.wales/sites/default/files/publications/2019-02/spsf-1-core-guidance.PDF [accessed 5 May 2021].
Welsh Government (WG) (2017a) *Education in Wales: Our National Mission, Action Plan 2017–2021*. Cardiff: Welsh Government.
Welsh Government (WG) (2017b) *Revised Professional Standards for Education Practitioners in Wales*. Cardiff: Welsh Government.
Welsh Government (WG) (2017c) *Prosperity for All: Economic Action Plan*. Cardiff: Welsh Government.
Welsh Government (WG) (2017d) *Childcare, Play and Early Years Workforce Plan*. Cardiff: Welsh Government.
Welsh Government (WG) (2019) *Childcare for 3 and 4 Year Olds*. Available: https://gov.wales/childcare-3-and-4-year-olds [accessed 30 June 2021].
Welsh Government (WG) (2020a) *Additional Learning Needs Transformation Programme*. Available: https://gov.wales/sites/default/files/publications/2020-03/additional-learning-needs-aln-transformation-programme-v3.pdf [accessed 5 May 2021].

Welsh Government (WG) (2020b) *Education in Wales–Our National Mission: Update October 2020.* Cardiff: Welsh Government. Available: https://gov.wales/sites/default/files/publications/2020-10/education-in-Wales-our-national-mission-update-october-2020.pdf [accessed 30 June 2021].

Welsh Government (WG) (2021a) *The Additional Learning Needs Code for Wales.* Available: https://gov.wales/sites/default/files/publications/2021-03/210326-the-additional-learning-needs-code-for-wales-2021.pdf [accessed 5 May 2021].

Welsh Government (WG) (2021b) *Curriculum for Wales: The Journey to 2022.* Cardiff: Welsh Government. Available: https://hwb.gov.wales/api/storage/0be87463-ba5a-4c88-882e-c293898cb67b/curriculum-for-wales-the-journey-to-2022.pdf [accessed 22 March 2021].

Welsh Government (WG) (2021c) *The Curriculum for Wales.* Available: https://hwb.gov.wales/curriculum-for-wales [accessed 10 May 2021].

Welsh Government (WG) (2021d) *Black, Asian and Minority Ethnic Communities, Contributions and Cynefin in the New Curriculum Working Group: Final Report.* Cardiff: Welsh Government. Available: https://gov.wales/sites/default/files/publications/2021-03/black-asian-minority-ethnic-communities-contributions-cynefin-new-curriculum-working-group-final-report.pdf [accessed 5 May 2021].

Wood, E. (2007a) New directions in play: consensus or collision? *Education 3–13*, 35(4): 309–320.

Wood, E. (2007b) Reconceptualising child-centred education: contemporary directions in policy, theory and practice in early childhood, *FORUM*, 49(1&2): 119–133.

2 Placing inclusion at the heart of things

The 'tricky challenge' for educational leadership

Matt Hutt

Introduction

It would be something of a banal truism to state that educational leadership is challenging on many levels. That the daily experience of leaders, irrespective of phase or national context, is demarcated by challenges large and small should surprise no one. Indeed, building the capacities of individuals and groups of individuals to find ways of meeting challenges is a task that the formal study of leadership sets itself, and a task that it confronts head-on. Research that explores *how* school leaders work successfully to negotiate the challenges they face is plentiful and extensive, and is often able to set out strategies for positive, future, practical implementation. With this backdrop in mind, what are the distinctive challenges that inclusive pedagogy presents in the context of leadership in early childhood education? Discussion of this important question is the focus of this chapter, and, as we shall see, it is a discussion that can be conducted at different levels of complexity and with different terms of reference, ranging from the pragmatic to the philosophical. Indeed, I will argue that inclusive pedagogy, as it is often constructed, sets a particular, tricky philosophical challenge to the *concept* and *idea* of leadership, and that this challenge is of a different order to the often-examined practical challenges that might be presented by conventional elements such as accountability pressures, resource management or organisational change.

To get to the discussion of this tricky challenge, the chapter will first consider the range of ideas covered by the term *inclusive leadership*, before considering the practical challenges of inclusion in early childhood education. We will then go on to briefly touch on more radical conceptions of inclusive pedagogy, discussed in more detail elsewhere in this book, in order to explore the kinds of leadership that might be implied. This will take us into the heart of the matter because, arguably, leadership that does not place inclusion at the core of its purpose may end up not really attending to it at all.

What is inclusive leadership?

Before we delve any further into an exploration of the potential impact of the concept of inclusion on the idea of leadership, it is worth considering the term

DOI: 10.4324/9781003163206-4

inclusive leadership, and identifying the different ways the term can be used. Research studies may use the term broadly to describe the ways in which organisations adopt leadership approaches that emphasise open and accessible interactions between formal leaders and their colleagues in order to, for example, attempt to foster employee creativity (Carmeli et al. 2010; Zu et al. 2020), or to develop innovative practices (Fang et al. 2019). Here, *inclusive leadership* refers quite specifically to the deliberate development of particular employee working relationships and conditions, and to the modification of organisational cultures to obtain identified positive effects within these employee communities. *Inclusive leadership* in this sense is all about creating an improved organisation by attending to the diverse experiences of employees. It can also have the additional aim of making sure that diversity within the workforce is acknowledged by leaders in such a way that 'individuals of diverse backgrounds at varying levels are treated fairly, valued for their contributions and included in decision making' (Kuknor and Bhattacharya 2020, 3). The emphasis on an inclusive approach towards the workforce, and on harnessing diversity across the spectrum of employees, can be applied to a wide variety of organisations. In this respect, it is as applicable to early years settings and schools as it is to other private and public sector organisations. However, because its point of focus is at the level of the organisation, and the people who *work* for that organisation, it is not directly concerned with inclusion in terms of learners. To consider this specific aspect of *educational* organisations, we need to move onto another potential use of the term *inclusive leadership*: leadership *for* inclusion.

Leadership for inclusion

In this use of the term, most often referenced in the research domains of school improvement, educational leadership and equity in education, the focus is more specifically on what leaders should do to develop inclusive practices and to build inclusive cultures within their settings, specifically in reference to the learners who attend them. This may or may not sit alongside their attempts to provide inclusive leadership for their teaching workforce, as described above: the two uses of the term could, in theory and in practice, be dealt with quite separately. What is important to note is that, in this second use of the term, the focus is on learners and on providing for their diverse contexts and experiences. This second interpretation of the term *inclusive leadership* directly references the world of education and the practice of leadership within educational settings. Here, *inclusive leadership,* describes an approach to leadership which meets the challenge of inclusion as an educational construct.

Yet even as the previous sentence is written and read, its formulation may give us pause for thought. As we have already noted, research into leadership practice, and leadership theories themselves, repeatedly explore how challenges may be overcome in pursuit of the creation of better places of learning, better curricula, better professional learning systems, better modes of practitioner collaboration, better forms of resource management and better means of self-evaluation. The list of challenges is broad and varied. Yet should *inclusion* be described as a *challenge*? By so doing, are we at risk of framing inclusion as a problem to be solved by leadership, and therefore to be added to the long list of educational problems and challenges? If we set inclusion as a problem to be solved by leaders or as a challenge to be strategically negotiated, are we in danger of translating inclusion into a language of problems and challenges that suits current modes of leadership, or, to put it another way, of taking something, a concept such as inclusion, and re-positioning it within the discourse of leadership? If we do this, are we really listening to the implications of inclusive pedagogy with its emphasis on diverse subjectivities (Osberg and Biesta 2008)? Are we rather, with maybe the best of ethical intentions, inserting inclusion into a leadership discourse so that it may be more easily understood and actioned in ways controlled and demarcated by leadership? We might conclude that if we end up doing this, we are ignoring the desire to develop inclusive pedagogy as a space of *emergent* subjectivity in which 'unpredictability, creativity and messiness ... [are] ... the results of good teaching, not a sign of its failure' (Osberg and Biesta 2008, 324).

This is the beginning of one of the tricky problems for leadership in respect of inclusion in its more radical construction. Since it is something of a theoretical and philosophical problem, we might be tempted to put it to one side for the moment, whilst still accepting it worthy of discussion and further exploration, and instead focus on the practical implications for leaders who wish to provide the best education possible for a diverse set of learners. We shall return to the theoretical complexities later in the chapter, and continue here to consider inclusion as a practical challenge for leaders. Even as we do this, we will note that dividing the discussion into a practical, evidence-based element, and a theoretical, philosophical domain, is not straightforward: time and again we shall see that inclusive pedagogy dislocates many of the core aspects of the concept of leadership. Nevertheless, the study of leadership is obliged to explore solutions and strategies to the real-world problem of education, even if it simultaneously questions the effects of this particular way of framing things.

On a practical level then, what does inclusive leadership, in the sense of leadership for educational inclusion, look like? To explore this in more detail, once again we must pause to distinguish between different ways of understanding the task. A *narrow* way of understanding it is to see it as including all children on one educational site. A slightly more expansive version focuses on integrating children from diverse contexts and backgrounds successfully into pre-existing education settings and systems, whilst an even *broader* understanding of the task focuses on providing a 'personalised educational response' for the diversity of learners (Ainscow 2020, 8). This final vision has been termed 'the inclusive turn', in which moves towards inclusion are about the development of organisations, rather than simply involving 'attempts to integrate vulnerable groups into existing arrangements' (Ainscow 2020, 9). Indeed, much of the recent research literature works from this more expansive vision, and embraces the concept of classrooms and other learning spaces as 'heterogeneous environments' (Morrissey 2020, 3), in which leadership engages 'constructively with issues of diversity' (Forde and

Torrance 2017, 107). Furthermore, this same literature has tended to include socio-economic diversity alongside other forms, and has therefore linked to a broader equity and social justice agenda (Liasidou and Antoniou 2015).

Since this has become quite a broad area to explore, it is helpful that the research base itself has mapped out various sub-domains. Research evidence into leadership for inclusion has tended to focus on four overlapping areas of enquiry:

1. What should leaders actually do to support inclusion and diversity?
2. How can leadership development programmes be improved to help future leaders support inclusion and diversity?
3. Which existing theories of leadership appear to support inclusion and diversity?
4. How does an understanding of inclusion and diversity modify the concept of leadership?

We shall explore these in turn.

Leadership activity to support inclusion

Starting from the premise that 'the mere presence of diversity, does not imply the presence of inclusion' (Kuknor and Bhattacharya 2020, 1), research studies have set about the task of identifying the actions that leaders could take proactively to develop organisational systems and cultures that meet a diverse range of individual needs. Research suggests that leaders should promote a positive vision of inclusive education (Agbenyega and Sharma 2014), and that the production of this vision should be formed through dialogue within the organisation (Nutbrown et al. 2013) 'to build a common philosophy' (Oskarsdottir et al. 2020, 524). Leaders should also support and develop collaborative professional cultures which would themselves foster 'a degree of consensus among adults around values of respect for difference' (Ainscow 2020, 12). The task can be summarised as one of building 'new understandings' regarding diversity across the school community, such that previously held negative assumptions may be challenged, and that diversity can be viewed as a norm in itself (Lumby 2019). Thus, there is much work for educational leaders to do in terms of developing the collective, organisational perception of the nature of diversity and inclusion. Without this broad, modified, framing consensus, it is unlikely that any more focused and specific actions to support inclusion will be embraced and enacted by the workforce (Lumby 2019).

Educational leaders are also advised to proactively involve parents from the diverse range of communities served by the institution (Ainscow 2020), but should *not* do so in terms solely demarcated by the needs and aims of the institution. Rather, leaders should work with parents in a spirit of humble reciprocity, and should avoid imposing norms and assumptions unduly (Lumby 2019). This commitment to involving the wider community should also be linked to a commitment to *all* learners within a system, not just the ones who attend the specific institution (Ainscow 2020). Here, commitment to inclusion requires leaders to take a broader perspective than the one defined by the horizons of their own organisation.

Some have argued that leadership *for* inclusion needs to encourage a teaching and learning culture that is supportive of professional risk-taking (Agbenyega and Sharma 2014; Ainscow 2020). The implication is that in a risk-averse culture, educational practitioners will be reluctant to engage with the *messiness* of inclusive pedagogy. The fact that this aligns with more general advice on powerful pedagogy is pointed out by some, such that 'inclusion becomes a way of achieving the overall improvement of education systems' (Ainscow 2020, 8): good teaching for inclusion is effectively good teaching for improvement of the organisation. Allied to this development of a *risk-taking* teaching and learning culture that embraces experimentation is a suggestion that leaders should invest in the kind of professional learning for practitioners that would help such a culture to grow (Agbenyega and Sharma 2014). This professional learning might then in turn help practitioners to develop the kind of reflective inquiry practices which would genuinely support inclusion: a model of *inclusive inquiry*, which would be built around the central idea of engaging with children's own views (Ainscow 2020).

This model of professional inquiry is deliberately formed upon generative, experimental dialogue between adults and children (Ainscow 2020). It is precisely *not* conceived as inquiry which is structured and organised according to adult preferences and assumptions, and is inclusive *because* it is developed and pursued at all stages in tandem with children: inquiry *done with*, rather than *enacted upon*. A similar philosophy underpins the leadership for inclusion approach to forging links with wider communities and other organisations. As part of an ecosystem for inclusion, the vision here is for leaders to listen attentively to perspectives that originate from beyond the four walls of the organisation, in order to form partnerships that are alive to different ways of thinking (Agbenyega and Sharma 2014; Ainscow 2020; Oskarsdottir et al. 2020). Leadership for inclusion does not dictate terms to wider communities. Rather, it works in conjunction with them to build relationships as 'democratic discussions' that in turn will 'attend to individual differences' between children (Oskarsdottir et al. 2020, 530).

It is also argued that leadership for inclusion needs autonomy for leaders to secure and deploy resources in more creative ways (Agbenyega and Sharem 2014). As is so often the case, arguments for increased autonomy are complemented by arguments for increased accountability (Grass 2017), as increased freedom to act comes with an increased responsibility to justify the effects of those same actions. Here too the academic literature surrounding leadership for inclusion often suggests that educational leaders should be subjected to accountability measures which track their ability to support inclusion (Agbenyega and Sharma 2014; Ainscow 2020; Liasidou and Antoniou 2015; Oskarsdottir et al. 2020). This is generally presented as an action to be undertaken by leaders at a system and institutional level, so that there would be 'school effectiveness indicators and accountability regimes to provide incentives for educational professionals to foster equitable and socially just provision for learner diversity' (Liasidou and Antoniou 2015, 353). Since the potential negative effect of some forms of accountability measuring on educational cultures is widely presented (Biesta 2010; Cochran-Smith et al. 2018; Sahlberg 2015), it is not surprising that those who argue for accountability evidence and data to play a role in leadership for inclusion also note that these data need to be used in a nuanced and detailed way, to avoid having 'a perverse effect on the behaviour of professionals' by concentrating on 'narrow, even inappropriate, performance indicators' (Ainscow 2020, 10). There is a real challenge here for leaders to use accountability to strengthen support of inclusion and diversity without being diverted into a set of simplistic metrics which then cease to become the proxy measures for an inclusive pedagogy, and become, themselves, the desired endpoint. Perhaps this is even more of a challenge when we remember that the aspiration of much work on inclusion and diversity is aimed at responding attentively to the qualitative differences between children as learners, whilst many accountability measures rest on the quantitative summation of exemplar similarities across learners. This is a tricky balancing act to perform, and within it, we can detect traces of the larger, more philosophical paradox that the idea of leadership encounters when it commits itself to becoming leadership for inclusion. We shall return to this conundrum later in the chapter.

Leadership development programmes to support inclusion

Having considered the range of suggested leadership activities that might support inclusion and diversity, we should now move on to a second, related, area of research enquiry: how can existing and aspiring leaders themselves be supported to realise these aims? On one level, this question is answered through the *ecosystem* model encountered above, in which a coherent and philosophically committed middle tier of organisations complements and enhances the work of individual settings (Ainscow 2020). This is viewed as a crucial aspect, since even if individual leaders are working to develop inclusion within their organisation, they are unlikely to be successful unless there are supportive structures and resources within the larger system (Liasidou and Antoniou 2015). Aside from this ecological perspective, attention has been focused on development programmes of professional learning for leaders, as a form of support (Liasidou and Antoniou 2015; Forde and Torrance 2017). This recognises that there needs to be something of a culture shift within leadership itself to move beyond a narrow focus on performance outcomes, evident some would argue even in early education settings (Roberts-Holmes 2020), and to concentrate rather on 'inclusive pedagogies which engage constructively with issues of diversity' (Forde and Torrance 2017, 107), a kind of culture shift for leaders. This type of ambitious professional learning for leaders should develop their *knowledge base* in respect of diversity and inclusion, should include an element of *conscious raising* and be *transformative* for the individuals themselves in respect of their ethical and moral perspectives, and should also help develop their skills in *political advocacy* so that they are able to bring about change within the system (Forde and Torrance 2017). These are significant and profound aspirations for any leadership development programme and, it is acknowledged, are only likely to be effective if they are placed at the core of such programmes; leadership development for inclusion and diversity cannot be a side issue or adjunct (Forde and Torrance 2017). This assertion, that inclusion and diversity need to be a core element of leadership development, is important to note. As we shall see, one of the challenges that inclusion presents to the concept of leadership is the need, repeatedly stressed, for it to be placed in a position of central importance. This is not simply an issue of coverage or capacity (where the difficulty might be easily resolved by incorporating more essential content into leadership development programmes). It is also an issue that begins to challenge the concept of what leadership is *for*, insofar as setting and prioritising the *purpose* of leadership has, traditionally, been something for leaders themselves to decide. In other words, deciding on which activity to prioritise, and which to downplay, has been an essential act of leadership itself. How open is the concept of leadership to a higher purpose that, to all intents and purposes, sets out transcendent priorities for leadership to pursue? What if school leaders decide that, in their context, there are other more pressing priorities than inclusion and diversity? Are they wrong if their leadership vision has a different set of priorities? This is another tricky conceptual question that we shall return to later.

Suitable leadership theories and approaches

It is possible of course that this problem can be addressed by identifying leadership theories or approaches which fit neatly with inclusive pedagogy. Much research into leadership for inclusion identifies distributed or shared leadership as a positive theoretical model explicitly (Agbenyega and Sharma 2014; Oskarsdottir et al. 2020), implicitly (Ainscow 2020; Kuknor and Bhattacharya 2020; Rayner 2009) or as part of a hybrid leadership arrangement, blended with managerial and teacher leadership approaches (Morrissey 2020) or with a servant leadership model (Kuknor and Bhattacharya 2020). It is not difficult to see the theoretical appeal of distributed leadership in this context, given that a truly inclusive approach aims to 'provide a personalised educational response, rather than expecting the student to fit the system' (Ainscow 2020, 8). There may be a suspicion that some (non-distributed) leadership approaches place emphasis on developing an effective and efficient *system* within an institution, and then focus on successfully *integrating* members of the institution into that system. Indeed, in this way, some leadership approaches can be viewed as 'practices of domination' (Agbenyega and Sharma 2014, 121), insofar as a select and discrete cadre of organisational leaders identifies an appropriate vision, culture and set of systems for the organisation, and then sets about developing and implementing them. Success here can be defined as an ability to get the rest of the organisation to agree with the vision, inhabit the culture and correctly enact the systems. Attention is drawn towards the expectations of a discrete leadership team, and not, potentially, focused specifically on the varied and diverse (non-systemic) pedagogical needs of children.

Of course, the appeal of a distributed or shared leadership approach in this context is its perspective on forms of leadership dispersed across the organisation (Harris 2008; Spillane 2006), and its movement away from top-down hierarchies. By embracing the leadership capital of a much broader spectrum of the workforce (Agbenyega and Sharma 2014), distributed leadership promises to take leadership action and place it much closer to the periphery, such that the periphery (if children in an early years setting should ever be described that way!) may benefit from nuanced and personalised leadership activity directly. In a distributed leadership approach, early years practitioners are not objects to be regulated, they are agents empowered individually to enact inclusive pedagogy in their own classroom (Agbenyega and Sharma 2014). This is the theoretical promise of distributed leadership and accounts for its sympathetic adoption into many leadership for inclusion models.

Modifying the idea of leadership

Of course, the alignment of two theoretical models does not solve all the issues. Noting that distributed or shared leadership approaches may well be more appropriate in terms of leadership for inclusion sets us off on a path, but the more detailed description of that path prompts further complex questions and tricky problems. Once again, the research literature has readily explored these problems. What kind of leadership practice, even within a distributed perspective, would successfully balance the need to provide some top-down, integrationist leadership direction with nuanced and variegated leadership decisions taken as close as possible to the diverse needs of children? The former, top-down aspect might be characterised by the question, *how can we adapt our learners successfully to processes designed to deliver excellent overall performance outcomes for the organisation?* The latter, bottom-up perspective might be characterised by the question, *how can we adapt our organisation in multiple and diverse ways to develop the potential of each child?* An overall answer may be that leaders will deliver a successful response to the first question by attending first and foremost to the detail of the second question. In this sense, it could be viewed that a commitment to inclusive pedagogy will, in turn, deliver improved overall organisational effectiveness, as noted earlier (Ainscow 2020), and there is likely to be some truth in this position. However, others have argued that leadership that takes inclusion seriously may need to be nudged from a preoccupation with the first question, towards the second, or, as Forde and Torrance (2017) put it, there may have to be less of a focus on 'effective practice to improve outcomes' and more of a focus on those 'inclusive pedagogies, which engage constructively with issues of diversity' (page 107).

However, suggesting that there should be less of a focus on one thing, and more emphasis on something else, does not mean that the first element could or should be ignored entirely. There is a balance to be struck through modifications perhaps to existing concepts of leadership which concentrate on whole-cohort outcomes as the key reference point for organisational improvement. Fortunately, the research literature on leadership for inclusion does explore *how* the concept of leadership can be modified. Many of these modifications attempt to dissuade leaders from being overly fixated on integrating all policies and practices into one all-enveloping totality. Leaders should be open to contradictions and not see them as 'an annoyance to be wished away' (Agbenyega and Sharma 2014, 126). They should warmly embrace complex empirical data as 'interruptions' that provoke fruitful 'self-questioning' (Ainscow 2020, 10). Leaders should develop a *critical mindfulness,* such that they 'regularly ask questions of themselves in order to avoid taking actions that may be domineering and meaningless' (Agbenyega and Sharma 2014, 129). They should also, it is suggested, become comfortable inhabiting a leadership space that is a continual 'problem-based dichotomy' of 'complex forces' which generate 'conflict and dilemma' (Rayner 2009, 443).

These suggestions, drawn from the literature on leadership for inclusion, are more than the simple assertions that leadership is frequently complex and problematic, or that good leadership does not avoid or duck organisational difficulties, or even that effective leadership practice revolves around rigorous, critical self-reflection. Although these are undoubtedly true and are fixtures in more general leadership research, there is something more profound going on here: it is the assertion that leadership for inclusion should not be aiming at systemic certainty and control, and that it should instead aspire to more contingent, locally varied practices which mirror, and are therefore more sensitively attuned to, the uncertainty, the 'unpredictability … [the] messiness' of effective inclusive pedagogy (Osberg and Biesta 2008, 324). The suggestion is that leadership will not get there unless it modifies its ways, unless it moves away from a reductive and simplistic fixation on the power of the integrated, problem-free organisation: as Rayner (2009) puts it, 'there is no easy solution or template even if one is claimed, and then conveniently called best practice' (page 438).

A number of tricky challenges

Thus, we have reached the point where we can step back and consider the challenges that inclusion presents to the concept of leadership. We have been led here by existing research into leadership for inclusion which has, alongside its mobilisation of more practical advice, necessarily articulated some key challenges and suggested modifications to the concept of effective leadership in response. Perhaps the most significant challenge is linked to the idea of leadership as *influence* and all that this implies. Often, the recognition that leadership is a form of influence is an acknowledgement that leadership can exist in distributed forms (Harris 2008): there are, after all, many formal and non-formal sites of influence in any early years setting. The link between influence and other leadership models has also been well established and Bush (2019) usefully distinguishes between influence and authority, with the latter being linked to *more formal* power structures. Yet to have influence is to exert power in the sense of deflecting or modifying the path of another. If we are influenced by a colleague we allow ourselves, however consciously or willingly, to adopt some of their professional behaviours, or their professional values, or their professional vision. In whichever domain their particular influence over us exists, we *integrate* ourselves a little more closely and smoothly into *their way of thinking*. In a common-sense way, this is how effective leadership works, and this process of influencing others need not be seen negatively. Indeed, it is the way that middle level leaders successfully ensure that their colleagues begin to adopt more effective teaching and learning practices, or the way that senior leaders get practitioners to buy in to their vision for the organisation. The point here is not to pretend that there is a negative, insidious aspect to the idea of influence (although it can manifest itself in this way). The point instead is to note that influencing another is, in part at least, about bringing them into some kind of alignment, or some kind of productive *integration* with your way of viewing, doing or dealing with things.

The idea of integration is, in turn, the key aspect for the discussion here. We may be reminded of the idea that inclusion aspires to be much *more* than a process through which diverse learners are integrated into a pre-existing culture and order (Ainscow 2020). Rather it aspires to be a situation in which children's diverse and varied subjectivities may emerge, and in which plurality is privileged, over the construction of 'common ground' (Osberg and Biesta 2008, 324). These aspirations:

> [challenge] the conventional logic of schooling whereby everything possible is done to *reduce* the differences between the teacher and those being educated on the one hand, and the differences between the various individuals being educated by the teacher (e.g. in terms of age, gender, ability, interests, etc.) on the other.
>
> (Osberg and Biesta 2008, 324)

Reducing difference, it is argued, actively '*prevents* education from taking place' (Osberg and Biesta 2008, 324).

If leadership implies a movement towards integration, as we have already noted, we should also consider that integration implies a partial erasure of difference, the very difference that is prioritised above. Does this mean that *leadership* for *inclusion* is being pulled in two opposing directions?

At this point it is worth pausing to avoid allowing ourselves to drop too neatly into a chasm of inaction created by a perceived binary opposition. Identifying a conceptual complexity in play here does not mean we should fall into the trap of thinking that *either* leadership and inclusion are completely aligned, *or* that they are mutually opposed, and that if they cannot be in one category, then they must be the other. The point is rather to consider the challenge that the notion of inclusion presents to the notion of leadership, and to begin to formulate an informed response to this challenge.

We know that educational settings still need to be led, and we would probably accept the idea that all organisations have to have an integrative function at *some* level, otherwise they would not really be institutions or organisations in any meaningful sense. The action of belonging to an educational community obliges the individual to willingly adapt themselves to some common ground, even if only at a relatively basic level. To deny any of this is to suggest that we are giving up on the idea of organisational coherence completely. Yet, we are probably also persuaded by the idea that a rich inclusive pedagogy will probably be constructed on an idea of emergent subjectivity that needs to resist, at some level, this integrative function. Where is the way forward?

A response to this might begin by asking another question: *what is leadership for?* This is a, perhaps worryingly, broad question, but it is similar to an important question that Biesta (2010) suggests has ceased to get sufficient attention: *what is education for?* As Biesta points out, discussion around the broader purposes of education has been largely replaced by discussion about the mechanics of effective learning. The result has been to bolster an assumption that, as long as learning is taking place, things are working well, without any real focus on what is being learnt or why. The concept of learning becomes detached from debate surrounding its purpose.

In a similar way, leadership is not simply a state of being, or an activity that must be carried out eternally and perpetually just because we happen to have organisations that need leading. Educational leadership should be conceptualised with a larger ethical, moral or political purpose, as has frequently been argued (Bottery 2019; Forde and Torrance 2017; Fullan 2003). This acknowledgement, that explicit discussion about the ends and purposes of leadership is necessary, is the starting point for a response to the tricky problem explored above; the productive re-conciliation of the integrationist tendencies of leadership, and the attention to difference implied by inclusion. The models of contingent, reflexive, *interruption-tolerant* leadership for inclusion explored above (Agbenyega and Sharma 2014; Ainscow 2020; Rayner 2009) all help to clarify *how* leadership for inclusion might modify the integrationist tendencies of leadership itself. All that is left is to incorporate discussion of the purpose of educational leadership.

I would argue that where inclusion and diversity are aspects of a *range* of purposes and priorities for leaders, the situation will always be problematic. It will be problematic because other purposes, other priorities, will emphasise themselves, and, in efforts to efficiently meet these other purposes, leadership will stop concerning itself with encouraging diverse learning subjectivities to emerge (Osberg and Biesta 2008), and will rather focus on common ground across the organisation to provide an effective organisational response to whichever challenge happens to be presenting itself. Perhaps the need to improve some key performance indicators will be prioritised, or it may be dealing with tighter resourcing, or even developing a new national curriculum. Arguably, unless leadership deliberately and consistently maintains a primary purpose of developing inclusion and diversity, it will be forever metaphorically *putting to one side* the tricky challenge that this entails, even if only for a period of time, to concentrate on aims and purposes that appear to be more tangible, more focused, more measurable and, crucially, more amenable to leadership activity that rests on shared and integrated identities and subjectivities.

It may seem, finally, that the key focus should be on persuading leaders that leading for inclusion and diversity is worthy of being placed as a top priority and purpose for leadership activity. There is much moral, ethical and political support for such a position, especially when links to social equity and social justice are emphasised. Yet perhaps we are not far away from a *challenger* priority that will persuasively and comprehensively justify its own need to be the primary purpose for learning and, therefore, for leadership in any learning organisation. As a society we may not be far from proclaiming that learning, and leadership for learning, should place ecological and economic sustainability at the heart of its endeavour, with all else as subsidiary. The concept of leadership may find this purpose irresistible, and leadership for inclusion may struggle, once again, to make its voice heard.

Key points

- Leadership for inclusion can refer to the workforce, learners or both.
- It can be considered as a practical problem, or as a theoretical and philosophical one.
- Leaders in educational settings can pursue a range of activities and approaches which support inclusion and embrace diversity.
- Leadership often sets itself the functions of solving problems, negotiating challenges, integrating disparate elements into a cohesive system, and developing networks of influence to build common identity. These may disrupt a thoroughgoing commitment to the implications of inclusive pedagogy.
- Leadership, without constant reference to a guiding purpose, articulated around inclusion, may not be as practically supportive of inclusion as it wishes to be.

Further reading

The following chapter explores many of the practical implications of inclusion for leaders:

Lumby, J. (2019) Leadership for diversity and inclusion. In Bush, T., Bell, L. and Middlewood, D. (eds.) *Principles of Educational Leadership and Management* (3rd edition). London: Sage.

References

Agbenyega, J. and Sharma, U. (2014) Leading inclusive education: measuring 'effective' leadership for inclusive education through a Bourdieuian lens. In Loreman, T. and Forlin, C. (eds.) *Measuring Inclusive Education*. Bingley: Emerald Publishing.

Ainscow, M. (2020) Promoting inclusion and equity in education: lessons from international experiences, *Nordic Journal of Studies in Educational Policy*, 6 (1), 7–16. doi:10.1080/20020317.2020.1729587 (accessed: 1 December 2020).

Biesta, G. (2010) *Good Education in an Age of Measurement*. Abingdon: Routledge.

Bottery, M. (2019) An ethics of educational leadership for complex and turbulent times. In Bush, T., Bell, L. and Middlewood, D. (eds.) *Principles of Educational Leadership and Management* (3rd edition). London: Sage.

Bush, T. (2019) Models of educational leadership. In Bush, T., Bell, L. and Middlewood, D. (eds.) *Principles of Educational Leadership and Management* (3rd edition). London: Sage.

Carmeli, A., Reiter-Palmon, R. and Ziv, E. (2010) Inclusive leadership and employee involvement in creative tasks in the workplace: the mediating role of psychological safety, *Psychology Faculty Publications* 43 [Online]. Available at: https://digitalcommons.unomaha.edu/psychfacpub/43 (accessed: 9 December 2020).

Cochran-Smith, M., Cummings Carney, M., Stringer Keefe, E., Burton, S., Chang, W., Fernandez, M., Miller, A., Sanchez, J. and Baker, M. (2018) *Reclaiming Accountability in Teacher Education*. New York: Teachers' College Press.

Fang, Y-C., Chen, J-Y., Wang, M-J. and Chen, C-Y. (2019) The impact of inclusive leadership on employees' innovative behaviors: the mediation of psychological capital, *Frontiers in Psychology* [Online]. doi:10.3389/fpsyg.2019.01803 (accessed: 9 December 2020).

Forde, C. and Torrance, D. (2017) Social justice and leadership development, *Professional Development in Education*, 43 (1), 106–120. doi:10.1080/19415257.2015.1131733 (accessed: 20 November 2020).

Fullan, M. (2003) *The Moral Imperative for School Leadership*. Thousand Oaks: Corwin.

Grass, D. (2017) Justification and critique of educational reforms in Austria: how teachers and head teachers (re-)frame new governance, *Journal of Social Science Education*, 16 (4), 6–74.

Harris, A. (2008) *Distributed School Leadership*. Abingdon: Routledge.

Kuknor, S. C. and Bhattacharya, S. (2020) Inclusive leadership: new age leadership to foster organizational inclusion, *European Journal of Training and Development* [Online]. doi:10.1108/EJTD-07-2019-0132 (accessed: 20 November 2020).

Liasidou, A. and Antoniou, A. (2015) Head teachers' leadership for social justice and inclusion, *School Leadership & Management*, 35(4), 347–364. doi:10.1080/13632434.2015.1010499 (accessed: 20 November 2020).

Lumby, J. (2019) Leadership for diversity and inclusion. In Bush, T., Bell, L. and Middlewood, D. (eds.) *Principles of Educational Leadership and Management* (3rd edition). London: Sage.

Morrissey, B. (2020) Theorising leadership for inclusion in the Irish context: a triadic typology within a distributed ecosystem, *Management in Education* [Online]. doi:10.1177/0892020620942507 (accessed: 20 November 2020).

Nutbrown, C., Clough, P. and Atherton, C. (2013) *Inclusion in the Early Years* (2nd edition). London: Sage.

Osberg, D. and Biesta, G. (2008) The emergent curriculum: navigating a complex course between unguided learning and planned enculturation, *Journal of Curriculum Studies*, 40 (3), 313–328.

Oskarsdottir, E., Donnelly, V., Turner-Cmuchal, M. and Florian, L. (2020) Inclusive school leaders–their role in raising the achievement of all learners, *Journal of Educational Administration*, 58 (5), 521–537.

Rayner, S. (2009) Educational diversity and learning leadership: a proposition, some principles and a model of inclusive leadership? *Educational Review*, 61 (4), 433–447.

Roberts-Holmes, G. (2020) Towards a pluralist and participatory accountability. In Cameron, C. and Moss, P. (eds.) *Transforming Early Childhood in England: Towards a Democratic Education*. London: UCL Press. doi:10.14324/111.9781787357167.

Sahlberg, P. (2015) *Finnish Lessons 2.0*. New York:Teachers College, Columbia University.

Spillane, J. (2006) *Distributed Leadership*. San Francisco: Jossey Bass.

Zhu, J., Xu, S. and Zhang, B. (2020) The paradoxical effect of inclusive leadership on subordinates' creativity, *Frontiers in Psychology* [Online]. doi:10.3389/fpsyg.2019.02960 (accessed: 9 December 2020).

3 Seeing children's learning subjectivities for inclusive pedagogy in early childhood education

Carmel Conn

Introduction

In his poem, 'What is play?', autistic poet and scholar Wenn Lawson describes adults and children exhorting him to go and play as a child, not realising that this was something in which he was already engaged. He describes the childhood pleasure he derived in a sensory-based experience of play, in 'all that glitters; blue, green and red' and a sparkly string that 'gives me such a feeling' (Lawson 2006, 19). What Lawson describes in this poem is a 'differential becoming' (Barad 2007) in his orientation to what was environmentally significant, but he also draws attention to the fact that this subjectivity was not well understood by those around him. Inclusive education is currently theorised as the ability of educational practitioners to recognise the differences children bring to their learning and to 'perceive more' about the ways in which children engage with learning (Florian and Graham 2014). Inclusive pedagogy is framed as enactments that flow from an ethics of responsibility and care, and belief in the ability of all children to learn (Hart and Drummond 2013). Lawson's poem serves to remind us that for some children this may be a more difficult accomplishment. Children's subjectivities are not always easily recognised and may appear to challenge the ability of practitioners to know how to adapt their practices, particularly where what is perceived by practitioners is 'complex embodiment', as Siebers (2017) describes it. The aim of this chapter is to explore how practitioners are able to perceive more when children's learning subjectivities are harder to see and are not well understood. I will propose that certain kinds of cultural practices are critical to the process of seeing learning subjectivities, most importantly, a willingness to affirm children, not according to universal standards, but as singular subjects who are engaged in making sense of the world in meaningful ways (Lenz Taguchi 2010). Following posthumanist theories of education, I will argue that close attention is needed to children's body-world experiences and to the existence of connections with human but also more-than-human aspects of their learning environment (Taylor 2013). It is through the practice of careful attention to children's orientation and activity, as well as of the active qualities of both human and nonhuman entities with which they engage, that a more inclusive gaze is achieved.

DOI: 10.4324/9781003163206-5

Posthumanist theories of education seek to locate children in a field of relational experience, seeing them as an intrinsic part of that experience and fully embedded within it (Moss 2019). What is articulated is nonhuman-centred relationships where one aspect of experience is not privileged over another and where material things are identified as having agency that foreground children's subjectivities (Holmes and Jones 2016). What is important is that practitioners attempt to see the world as it offers itself to children in terms of possibilities for action. Only in this way can they usefully know about directions for learning and how to support these (Kuby 2018). It is recommended that practitioners gain new ways of seeing children's subjectivities by taking steps to deconstruct practice (Allan 2008), and it is this process of deconstruction that will be explored here with reference to my own experience as educator and then researcher in inclusive education in relation to young autistic children. Autistic children often experience the most exclusion in our education systems today and I want to explore here an important and recurring motif of my educational practice across the years: young children's relational experiences of material objects in everyday classrooms. This is in order to illustrate how de-centring the human and attending to the material allows one to begin to understand what goes on in 'in-between relationships' (Lenz Taguchi 2011) and the possible nature of differential embodiment. The learning possibilities of a young autistic child's experience of the material in his classroom is hypothetically explored using personal accounts of childhood sensory-perceptual experiences produced by autistic writers. I will argue that acknowledging children's sense-making in relation to the more-than-human produces new knowledge for practitioners and supports different kinds of decisions about pedagogical action.

The need to widen our idea of 'what is' in children's learning

In perceiving more in early childhood education, it is important to consider *how* children are perceived. Children, particularly those who are marginalised, are often categorised according to a particular population, learning need or diagnostic group, but this tends to fix their subjectivities and flatten out their individual personalities. Describing someone according to a set of criteria or in terms of a developmental framework reduces them to the descriptors that are provided and constrains the ways in which they can be thought about. This often has the effect of seemingly allowing judgements to be made and conclusions to be reached about progress and what needs to be learned, but ones that do not feel satisfactory or even legitimate when thinking about the child one knows from everyday learning contexts. As Simmons and Watson (2018) point out in writing about disability, such reductionist ways of thinking give rise to ambiguous shifts in how children are perceived, for example, from communicative to non-communicative, from sociable to non-sociable, from able to disabled, as they move from more to less enabling environments.

Reducing anyone to a set of criteria is problematic, but for young children it can easily lead to assumptions about their abilities and the imposition of subjectivities that are wide of the mark. By contrast, seeing children in non-reductionist, dimensionally complex ways serves to open up the issue of subjectivity, allowing children to emerge as 'singular beings' (Lenz Taguchi 2010). It signals more possibilities in terms of children's learning trajectories and broadens out the ways in which human potential is conceived. Proper recognition of children's singularities as subjects implies seeing these as unfixed, often contradictory and contingent on unique sets of personal interests and concerns, individual histories and personal resources, in addition to social and cultural practices. The interest of the educational practitioner should be in what the child is interested in, how they individually engage, what they seek out and what they desire (Moss 2019). There needs to be an expansive view of children and a lightness of approach to offering propositions about their learning experiences and subjectivities. In early childhood education, a pedagogy of relationship and listening is infused with playful curiosity and an openness to children and what they do, practitioners not imposing assumptions about children, but formulating and rejecting ideas as they reflect on their own knowledge and practices (Rinaldi 2006).

In respect of the above, the concept of child-centredness requires some consideration. Being child-centred in the sense of focusing on children's activity and following their lead is thought to be an important practice in early childhood education (Siraj et al. 2019). The term child-centredness, however, can suggest that it is the child who is at the centre of experience, but, as Biesta (2014) points out, the key concept should be experience itself. It is experience rather than individual brains and minds that should be the focus of consideration in education, with learning characterised as children's inquiry, experimentation and sense-making in relation to social, material and spatial environments (Kuby 2018). Children's learning experiences take the form of transactions with what is of significance to them and what they see as possible in terms of action—what is sometimes termed *intra*-actions as a way of emphasising the emergent nature of the experience (Barad 2007). Learning comes about through a capacity to see connections between things and by finding meaning in learning activities, a process that is supported by pedagogical actions taken by practitioners (Biesta 2014). Increasingly, the notion of the child as a separate and autonomous learner is challenged. Children have agency, but this does not exist as an innate capacity, detached from the immediacy of their environments and something that they bring with them. Rather agency emerges as a result of children's engagement with what is outside of themselves, shaped by the interplay of the individual child and environmental affordances and constraints (Tudge 2008). Brain, body and environment, moreover, exist in non-hierarchical ways so that it is never the case that the child is simply the superior and intentional subject who causes events to happen.

Children's common worlds

In trying to perceive more it is important to consider *what* is the focus of our thinking about children. Following the work of Bruno Latour, Taylor (2013) draws our attention to children's 'common worlds' which she describes as composed of entities that are at once discursive and material, living and inert, human and more-than-human. She argues that much of what gets lost in trying to represent children's life-worlds is the fullness and intra-active quality of children's experiences in relation to the many different entities that make up their environments, that is, what is experienced by them as *real*. For Taylor and others, it is not individual minds, but children's relations with 'things' that constitute their common worlds and therefore the basis of their learning. Supporting children's learning is first about seeing what these things are. In common worlds, children's modes of thinking are embodied and very often sensory, affective, contingent and experimental. The challenge for practitioners is to *see* these ways of being in order to know when to intervene in children's activities and what support to offer.

The posthumanist turn in education has meant much greater attention to material things in learning contexts and the ways in which they influence children's learning experiences. Lenz Taguchi (2009) argues that we need to think about the impact of the nonhuman as well as the human in learning, as she writes, the impact of chairs, the feel of dots and floors, and the quality of sound. Experiences of material things often constitute the foreground for children, particularly for young children for whom representing experience in language is probably a reduction of the vitality of that experience. Children's learning subjectivities are often discursively produced by adults, but this may be prematurely done (Jones et al. 2010). The need is to think about their lived experiences and not leap to representing these through discursive practices that quickly draw conclusions for the purpose of completing assessments and writing reports. Assessment practices should be seen as partial and provisional in that respect, and of necessity ongoing (Osberg and Biesta 2010).

In stepping away from the human and seeing children as located in a field of human and more-than-human relational experience, it is important to contemplate the liveliness of objects or 'thing power' as van Goidsenhoven and Schauwer (2020) describe it. Presenting one child's experience of playing with a stone, Jones (2016) notes that the child's attention is not 'to', but with, toward, in and around the object. She writes that in talking to the child about his stone play, she had the sense of asking him to subtract from the intensity of his experience of the stone and lose its 'emergent multiplicity' (page 117). Jones argues that it is better to spend time following the 'and ...' within children's experiences, that is, tracing all its many parts or connections, rather than foreclosing it by seeking meaning too soon. In doing this, it is essential not to privilege one aspect of experience over another, seeing the child, for example, as the driver of the experience or sole performative agent. Children are an intrinsic part of their educational experience and are fully entangled with it. It is important therefore to see how matter and artefacts are performative agents too in the way they have an energy and determine how a learning event unfolds. It is important to focus on the 'in-betweenness' for children and entities within their environments in order to know more and begin to understand their learning experiences (Lenz Taguchi 2011).

This is what Lenz Taguchi (2010) has described as an inclusive gaze. She calls for teachers and theorists to adopt a 'much wider expanded gaze' that shifts away from interpersonal and hierarchical interactions towards the inclusion of the performative agency of matter and the intra-active processes that take place in-between the material, the child's emotional response and their sense-making. If we move our gaze in this way, she argues, it becomes possible to see the world *as it offers itself to the child* as well as possibilities in terms of directions for learning. Children's learning can begin anywhere and go any place, 'as in a centrifugal movement around a specific problem and theme of investigation' (Lenz Taguchi 2010, 27). Educational practitioners need to pay attention and grasp that fact for all children, with all of the differences they bring to their learning. In this way, practitioners are able to know when and how to challenge learning processes as they unfold and to judge achievement when it happens. Such an approach to practice should counteract an over-reliance on pre-ordained learning outcomes and normative assessment frames. These practices speed up the process of making judgements about children, but reduce the possibility of a contemplative gaze, making it more likely that learning will be judged before it even takes place (Clark 2020).

Binary relationships in children's learning experiences

Lenz Taguchi and others writing in the posthumanist turn have argued that adopting an inclusive gaze involves moving ourselves from a position of knowing to one of *not yet knowing*. Allan (2008) describes this shift as requiring a certain determination by practitioners to shed familiar ways of thinking about children and take up the challenge to think within confusion. She comments that educational practitioners need to become literate by unravelling pre-existing knowledge and assumptions and deconstructing practice. This is a process that has been associated with a specific set of steps, beginning with the identification of important sets of binary relationships that operate within pedagogy (Lather 2013). In my own research, I have sought to deconstruct inclusive educational practices by examining the binaries of teacher-pupil dialogic relationships (Conn et al. 2020) and social-material practices (Conn 2019a). A focus on binary relationships allows greater understanding of the ways in which entities come together to shape pedagogical practices and produce learning. In this chapter, I explore the binary of human and material relationships further by providing an account of the intra-activity of one child's subjectivity and the performative agency of a material object. I describe the ways in which the material can exert force within learning and allow or constrain certain actions by the child. Reversing dominant hierarchies–from human-nonhuman to nonhuman-human relations–opens up

48 *Carmel Conn*

new vistas in terms of what is real within learning experience and the nature of pupil agency and sense-making. So central is this process of deconstructing practice for inclusive pedagogy that I am going to use the remainder of the chapter to examine it in more detail.

On light, learning and play: a child is distracted by the interactive whiteboard

Deconstructing practice is what expands our pedagogical gaze and makes it properly inclusive. This is what allows children's learning subjectivities really to be seen and to be properly engaged with. It is a process that requires a complex understanding of causality within learning experiences, however, and the bringing together of important but hard to see body-world experiences, personal ways of knowing and the role of emotion in this. Some children's subjectivities are harder to see and require more imaginative work and inner confidence on the part of the practitioner, and this is what I want to explore next in relation to one child's learning experience in an early years classroom. I want to present a plausible account of the ways in which a practitioner can 'think through teaching' (Hart 2000) by taking steps to deconstruct their practice in relation to learning.

In my experience as a practitioner and, later, as a researcher of inclusive education, I have come across many moments of practice when I have found it hard to understand children's learning subjectivities. In this part of the chapter, I explore a hypothetical situation which nevertheless provides, I hope, an authentic and credible illustration of the argument presented here. The situation is that of a young boy, who has recently received a diagnosis of autism, being highly distracted by the glowing screen of the interactive whiteboard in his classroom, not able to turn his gaze away from it when it is switched on. Such a situation serves to emphasise the importance of the human-material binary in education and the connectedness that children experience in relation to material things, but it also illustrates the way in which the nature of this connection is not easily understood by adults. In this case, it is imagined that the boy's teacher has tried to gain his attention by calling his name gently, but also by telling him more authoritatively to listen, but these instructions have been ignored, or so it seems to the teacher. It is understandable perhaps that such a conclusion should be reached if the view taken of the child is that their intentionality is what always drives their action. Such an interpretation may lead to the issue being seen as one of compliance and provoke irritation or even anxiety in the teacher, who may see the child's unresponsiveness as a challenge to her authority. It may give rise to feelings in the teacher of being 'cast off' by a child, as Jones et al. (2010) write, causing a professional crisis of belief in her ability to teach this particular child. The apparent strangeness of a child's compulsion to look at the interactive whiteboard and seeming obliviousness to everything around, moreover, may lead a teacher to feel out of her depth and conclude that the child's needs exceed what she is able to support

(Florian and Graham 2014). If the only solution is to turn off the interactive whiteboard, then the presence of this child in the classroom becomes a threat to the teacher's accountability to teach all her pupils.

The belief that any difficulty in learning is a problem of the child is a potent one in educational practice that supports the development of ideas about children who are different from other children and able to achieve only in limited ways (Hart and Drummond 2013). This in turn can result in practitioners concluding that they lack the capacity to teach a child using appropriate pedagogies, which they may believe exist somewhere else and are different in some way to how other children are taught (Florian 2019). By reversing the binary that is operating however–in the instance described above, that of the subjectivity of the child and the interactive whiteboard as the material object of his attention–one can see that another interpretation is possible. By emphasising the presence of the material in the child's subjective experience and considering what it *does* for the child, it is possible to see that powerful agency exists in the material properties of the interactive whiteboard when it is switched on. This, perhaps, is the most vital aspect of the child's experience. Such an interpretation fits well with current explanations of autism, particularly those provided by autistic people themselves. These emphasise difference in sensory-perceptual processing and present being autistic as a matter of attention to different 'saliences' in the environment, that is, what stands out as of significance in perception (Milton et al. 2018). People orient perceptually in different ways and are attentive to different aspects of their environment. Autistic people tend to orient themselves more strongly perceptually according to their interests and the personal ways in which they experience stimuli, more than to shared social meanings (Murray et al. 2005). Very often, autistic people have different sensory responses in their perceptual experience, some reporting heightened sensitivity in terms of what they can see, hear, smell, touch and taste, and others seeking out sensory stimulation. Autistic people may experience difference in coordinating their own internal responses to experience and their ability to inhibit incoming stimulation. It may be the case that they get 'pulled in' by an experience and become unable to shut off from it or even become overwhelmed and experience a kind of sensory overload (Lawson 2011).

Differences in sensory processing are important since these can mean a stimulus is experienced more intensely and with greater fixity of focus, creating an 'attention tunnel' that makes it hard to attend to other stimuli (Murray 2018). Autistic writers describe being captured in their attention by objects in their environment. Naoki Higashida (2013), for example, writes of details 'jumping out' at him and claiming his attention so that he is not able to concentrate on anything else, whilst Camille Pang (2020) describes being mesmerised as a young child, aged 5, by dust particles floating across the sunlight that streamed in through her bedroom window, something she could have done all day if allowed. Autistic writers describe the intensity of their experience as one of a single sense going into overdrive so that they lose track of their other senses and become 'deaf' to what is going on around them (Murray 2018). The intrusion of other stimuli, moreover, such as a sudden loud noise or someone being addressed, can be experienced as a shock that can feel both shattering and even painful (Tammet 2006).

Considering a child's experience in terms of the impact of perception of the material makes it possible to see that it is the liveliness of an object, rather than the subjectivity of the child, that could be the positive force controlling an event. For an autistic child looking at an interactive whiteboard, this may be described in terms of the intensity of the light to pull his or her attention to it, to the exclusion of everything else that is going on around in the classroom. It is this aspect of the environment that has powerful agency and exerts the most influence by virtue of the child's neurodivergent cognition. It is not that a child is distracted by the interactive whiteboard, but that the interactive whiteboard mesmerises a child.

Such an explanation of one child's experience in the classroom could provide a watershed moment in the thinking of a practitioner. It becomes possible to see all children's experience in this way, to think less about their actions and intentions, and more about the ways in which material objects and other aspects of learning environments present themselves and create an impact. It is possible to see, for example, that a large empty space such as the school hall calls out to children to run, but without clearly indicating where they should stop, or alternatively, that a space crowded with people offers no suggestion of a way through. It becomes possible to imagine that the sounds one experiences as being in the background are in the foreground for some children and indistinguishable to them in terms of their meaning and relevance. Visual sequences of things that 'pop out' at the practitioner may stay hidden for some children and require clues as to their whereabouts. The motor feedback loop of child, hand, brush and paper may constrain the making of recognisable pre-writing shapes and require a much larger scale for an accessible learning environment. For children who experience difficulty in gripping, grasping and stepping, it is possible to see that the prospect of using scissors, doing up buttons and walking down the stairs evoke feelings of nervousness, panic and a strong 'flight' response. Any expectation that these feelings are easily controlled lacks the understanding that it is not necessarily the child who is the superior agent and the one who is 'in control'.

Pedagogical possibilities of 'in-between' relationships

Any sense that material objects and spatial arrangements exert force within learning may lead practitioners to re-arrange or remove something so that it is not a distraction. In the case of the child who is unable to look away from the interactive whiteboard, this might involve screening off the board from the child's view as a way of counteracting his inability to inhibit this stimulus and enable him to focus on his learning. But more focused attention to what goes on between children and entities within learning environments–their experience of 'in-between relationships', as Lenz Taguchi (2011) describes it–may lead to another direction in terms of support. Closer attention to children and to the ways in which they respond within intra-actions could lead practitioners to conclude that the experience is a positive one and something to encourage rather than control. An ethics of responsibility and care tends to operate within early childhood education and this requires attentiveness to children's responses in learning and an open-ended approach to interpreting children's behaviour (Moss 2019). When a child is happy, relaxed and thoroughly absorbed, then the decision may be made to see what unfolds and not to interrupt the flow of the experience.

Such a decision may be more likely for practitioners who are confident in their abilities to support children. To remain in a state of not fully understanding learning subjectivities, but to allow events to unfold anyway, requires self-belief on the part of the practitioner and a set of values centred on the capability of all children to learn (Conn 2019b). Important in this would be wider institutional values and the existence of a responsive culture of inclusion invested in raising achievement in the context of all children (Nutbrown and Clough 2013). Where difference is seen as a virtue in children's learning and where deficit is deemed an unacceptable term to use to describe children, a culture of pedagogical experimentation may be a highly valued one (Florian and Black-Hawkins 2011). A belief may operate that children's differing engagement with learning is a pedagogical challenge to be met with the finding of creative solutions. Appreciation of children's competencies in learning and trust that their activity is meaningful, even when that meaning is not well understood, would be key underpinning pedagogical principles here (Hart and Drummond 2013).

A decision to stay with the 'in-between' leads to new possibilities in learning. To use the example of the boy and the interactive whiteboard once again, consideration of personal accounts written by autistic people suggest that 'in-between' relationships are of value. Many autobiographical accounts have been published by autistic people and often these include descriptions of childhood sensory-perceptual experiences. Some focus specifically on the perception of light, invariably describing it as a pleasurable experience that brought feelings of happiness and relaxation. Daniel Tammet (2006) describes his fascination with the 'shiny, wet surface' of bubbles in his nursery (page 27), for example, and with light reflected off the polished surface of leaflets he collected as a child. Naoki Higashida (2013) comments that direct daylight could sometimes 'feel like pins', but that his flapping hands filtered the light and made it feel pleasant. He says of autistic people, 'when we're bathed in light, we're happy' (page 102). Autistic perception is defined by Lucy Blackman (1999) as her experience of 'light, shade, colour and movement' that created an 'enchanted world of light and sudden gaps into which people and objects moved' (page 26). Blackman describes how the world was perceived by her, not in terms of dimensionality and depth, but as flickerings and fluctuations caught at the edge of her vision. As a child, morning light made the air feel as if it was 'like spun sunshine, but soft enough to stun me' so that she could only see that and not hear anyone speaking to her (page 116).

In autistic accounts, the perception of light is often described as releasing strongly positive feelings of contentment, safety and aliveness. Daniel Tammet writes that it was being surrounded by 'shiny, trembling towers' of stacked coins that allowed him to feel 'calm and secure inside' (2006, 78). According to Tammet, it was this kind of experience that enabled him to manage the 'daily hubbub' and social pressures of being the oldest of nine siblings in a small family home. A similar sense of well-being is described by Wenn Lawson (2000) in recalling the childhood experience of spinning the wheel of his bike, watching the light gleam off the mudguards. 'It seemed to go on forever,' he writes, 'it was so intoxicating and I felt so alive' (page 2). Lawson comments that it was this experience that made him feel safe as a child and gave him a sense of connection to 'life and feeling'.

As with many autistic writers and scholars, Jasmine Lee O'Neill (1999) declares that it is her inner world of heightened sensitivity that allows her to feel grounded and gives her 'private fortitude'. 'I, myself, love all my senses', she writes, 'and cherish the profound experiences they bring to my life' (page 28). For O'Neill, these support creativity and 'provide a lovely feeling to me'. She describes the pleasurable 'entire body stimulus' that comes from looking at something and allowing oneself to be drawn to it, but points out that this is something non-autistic people are able to experience too. Writing about autistic perception, Manning and Massumi (2014) also describe the joy of attention that senses colour, sound, smell, rhythm and emotion in intense, non-hierarchical and non-representational ways. They argue that autistic perception is a more complete engagement with the world as it presents itself in the field of perception. Attention is distributed more equally amongst all stimuli for autistic people and modes of being are not necessarily centred on language. As Manning and Massumi argue, non-autistic people are able to attend in this way too, but differences in socio-linguistic development mean they are more likely to subtract from their sensory-perceptual experience at speed and attend more immediately to social meanings beyond the immediate milieu.

Such accounts of autistic perception help us think about what kinds of subjectivities are produced in the 'in-between' relationships described. It is not hard to see, perhaps, that what is produced are *autistic subjectivities* and the healthy emergence of children who are able to be themselves and experience emotional well-being. Pedagogical possibilities begin to open up when it is considered that conditions for learning are robustly present, in the form of feelings of safety and security, positive emotional states, absorption and creativity. Thinking about the boy's experience of the interactive whiteboard once more, being allowed to experience such a positive flow experience may provide him with a way of managing a challenging social environment and give him some important downtime. In an educational system, where environmental conditions are often cited as mitigating against learning and as producing increased levels of stress for autistic children (Jones et al. 2014), opportunities for downtime may be critical to the success of a child's school placement.

In addition to providing an experience of well-being, however, it is possible to see that the in-betweenness of boy and interactive whiteboard could also be a site of learning and development. Following autistic accounts of the perceptual experience of light, embodiment that involves feelings of pleasure, excitement and absorption could be suggestive of an episode of play for example. Play is defined in terms of its spontaneity, intrinsic motivation, positive emotion and relaxed state (Sutton-Smith 2001). Feelings of enjoyment and creativity, flow-states and affirmative experiences of self are all characteristics of play (Brown 2009). In describing sensory-perceptual experiences in childhood, some autistic writers do indeed describe this as a playful mode of being that reflected their experience of the world and ways of making sense. Play is theorised as a form of adaptive behaviour that supports exploration of the environment and the trying out of new possibilities (Pellegrini et al. 2007). For young autistic children, this may take an appropriately neurodivergent form, one better suited to sensory- rather than linguistic-based sense-making (Conn 2015).

A neurodivergent developmental pathway probably means that autistic perception and sensory responses support sense-making in relation to the world as it is experienced autistically, but, as Mottron (2017) argues, it could also support social cognition and the development of social understandings. It is not clear that intersubjectivity supports cognitive development for autistic children in the same way that it does for non-autistic children, and it may be the case that some understandings about the world are produced more individualistically. For example, in his award-winning book *Diary of a Young Naturalist*, Dara McAnulty writes that, much more than talking to others, it is his 'daydreaming and thinking' and letting his mind wander that best provides him with opportunities to know and understand the world (McAnulty 2020). Interestingly, some autistic writers state that they gained understandings about the social world from their individualistic sense impressions. Dawn Prince-Hughes (2004) writes about how she kept copious ethological-type notes on the outer observable actions of her peers as a way of trying to make sense of them as people. Similarly, Donna Williams (1992) describes how it was her 'felt sense' of other people, one that was sensorily attentive to their distinctive bodily qualities and the sensory impression of things they owned, that gave her reliable insight into people's personalities. Specifically in relation to the experience of light, autistic writer Camille Pang (2020) describes how observing light refraction from her mother's crystal oyster shell, and the way in which it broke into 'its full spectrum of colours' in the sunlight, helped her think about complexity within the social world. Like other autistic writers, she notes that her formulation of theories about people and social phenomena often arise from her close observations of the natural and material world.

Thus, consideration of the interactive whiteboard in terms of what it does for the child allows us to see that it may perform many actions. It may 'dance' in the quality of its light and mesmerise and pull the child to it. It may block out other stimuli and command the child's capacity to attend. It may also provide feelings of pleasure and entertainment as an experience of play, with associated benefits of personal well-being, safety, absorption and a sense of wholeness. Finally, it may allow the autistic child to create meanings in relation to the world, including the world of people and language. What is clear is that for the thoughtful practitioner, curious about the binary relationships that operate in their classroom, it is close attention to children's individual responses and openness to other ways of being in the world that allows engagement with these kinds of differential embodiments. Above all, the ability to take a stance as a 'modest witness' (Blaise et al. 2017) is key. This is an understanding of knowledge creation taken from feminist and ecological studies that emphasises the importance of not standing in judgement of others and of accepting the partial ways in which we can know someone. Seeking to understand others is an ongoing accomplishment that requires a level of humility in relation to what we think we know and a slower, more hesitant process of attunement (van Goidsenhoven and Schauwer 2020). This may lead to uncomfortable feelings of 'not knowing' which, however, result ultimately in greater discernment and more inclusive pedagogy.

Conclusion

By using the recurring motif of one young boy's body-world experience of the interactive whiteboard in his classroom, I have illustrated the way in which inclusive pedagogy involves a process of practitioners becoming literate, as Allan (2008) describes it. It is by focusing on all aspects of children's experience, I have argued, that it becomes possible to see more clearly the differences they bring to their learning. My interest has been in how the material–in this instance, the quality and experience of light–can both produce and enable children's learning subjectivities. My argument has been that the process of inclusive pedagogy is aided by the practice of de-centring the subjectivity of the child as the locus of learning and attending more to their *experience* of learning, specifically to the *material and spatial* as well as the social and discursive. This provides a strong case for treating with more caution ideas about children that seek to reduce the complexity of their learning, by viewing it against a certain set of standards for example. Such an approach tends to gloss over critical aspects of children's learning experiences, but perhaps more importantly, it prematurely cuts short what should be an extended process of practitioners trying to *perceive more*.

Key points

- Understanding children's body-world experience is essential to supporting their learning.
- This requires attentional practices that support consideration of how children are making sense of the world and of the quality of their interactions with learning environments.

- For some children, practitioners need to work harder at understanding this body-world experience and need to be able to 'perceive more' about children's learning interactions in order to achieve a more inclusive gaze.
- It is important not to stand in judgement of children, but to seek to comprehend how they are engaging with material as well as social features of learning environments.
- Material things should be seen as suggesting possibilities for action and contributing actively, therefore, to the outcomes of children's learning.

Personal accounts written by autistic people are the best source of information for understanding the kind of first-person experience of the world that is described in this chapter. Many of these are published and include chapters focused on childhood and early experiences of learning. Two books that are particularly interesting in this respect are as follows:

Further reading

Pang, C. (2020) *Explaining Humans: What Science Can Teach Us about Life, Love and Relationships*. UK: Viking/Penguin Books.

Tammet, D. (2006) *Born on a Blue Day: A Memoir of Asperger's and an Extraordinary Mind*. London: Hodder.

References

Allan, J. (2008) *Rethinking Inclusive Education: The Philosophers of Difference in Practice*. Dordrecht: Springer.

Barad, K. (2007) *Meeting the Universe Halfway: Quantum Physics and the Entanglement of Matter and Meaning*. Durham and London: Duke University Press.

Biesta, G. J. J. (2014) Pragmatising the curriculum: bringing knowledge back into the curriculum conversation, but via pragmatism, *Curriculum Journal*, 25 (1): 29–49.

Blackman, L. (1999) *Lucy's Story: Autism and Other Adventures*. London and Philadelphia: Jessica Kingsley Publishers.

Blaise, M., Hamm, C. and Iorio, J. M. (2017) Modest witness(ing) and lively stories: paying attention to matters of concern in early childhood, *Pedagogy, Culture and Society*, 25 (1): 31–42.

Brown, S. (with C. Vaughan) (2009) *Play: How It Shapes the Brain, Opens the Imagination, and Invigorates the Soul*. New York: Avery.

Clark, A. (2020) Towards a listening ECEC system. In: Cameron, C. and Moss, P. (Eds), *Transforming Early Childhood in England: Towards a Democratic Education*, pp. 134–150. London: UCL Press.

Conn, C. (2015) 'Sensory highs', 'vivid rememberings' and 'interactive stimming': children's play cultures and experiences of friendship in autistic autobiographies, *Disability and Society*, 30 (8): 1192–1206.

Conn, C. (2019a) Socio-material realities of inclusive pedagogy for autistic pupils in mainstream primary schools in the UK, *Scandinavian Journal of Disability Research*, 21 (1): 262–270.

Conn, C. (2019b) *Autism, Pedagogy and Education: Critical Issues for Value-based Teaching*. Switzerland: Palgrave Macmillan.

Conn, C., Lewis, M. and Matthews, S. (2020) An analysis of educational dialogue as support for learning for young pupils with autism in mainstream schools, *International Journal of Inclusive Education*, 24 (3): 251–265.

Florian, L. (2019) On the necessary co-existence of special and inclusive education, *International Journal of Inclusive Education*, 23(7–8): 691–704.

Florian, L. and Black-Hawkins, K. (2011) Exploring inclusive pedagogy, *British Educational Research Journal*, 37 (5): 813–828.

Florian, L. and Graham, A. (2014). Can an expanded interpretation of phronesis support teacher professional development for inclusion? *Cambridge Journal of Education*, 44 (4): 465–478.

Hart, S. (2000) *Thinking Through Teaching: A Framework for Enhancing Participation and Learning*. London: David Fulton.

Hart, S. and Drummond, M. J. (2013) Learning without limits: constructing a pedagogy free from determinist beliefs about ability. In: Florian, L. (Ed.), *The Sage Handbook of Special Education*, pp. 439–458. Los Angeles, London, New Delhi, Singapore, Washington DC: Sage.

Higashida, N. (2013) *The Reason I Jump*. Translated by K. A. Yoshida and D. Mitchell. London: Sceptre.

Holmes, R. and Jones, L. (2016) Flickering, spilling and diffusing body/knowledge in the posthuman early years. In: Taylor, C. A. and Hughes, C. (Eds.), *Posthuman Research Practices in Education*, pp. 108–127. Basingstoke, Hampshire: Palgrave Macmillan.

Jones, G., Milton, D., Bradley, R., Guldberg, K., MacLeod, A., Thomas, G., Simpson, P., Stanyer, A. and Wiseman, A. (2014) *AET Early Years Standards*. London: Autism Education Trust.

Jones, L. (2016) A practice in materialized refiguration. In: Reinersten, A. B. (Ed.), *Becoming Earth: A Post Human Turn in Educational Discourse Collapsing Nature/Culture Divides*. Rotterdam: Sense Publishers.

Jones, L., Holmes, R., MacRae, C. and MacLure, M. (2010) 'Improper' children. In: Yelland, N. (Ed.), *Contemporary Perspectives on Early Childhood Education*, pp. 177–191. Berkshire: Open University Press.

Kuby, C. R. (2018) Rhizomes and intra-activity with materials. In: Iorio, J. M. and Parnell, W. (Eds.), *Meaning Making in Early Childhood Research: Pedagogies and the Personal*, pp. 146–165. New York: Routledge.

Lather, P. (2013) Post-critical pedagogies: a feminist reading. In: Luke, C. and Gore, J. (Eds.), *Feminisms and Critical Pedagogy*, pp. 120–137. London and New York: Routledge.

Lawson, W. (2000) *Life Behind Glass: A Personal Account of Autism Spectrum Disorder*. London and Philadelphia: Jessica Kingsley Publishers.

Lawson, W. (2006) *ASPoetry: Illustrated Poems from an Aspie Life*. London and Philadelphia: Jessica Kingsley Publishers.

Lawson, W. (2011) *The Passionate Mind: How Pupils with Autism Learn*. London and Philadelphia: Jessica Kingsley Publishers.

Lenz Taguchi, H. (2009) *Going Beyond the Theory/Practice Divide in Early Childhood Education: Introducing an Intra-active Pedagogy*. London and New York: Routledge.

Lenz Taguchi, H. (2010) Rethinking pedagogical practices in early childhood education: a multidimensional approach to learning and inclusion. In: Yelland, N. (Ed.), *Contemporary Perspectives on Early Childhood Education*, pp. 14–32. Berkshire: Open University Press.

Lenz Taguchi, H. (2011) Investigating learning, participation and becoming in early childhood practices with a relational materialist approach, *Global Studies of Childhood*, 1 (1): 36–50.

Manning, E. and Massumi, B. (2014) *Thought in the Act: Passages in the Ecology of Experience*. Minneapolis and London: University of Minnesota Press.

McAnulty, D. (2020) *Diary of a Young Naturalist*. Dorset: Little Toller Books.

Milton, D., Sasson, N. J., Sheppard, E. and Yergeau, M. (Chair C.Nicolaidis) (2018) An expert discussion on autism and empathy, *Autism in Adulthood*, 1 (1): 4–11.

Moss, P. (2019) *Alternative Narratives in Early Childhood: An Introduction for Students and Practitioners*. London and New York: Routledge.

Mottron, L. (2017) Should we change targets and methods of early intervention in autism, in favor of a strengths-based education? *Journal of European Child and Adolescent Psychiatry*, 26 (7): 815–825.

Murray, D., Lesser, M. and Lawson, W. (2005) Attention, monotropism and the diagnostic criteria for autism, *Autism*, 9 (2): 139–156.

Murray, F. (2018) Me and my monotropism: a unified theory of autism. *The British Psychological Society (The Psychologist)*, November. Available: https://thepsychologist.bps.org.uk/volume-32/august-2019/me-and-monotropism-unified-theory-autism [accessed 2 June 2020].

Nutbrown, C. and Clough, P. (with F. Atherton) (2013) *Inclusion in the Early Years*. London, Thousand Oaks, New Delhi, Singapore: Sage.

O'Neill, J. L. (1999) *Through the Eyes of Aliens: A Book about Autistic People*. London and Philadelphia: Jessica Kingsley Publishers.

Osberg, D. and Biesta, G. (2010) The end/s of education. Complexity and the conundrum of the inclusive educational curriculum, *International Journal of Inclusive Education*, 14 (6): 593–607.

Pang, C. (2020) *Explaining Humans: What Science Can Teach Us about Life, Love and Relationships*. UK: Viking/Penguin Books.

Pellegrini, A. D., Dupuis, D. and Smith, P. K. (2007) Play in evolution and development, *Developmental Review*, 27 (2): 261–276.

Prince-Hughes, D. (2004) *Songs of the Gorilla Nation: My Journey Through Autism*. New York: Three Rivers Press.

Rinaldi, C. (2006) *In Dialogue with Reggio Emilia: Listening, Research and Learning*. London and New York: Routledge.

Siebers, T. (2017) Disability and the theory of complex embodiment: for identity politics in a new register. In: Davis, L. J. (Ed.), *The Disability Studies Reader*, pp. 313–332. Fifth edition. New York and London: Routledge.

Simmons, B. and Watson, D. (2018) *The PMLD Ambiguity: Articulating the Life-Worlds of Children with Profound and Multiple Learning Disabilities*. London and New York: Routledge.

Siraj, I., Taggart, B., Sammons, P., Melhuish, E., Sylva, K. and Shepherd, D.-L. (2019) *Teachers in Effective Primary Schools: Research into Pedagogy and Children's Learning*. London: UCL-IOE Press and Trentham Books.

Sutton-Smith, B. (2001) *The Ambiguity of Play*. Cambridge, MA and London: Harvard University Press.

Tammet, D. (2006) *Born on a Blue Day: A Memoir of Asperger's and an Extraordinary Mind*. London: Hodder.

Taylor, A. (2013) *Reconfiguring the Natures of Childhood*. London and New York: Routledge.

Tudge, J. (2008) *The Everyday Lives of Young Children: Culture, Class, and Child Rearing in Diverse Societies*. Cambridge: Cambridge University Press.
van Goidsenhoven, L. and Schauwer, E. (2020) Listening beyond words: swinging together, *Scandinavian Journal of Disability Research*, 22 (1): 330–339.
Williams, D. (1992) *Nobody Nowhere*. London: Corgi Books.

4 Children's agency and negotiation of space for enabling environments

The use of Tuff spots for practitioner education

Claire Pescott

Defining the learning environment

Active engagements with classroom spaces and provision for play within early years settings date back as far as Dewey (1916) who placed significant value on the contents and arrangements of the 'physical classroom'. Similarly, McMillan (1919), the pioneer of British nursery schools, stipulated that creating an environment that is enabling makes learning almost inevitable and that first-hand, active learning is central to this. This notion of enabling environments resonates more recently with Montessori (1949) education where the 'prepared environment' allows children to access real life tools, open-ended toys, and a holistic and child-centred approach to learning. The centrality of the relationship between space and place in the UK early years curricula is often presented as having significant importance (Swift 2017). Rather than being a neutral and benign environment, the classroom and the space it engenders take on a reciprocal relationship with those that inhabit it, with both the children and the adults simultaneously producing and reproducing it (Lyttleton-Smith 2017). The need for inclusive and equitable spaces for teaching and learning in the early years is an area of ongoing educational debate, though inclusion often remains elusive and opinions about how best to achieve this continue to be divided (Laurie et al. 2017). Practitioners seek to provide high quality and meaningful experiences for all children and endeavour to implement the curriculum in a way that enables children to be capable and masterful learners and find their own meaning making through a context rich and enabling environment (Hayes and O'Neill 2019).

Defining the learning environment is a complex and multidimensional process which involves consideration of the physical space, material resources, planned learning experiences and how children respond to these. Ephgrave (2018) describes the early years setting as a multi-layered organisation, with the environment being a piece of this jigsaw. It is crucial, therefore, to look at this environment with a child's eye. In a practical sense, resources need to be clearly labelled and easily accessible, thus enabling children to develop independence and appreciate print in the environment (Burnham 2016). Furthermore, learning

DOI: 10.4324/9781003163206-6

environments need to be multi-faceted, dynamic, evolving and viewed as a part of children's socio-cultural worlds (Jechura et al. 2016; Selbie and Wickett 2010). Drawing upon Reggio Emilia pedagogy, the definition of the environment as the 'third teacher'–a space that motivates and supports relationships between teachers and peers–is a useful way to contextualise this (Hayes and O'Neill 2019). To add further complexity, an enabling environment needs to be a democratic one, where all children are valued equally, where their experiences and cultural practices are celebrated, and where multicultural and multi-ethnic resources are provided (Johnston et al. 2018). To foster inclusivity, environments need to be developmentally appropriate for a wide range of abilities, and nurturing in the sense that effective responses are made to accommodate children's diverse and emerging needs (Jechura et al. 2016). Environments do not simply support academic learning, however, but also reinforce social and emotional development and contribute to a developing awareness of self as competent and capable of decision-making (Parker-Rees et al. 2010).

The learning environment is above all a social environment where children and adults operate within dynamic structures, with each individual bringing their uniqueness and personal ways of knowing (Ephgrave 2018). Daniels (2016) emphasises young children's agency when interacting with the environment and the fact that they draw upon space and materials in order to make meaning. Space and materials are continually claimed and re-claimed as they are made meaningful or assigned meaning by both children and teachers. This may be viewed as a form of enacted pedagogy and can both enable and constrain children's learning. The way the resources are organised can allow children to move around these spaces, both physically and metaphorically, and allow them to create different meanings (Daniels 2016). Children's development is supported by the environment when they are allowed to explore, exercise choice, take risks and be agentive (Canning 2010). Hilppö et al. (2016) advocate that there is both a situative and discursive take on this sense of agency and that this feeling of empowerment through controlling one's actions is a key endeavour in early years settings. It is then, arguably, the extent to which educational practice enables this sense of agency that the quality of engagement resides. Hilppö et al. (2016) further argue that, in practice, children get little opportunity to express, reflect on and develop their own engagement with and enactment of learning. It is therefore essential that practitioners afford children agency through the environment and through the provision of meaningful opportunities for demonstrating control and initiative, whilst respecting children's interests. This Siraj et al. (2016, 13) describe as the 'dance of agency and structure', which is a useful definition in orientating to how children frame social order, co-construct interactions between teachers and other children, and essentially shape the way in which they experience agency.

In this chapter, the learning environment is explored as an important layer for inclusivity within early years practice and as a way of taking account of children's diverse needs in planning and practical implementation. It is essential that practitioners consider their own and the children's subjectivity when planning for learning environments to ensure that co-construction exists and to recognise children's agency within this pedagogy. As well as the practical implications of ensuring resources are accessible and labelled, practitioners need to consider the space and resources in relation to children's interests and plan for these in response to their observations. Practitioners need the autonomy and the confidence to challenge dominant discourse in relation to deterministic ability driven agendas and summative accountability. Through the use of student teachers' work, this chapter endeavours to illustrate how a holistic approach can be facilitated by the employment of Tuff spots for enhanced provision that provides children with rich experiences and links naturally to literacy and numeracy learning as well as appealing to children's curiosity. Adopting an open-ended approach ensures that children access provision at their own pace and with their own agenda, and ensures too that rich play experiences accommodate their differences in learning and development.

Inclusive pedagogy and the role of the environment

Devarakonda (2013) suggests that inclusive education is concerned with removing barriers to learning and is a strategic approach designed to facilitate success for all children. She highlights that it is not simply concerned with children who have special educational needs or who are disabled however. Rather the view taken is that diversity is key, defining this in terms of individual strengths and desires within a community where each member is valued. Viewing inclusivity in this way challenges individual biases of gender, ethnicity, race, class and religion and engenders a thinking stance on the environment that individuals occupy together. Plows and Whitburn (2017) comment that underpinning the notion of inclusive education is the idea that everyone can participate in learning and teaching, and that this requires practitioners to reflect on their everyday practice to ensure they respond to the individual needs of children. As part of professional reflection, it is imperative that practitioners consider ways of reducing attitudinal, institutional and environmental barriers. Small everyday changes in how we conceptualise humanity and make judgements about other people can have a profound effect on inclusive practice (Plows and Whitburn 2017). This includes the rejection of deterministic beliefs about ability and adoption of a non-deficit perspective on learning, practitioners starting instead from the premise of what the child knows (Welsh Government 2015). Consequently, an inclusive pedagogical approach necessitates practitioner focus on how to make rich learning opportunities available for all children so that they can participate in the community of the classroom environment (Johnston et al. 2018). This notion, Howard and McInnes (2013) highlight, is an important component of a wider move towards an enabling environment and the development of positive relationships to ensure that each child can fulfil their potential. It is also important to consider that children have their own views of inclusion and sense of belonging, which may be different from those held by adults (Nutbrown and Clough 2009). For best practice, a combination of child-led and adult-led activities can provide the best outcome for children, though a play-based pedagogy can make this a difficult balance to strike since children do not always accept adults as play partners. How practitioners view planned purposeful activities is not necessarily how these are perceived by the child (Woods, 2017).

Children's play and the environment

The importance of play and how this influences children's development is well documented. However, even though play is viewed as synonymous with childhood, it is difficult to define because of its dynamic and ever evolving nature, but also because differing pedagogic principles operate in relation to play (Breathnach et al. 2017). Moyles (2010, 4) highlights this complexity of play and describes it as 'trying to seize a bubble'. The United Nations Convention on the Rights of the Child (UNICEF 1989) is enshrined within play policies across the UK and promotes the values of choice, agency, inclusivity and freedom. Learning through play is the common denominator of the four UK early years curricula, though each curriculum model has slightly different values and beliefs that underpin their pedagogy (Pescott 2017). Practitioners have both a professional and ethical responsibility to interpret these frameworks and consider children's responses to these based on multi-faceted dimensions of diversity, which include religion, culture, social class, gender, ethnicity and any additional needs (Wood 2013). However, there are increasing tensions between 'play-based' pedagogy and the structured curriculum outcomes in national frameworks. Chesworth (2018) highlights the fact that global perspectives of early childhood education are increasingly reliant on discourse associated with standardised notions of knowledge acquisitions and developmental milestones. He argues that a tension exists for practitioners who are held both accountable for the instrumental measurement of this learning, whilst still subscribing to play-based approaches to learning. Wood (2014) further asserts that it is often practitioners' beliefs that are the main determinant in facilitating play. Consequently, child-centred theories and belief systems of the values of play can be at odds with policy frameworks that maintain a discourse of universalism and a one size fits all response not conducive with inclusive opportunities. Wood and Hedges (2016) argue that an emphasis on processes of learning through play can sometimes be unfavourably associated with *laissez faire* approaches. This continues to make the extent to which children should engage with taught skills and concepts a contentious issue in early childhood education. Malone (2016) disputes this and argues that, rather than a *laissez faire* approach to pedagogy, the practitioner must continually make important decisions about how space and materials are utilised, allowing an element of fluidity that accommodates all children. Participation may be influenced by the child's interests as well as gender, social class and ethnicity.

Early experiences should enrich children's lives within meaningful and authentic contexts and take the form of integrated learning experiences within play-based environments (Jechura et al. 2016). Canning (2010) points out though that children's play is influenced by the environment and can be both accommodated and limited by it. The notion of play and the importance of this cannot be differentiated from the cultural context of our society since childhood is not a static or universal concept (James and James 2004). Different opportunities need to be facilitated, therefore, within both the indoor and outdoor environment, and for planned for and unexpected learning that reflects children's interests, culture and ethnicity. Heuristic play, where children are encouraged to use materials in an organic process of trial and error, without set rules or a specified outcome, is one such way that this can be accommodated (Canning 2010). Children are given the time, confidence and space to become deeply engaged, with their wellbeing high on the agenda for this free flow type of activity (Ephgrave 2018). Johnston et al. (2018) note that play that occurs within an early years setting is inextricably linked to opportunities within the environment and there needs to be appropriate resources and activities available to necessitate this. Andrews (2012) suggests the use of 'loose parts' within an early year's environment, which are defined as 'open-ended' materials that do not have a specific purpose and allow imaginative responses. These may take the form of, for example, cardboard boxes, fabric, junk materials as well as items found in the natural environment. Such items give children choice and offer imaginative opportunities. As well as engaging with materials, it is often seemingly mundane experiences, such as helping a friend or climbing on a frame, that play a central role in shaping children's agency, rather than planned for experiences (Hilppö et al. 2016). Play and learning are intrinsically linked, and play-based learning supports children as active social agents who are constantly framing and re-framing their knowledge and understanding of the world (Plows and Whitburn 2017). Play acts as a vehicle to support creativity as well as divergent thinking (Woods 2017) and is therefore integral to effective practice within an early years environment.

A post-structuralist perspective on inclusive pedagogy

A Foucauldian lens allows us to critically analyse the ways in which policy produces particular regimes of truth about young children (Lewis 2018). Foucault (1982) suggests that as well as producing dominant discourses, the mind set of 'governmentality' means we essentially internalise these discourses so that they become our own truth. Subjectivity, an enduring Foucauldian theme, extends beyond identity and personal responses to situations. Early years pedagogy needs to be viewed as embedded within the specific socio-political context (MacNaughton 2005). Importantly therefore, practice needs to take account of the particular context within which the child is operating, for example, in relation to gender, class, race and ethnicity, since privileging child development exclusively does not allow practitioners to consider social practices from the home environment (Cohen 2008). Such a perspective challenges the ways in which the curriculum is often framed by emphasising the fact that pedagogy requires time for children to repeat, embody and make connections to their world (Wood and Hedges 2016). Adopting this philosophy suggests that power circulates between people and within systems.

Indeed, child development as a regime of truth can be disrupted in early years environments through critical reflection and open dialogue between practitioners and between practitioners and children. Policy is often presented as being factual and logical, but Lewis (2018) highlights the fact that there are five levers generating these widely held dominant discourses which are: funding, targets, initiatives, planning and inspections. Political as well as developmental truths are underpinned by the basic assumption that all children, regardless of their culture, are largely the same and follow the same normative scale (Wood and Hedges 2016). Post-structuralism challenges developmental psychology and its normative discourse about how children understand and should be positioned (Dahlberg et al. 2013). Often, this does not consider subjective experience and equitable approaches (Laurie et al. 2017). Furthermore, this homogenised view of childhood risks labelling children who do not neatly fit a normative developmental pathway and risks as well perpetuating a deficit model (Lewis 2018). Bradbury and Roberts-Holmes (2018) stipulate how the 'datafication' of early childhood education affects everyday practices and in turn impacts on young children's identity, relationships and individual learning. Lewis (2018) theorises this in Foucauldian terms and suggests that this data-driven culture acts as a form of disciplinary power and likens children to being on a conveyor belt of education. Particular constructs of young children, which are driven by political and economic priorities, silence more nuanced understandings of children as unique individuals who cannot be quantified by standardised measures or reduced to league tables or levels on a standardised test (Lewis 2018).

Alternatively, rather than being driven solely by deterministic ideas about children's abilities, Wood (2014) theorises children's agency in the context of institutional power structures and argues that planning and implementing a play-based curriculum empowers children. Essentially, rather than being free from power, children are influenced by the adult's agenda, but how they frame these experiences may be different from adult understandings. This arguably makes the opportunity for 'free play' an even more important aspect of democratic practices since, in this way, children are able to exercise power over space and resources as well as negotiate this with peers and adults (Wood 2014). Sellers (2013) draws on the work of Deleuze and Guattari (1994) to understand children's complex relationship with the curriculum, situating this within the milieu of being/becoming. This argument suggests that rather than being controlled by adults, children can enact their subjectivities and demonstrate a form of performativity in response to the curriculum. Inclusivity is facilitated by children's responses to the curriculum that emerge from their own expressions of understanding. Children's subjectivities, including culturally and ethnically situated learning experiences, ensure individual curatorship, co-constructed with others (Sellers 2013). Wood and Hedges (2016) extend this argument by suggesting that children's engagement and participation with the environment is extremely important for them and helps facilitate their own thinking and actions. Ailwood (2010), however, cautions against trading one discourse too easily for another without critical examination of claims to truth that post-structuralists challenge. Also, it should be considered that post-structuralism does not provide a practical theory but rather a critique around which deconstruction takes place.

Practical approaches to planning for an enabling environment

Professional learning is the cornerstone in ensuring effective practice within the early years (Envy and Walters 2013). Research demonstrates that the skills and qualifications of early years practitioners are a significant contributory factor in determining quality within early years settings (Envy and Walters 2013). There was a call for the early years workforce to be of a high quality as far back as England's Green Paper 'Children's Workforce Strategy' (HM Government 2005), with this seen as creating long-term benefits for children. However, disparity still exists between the extremes of low-status childcare workers compared to graduate teachers (Cameron 2020). In Wales, a national approach to professional learning has been advocated with a vision that fits with an evolving education system. This is typified by a co-constructed professional learning journey which gives autonomy to the practitioner. There are also professional standards that set clear expectations to support practitioners themselves individually and collectively to identify and reflect on areas of future development (Welsh Government 2018). In response to the OECD's (2017) review of the current school system, the education reform programme in Wales has become a national priority. This involves sustained investment in key policy, the co-construction of policies with key stakeholders and an improvement to communication and evidence gathering within this reform journey. Currently, Wales is in a transitory position in terms of curriculum implementation and consequently some schools are still utilising the current Foundation Phase framework (Welsh Government 2015) while pioneer schools are implementing the new Curriculum for Wales 2022, which will be implemented in all settings by September of that year. Despite the evolution of the curriculum in response to political and social needs, both curricula are based on an active learning approach and the commitment to play remains central for the early years. Additionally, the new curriculum will give more autonomy to practitioners to develop the curriculum in response to the particular needs of the children in their settings (Welsh Government 2020).

At the University of South Wales, students on the BA (Hons) Early Years Education and Practice undertake a variety of modules over the three years of their course. These include a module titled 'Professional Practice', which seeks to support reflection on their experiences in placement (early years settings, Flying Start, state nurseries and creches) and to combine theory and practice with further modules on child development, play and wellbeing, and on literacy and numeracy teaching. In their second year, students have a compulsory module, titled 'Curriculum Matters', which introduces them to how the curriculum works in practice and how they can enact this in a practical way within their placement. The course has recently added a 'practitioner status' component which has been endorsed by the Care Council Wales (CCW), which requires a number of 'competencies' to be evidenced by students and then signed off by the mentor in their early years placement setting. This allows the requirements for the students' practice to be demonstrated in terms of 'leading' certain areas of planning and group activities. Consequently, undertaking practical ways of implementing an enabling environment within their university experience allows for this to be implemented within their practice. Planning an enabling environment is fundamental to providing rich, authentic learning experiences for all children to flourish in (Wood 2014). Within the current Foundation Phase in Wales (Welsh Government 2015), play pedagogy is held central to practice and is structured through the use of continuous and enhanced provision (Thomas and Lewis 2016). Drawing upon this curriculum framework, practitioners plan in accordance with policy in their settings to ensure that the 'range' (the what) and 'skills' (the how) are met and are progressive across year groups. The students are encouraged to facilitate their own planning as a way of more thoroughly understanding the implications of teaching and learning (Wood 2013). The planning allows opportunities for scheduled as well as informal observations which enable pertinent lines of inquiry to be pursued, open-ended questioning and consideration of key terminology (Thomas and Lewis 2016). Differentiation is carefully considered and planned for, with reflection of how the environment needs to be adapted to accommodate all learners. This could include labels that have writing as well as pictorial depictions, the opportunity for more or less complex instructions on laminated cards for the children to pursue at their own pace, and templates for writing with varying degrees of scaffolding. The planning process is cyclical and continuous and involves a circle of observation, assessment and planning, with continual adjustment made to include the children's responses and interest levels before the whole process begins again (Bryce-Clegg 2015). This then essentially gives the practitioner the autonomy to develop their plans in a creative and innovative way that draws upon their own strengths, motivation and interests as well as considering the collective and individual needs of their learners (Burnham 2016; Moyles 2011). Students are given support to plan using the Foundation Phase framework (Welsh Government 2015) and are encouraged to think creatively in terms of topics and themes that may interest children. The four purposes of the new Curriculum for Wales 2022 are also considered and how the environment can help to realise this vision through co-construction with both practitioners and the children (Sellers 2013).

Creating enabling environments and the importance of this to child development and curriculum delivery is held central to the 'Curriculum Matters' module and students are expected to undertake practical ways of demonstrating this as well as relating it to theory. Assessment within this degree programme takes not only the form of academic essays, but also of opportunities for students to showcase practically how they are able to make robust links between theory and practice. Assessment of the 'Curriculum Matters' module requires students to produce a Tuff spot (a large, heavy duty receptacle) in a theme of their choice as a way of demonstrating their understanding of play-based pedagogy and holistic learning. This is with specific reference to enhanced provision planning, where a small group of children would access the resource at any one time. Enhanced provision is defined as how physical resources and space are developed with objects or prompts that support a range of interests and encourage investigation and experimentation (Bryce-Clegg 2015). Foundation Phase (Welsh Government 2015) pedagogy includes continuous provision, enhanced provision and focused teaching, which together are represented by a triangle to demonstrate how they link together. Continuous provision, situated at the bottom of the triangle, are the resources that are always available (such as sand, water and the home corner). At the top of the triangle is the focused teaching which is the discreet skills taught to small groups of children with a specific focus on skills that need developing that have been observed through the children's play experiences (Thomas and Lewis 2016). Enhanced provision, in the middle of the triangle and central to the pedagogy, is an essential component of establishing an enabling environment and allowing all children autonomy and agency in accessing provision (Johnston et al. 2018). Establishing a well-planned environment allows children to problem solve and experiment with minimal input from adults (Swift 2017). So, for example, the construction area that is always available for the children within a setting (continuous provision), which has resources such as wooden blocks, multi-link and foam blocks, can be developed (enhanced provision) with several additions. This may involve resources such as tape measures, a measuring stick and string, which would encourage mathematical development and using standard or non-standard types of measurements. Hard hats and appropriate dressing-up clothes could be included which would encourage language, literacy and communication skills through role play and giving instructions to others. Similarly, labels with pictures and words could be utilised, which could promote reading strategies. There would also be the opportunity for physical development through manipulating the blocks which would develop fine motor skills as well as balancing skills and hand-eye coordination. Personal and social development could also be encouraged through turn-taking and establishing the need for negotiated interaction. This holistic way of enhancing the environment allows for children's individual responses and the opportunity for decision-making, initiative and agency (Breathnach et al. 2017).

In the student's Tuff spot, they are required to demonstrate differentiated teaching through the way they organise the resources and scaffold learning in the learning opportunities it provides. Working in small groups, students are required to specify in their planning how their Tuff spot links to the curriculum requirements and how it provides open-ended play and learning opportunities. This summative assessment is incorporated into an academic poster to demonstrate their understanding of how the three areas of the Foundation Phase triangle (continuous provision, enhanced provision and focused teaching) operate in practice. From student feedback for the module, this has proved to be an invaluable way of encouraging hands-on practice and many students have replicated this Tuff spot within their own placement setting. The following examples showcase some of their work.

In Figure 4.1, the Tuff spot was designed to be multisensory and different textures were provided (soil, fake grass, leaves, sticks and wood shavings) as a replica of the environments where minibeasts might be found. The students had noticed within their placements that the children were interested in wildlife and wanted to encapsulate this within their enhanced provision. The students also highlighted how their own interests in the outdoor environment were a way to share their passion for this and to encourage a better understanding of the importance of being respectful of the outdoors as a home to many animals. The book *Mad about Minibeasts* (Andreae and Wojtowycz 2011) was provided as an initial context for learning and would have been read to the children prior to setting up the Tuff spot. The planning for this Tuff spot was primarily concerned with the area of 'Knowledge and Understanding of the World' (Foundation Phase, Welsh Government 2015); however, the students have provided many open-ended opportunities for literacy, numeracy and social development. For example, the book encourages specific vocabulary use and there are opportunities to read the identification sheet that has pictures to help with reading strategies. The children were encouraged to locate specific replica minibeasts using the tweezers and magnifying glasses provided (which also promotes fine motor skills). Mathematical development was promoted through classification, touch counting, and basic addition and subtraction of the minibeasts. Whilst the students provided intentional learning opportunities, their Tuff spot also allowed for child-led learning and open-ended play opportunities and meaning making for individuals. There was no set time limit to explore the area and no forced learning outcomes, the child free to experiment and respond imaginatively to the stimulus in their own way (Bryce-Clegg 2015).

Figure 4.1 Example of a minibeast Tuff spot. (Photograph taken by the author)

Figure 4.2 shows how the students designed their Tuff spot to encourage children to make their own potions. As with the previous example, a book was used as a stimulus, in this case *Winnie and Wilbur: The Amazing Pumpkin* (Thomas 2016) which was intended to be read to the children prior to the introduction of this enhanced provision. This was topical since it was made at the time of Halloween and would appeal to the children's interest. In their placements, the students had noted that children enjoyed experimenting and mixing different ingredients whilst outside. In terms of literacy, this Tuff spot provided a rich context for the use of adjectives and descriptive vocabulary with the inclusion of vibrant colours, interesting shapes and textures of the various dried ingredients such as lentils, pasta and glitter. The use of time connectives was also encouraged. These words were stuck around the base of the Tuff spot and children were provided with differentiated sheets which had variously scaffolded templates to record their potion if they wished. Using this enhanced provision, children could select the quantity of each ingredient and this promoted non-standard measurement, estimation skills as well as sequencing. This was designed to also encourage fine motor skills and manipulation as well as the opportunity to use real cooking utensils, such as measuring jugs and wooden spoons. For children with difficulties in these areas, it allowed for learning at their own pace and being able to revisit learning to consolidate skills. To make for an authentic learning experience, the children were provided with safety googles and science lab coats. This, the students noted, facilitated group management techniques since the number of children allowed to use the Tuff spot at any one time needed to correspond with the equipment available. This is an important consideration when planning enhanced provision as a child-led approach is advocated and children need to demonstrate autonomy and responsibility when utilising the areas (Bryce-Clegg 2015).

In the final example (Figure 4.3), a more specific mathematical focus is provided. The students expressed a desire to move away from worksheets and provide children with a stimulus that could be differentiated to encourage mathematical skills such as number recognition, one to one correspondence,

Figure 4.2. Example of a potion-making Tuff spot. (Photograph taken by the author)

Figure 4.3. A Tuff spot with a mathematical focus. (Photograph taken by the author)

and simple addition and subtraction. The relationship between these operations is considered and by providing objects based on the theme of water encourages a tangible experience of abstract concepts. Mark making and the inclusion of shaving foam encouraged larger movements for number formation and the non-permanence of the medium provided an environment of experimentation where wrong answers could easily be eliminated. Similar to the Tuff spots described above, the use of tweezers encouraged fine motor skills, whilst handling orbezz (water beads, as pictured in the fishbowl) provided a sensory experience. The use of the measuring jugs, with easily changed labels, made the provision suitable for all children, irrespective of their mathematical ability. Furthermore, it encouraged practical exploration of concepts such as capacity and measure, which the children naturally investigated using the equipment provided.

Evaluation of the enabling environments

In all the examples provided above, and others that have not been showcased in this chapter, open-ended approaches were actively demonstrated. Students viewed children holistically and tried to appeal to their senses to stimulate active participation. A consideration of visual, gestural and spatial modes of learning were particularly apparent which facilitated an exploration of the material world and multi-modal play (Daniels 2016). As advocated by Hayes and O'Neill (2019), this pedagogical framing includes arrangements of space, provision of materials to promote active learning environments and rich opportunities to learn. Ephgrave (2018) emphasises that children respond to authentic resources and experiences and this can be seen through the students' examples in the form of the natural literacy and numeracy learning enabled by the use of the space, alongside encouragement to explore through, for example, minibeasts and potions. The students' work demonstrates that a well-planned environment facilitates experimentation, problem solving and communication with minimal input from practitioners (Swift 2017).

In addition to the summative assessment, the students were encouraged to reflect upon their experiences, which is essential for their development as effective early years practitioners (McKeon and Harrison 2010). The following questions were utilised: How did you work as a group? What were the issues you faced? What went well? How can you use the Tuff spot in your practice? What have you learnt about enabling environments? How could you adapt the Tuff spot to suit a different theme? On reflection, this activity allows a hands-on approach to enacting an enabling environment and allows students to experience theory into practice in a meaningful way. Teaching about curricula utilising practical examples is a useful way of challenging students' deterministic views about ability, and misconceptions and biases in relation to individual needs. It also encourages them to question dominant discourses surrounding standardised notions of learning (Moss 2019). It encourages them to appreciate the non-human aspects of the environment and appreciate how educational practices are affected by materials (Hackett and Rautio 2019). For student practitioners, as with those who are qualified, it is essential that reflective practice takes place, with time taken to reflect and consider their role in creating, maintaining and designing the learning environment (Hayes and O'Neill 2019). A dynamic and interactive context, high quality resources and accessibility are key to providing rich play experiences where children are respected as cultural agents (Daniels 2016).

Through these examples, it has been demonstrated that context is important to curriculum co-construction and that examining this in a practical way produces a more reflexive approach which is participatory in nature (Trevor et al. 2020). Allowing students to have practical experience of negotiating the curriculum within a physical space allows for a deeper understanding of pedagogy and the ways in which complex learning interactions unfold (Moyles 2010). This facilitation of a pedagogical space allows students to consider children's diversities in a more holistic way that are not bound by perceived ability levels or normative goals. How the curriculum is unpacked by the practitioner and co-constructed with children is influenced by this pedagogical knowledge with practical implications (Trevor et al. 2020). Through first-hand experiences, the students recognise the reciprocal relationship between the learning environment and their pedagogical actions and come to see learning, not as a straightforward endeavour, but rather as a process requiring deconstruction and reflection in response to the differences children bring to learning (Moss 2019). Furthermore, from a post-structuralist perspective, it also challenges dominant discourses about the linearity of learning and the need for continually fulfilling set outcomes. It allows for a more organic response from children that enables them to thrive in a respectful way (Ephgrave 2018).

Key points

- Children learn by experimenting and an enabling environment is a way to ensure they have the opportunity for rich, open-ended experiences that support their development.

- This chapter has presented practical examples in the form of student teachers' Tuff spots to illustrate how the environment is an integral element in children's learning.
- Through careful observation and planning, practitioners can provide rich contexts for learning and purposeful play that encapsulate an inclusive environment for all children to thrive in.
- These spaces and the materials in the environment are continually claimed and re-claimed by children and adults as they seek to make meaningful experiences.
- Reflecting on the environment through a post-structuralist lens challenges dominant discourses about learning and education and allows practitioners to deconstruct practice, question deterministic views of learning and recognise children's agency.

Further reading

Bryce-Clegg, A. (2015) *Best Practice in the Early Years*. London: Bloomsbury.
This book offers practical ways to ensure the environment is enabling and inclusive for all children.

Moss, P. (2019) *Alternative Narratives in Early Childhood. An Introduction for Students and Practitioners*. Oxon: Routledge. This book challenges accepted beliefs around educational discourse and encourages the reader to think about issues and challenges in a more holistic way.

Acknowledgements

Thank you to the students who gave me the permission to showcase their work in this chapter and for providing illustration of the arguments discussed.

References

Ailwood, J. (2010) Playing with some tensions: Poststructuralism, Foucault and early education. In Brookes, L. and Edwards, S. (eds.) *Engaging Play*. Maidenhead: Open University Press, pp. 210–222.
Andreae, G. and Wojtowycz, D. (2011) *Mad about Minibeasts!* London: Orchard Books.
Andrews, M. (2012) *Exploring Play for Early Childhood Studies*. London: Sage.
Bradbury, A. and Roberts-Holmes, G. (2018) *The Datafication of Primary and Early Years Education: Playing with Numbers*. Abington: Routledge.
Breathnach, H., Danby, S. and O'Gorman, L. (2017) 'Are you working or playing?' Investigating young children's perspectives of classroom activities, *International Journal of Early Years Education*, 25 (3): 439–454.
Bryce-Clegg, A. (2015) *Best Practice in the Early Years*. London: Bloomsbury.
Burnham, L. (2016) *How to be an Outstanding Early Years Practitioner*. London: Bloomsbury.
Cameron, C. (2020) Towards a 'rich' ECEC workforce. In Moss, P. and Cameron, C. (eds.) *Transforming Early Childhood in England: Towards a Democratic Education*. London: UCL Press, pp. 67–82.
Canning, N. (ed.) (2010) *Play and Practice in the Early Years Foundation Stage*. London: Sage.

Chesworth, L. (2018) Theorising young children's interests: Making connections in-the-moment happenings, *Learning, Culture and Social Interaction*, 23 (1): 83–96.

Cohen, L. (2008) Foucault and the early childhood classroom, *A Journal of the American Educational Studies*, 44 (1): 7–21.

Dahlberg, G., Moss, P. and Pence, A. (2013) *Beyond Quality in Early Childhood Education and Care*. 3rd edn. London: Routledge.

Daniels, K. (2016) Exploring enabling literacy environments: young children's spatial and material encounters in early years classrooms, *English in Education*, 50 (1): 12–34.

Deleuze, G. and Guattari, F. (1994) *What is Philosophy? European Perspectives: A Series in Social Thought and Cultural Criticism European Perspectives*. Columbia: University Press.

Devarakonda, C. (2013) *Diversity and Inclusion in Early Childhood. An introduction*. London: Sage.

Dewey, J. (1916) *Democracy and Education*. New York: MacMillan.

Envy, R. and Walters R. (2013) *Becoming a Practitioner in the Early Years*. London: Sage.

Ephgrave, A. (2018) *Planning in the Moment with Young Children. A Practical Guide for Early Years Practitioners and Parents*. London: Routledge.

Foucault, M. (1982) The subject and power, *Critical Inquiry*, 8: 777–795.

Hackett, A.and Rautio, P. (2019) Answering the world: young children's running and rolling as more-than-human multimodal meaning making, *International Journal of Qualitative Studies in Education*, 32 (8): 1019–1031.

Hayes, N. and O'Neill, S. (2019) Little changes, big results: the impact of simple changes to early years learning environments, *Early Years*, 39 (1): 64–79.

Hilppö, J., Kumpulaune, K. and Rainio, A. (2016) Children's sense of agency in pre-school: a sociocultural investigation, *International Journal of Early Years Education*, 24 (2): 157–171.

HM Government (2005) *Children's Workforce Strategy*. Available at: https://www.nscap.org.uk/doc/childrens%20workforce%20strategy.pdf (Accessed: 18 March 2021).

Howard, J. and McInnes, K. (2013) *The Essence of Play: A Practice Companion for Professionals Working with Children and Young People*. London: Routledge.

James, A., & James, A. (eds.) (2004) *Constructing Childhood: Theory, Policy and Social Practice*. Basingstoke: Palgrave MacMillan.

Jechura, J., Woolridge, D., Bertelsen, C. and Mayers, G. (2016) Exploration of early childhood learning environments, *Early Learning Environments*, 82 (3): 9–15.

Johnston, J., Nahmad-Williams, L., Oates, R. and Wood, V. (2018) *Early Childhood Studies: Principles and Practice*. 2nd edn. London: Routledge.

Laurie, G., Marquis, E., Fuller, E., Neuman, T., Qui, M., Roelof, F. and van Dam, L. (2017) Moving towards inclusive learning and teaching: a synthesis of recent literature, *Teaching and Learning Inquiry*, 5 (1): 1–13.

Lewis, Z. (2018) Policy and the image of the child: a critical analysis of drivers and levers in English early years curriculum policy, *Journal of Early Years*, 17 (2): 1–15.

Lyttleton-Smith, J. (2017) Objects of conflict: (re) configuring early childhood experiences of gender in the preschool classroom, *Gender and Education*, 31 (6): 655–672.

MacNaughton, G. (2005) *Doing Foucault in Early Years Childhood Studies*. London: Routledge.

Malone, K. (2016) Reconsidering children's encounters with nature and place using posthumanism, *Australian Journal of Environmental Education*, 32 (1):42–56.

McKeon, F. and Harrison, J. (2010) Developing pedagogical practice and professional identities of beginning teacher educators, *Professional Development in Education*, 36 (1): 25–44.

McMillan, M. (1919) *The Nursery School*. London: J.M. Dent and Sons.

Montessori, M. (1949) *The Absorbent Mind*. Chennai: The Theosophical Publishing House.

Moss, P. (2019) *Alternative Narratives in Early Childhood. An Introduction for Students and Practitioners*. Oxon: Routledge.

Moyles, J. (ed.) (2010) *Thinking about Play: Developing a Reflective Approach*. Maidenhead: Open University Press.

Moyles, J. (2011) *Beginning Teaching–Beginning Learning*. 4th edn. Maidenhead: Open University Press.

Nutbrown, C. and Clough, P. (2009) Citizenship and inclusion in the early years: understanding and responding to children's perspectives on 'belonging', *International Journal of Early Years Education*, 17 (3): 191–206.

OECD (2017) *The Welsh Education Reform Journey. A Rapid Policy Assessment*. Available at: http://www.oecd.org/education/The-Welsh-Education-Reform-Journey-FINAL.pdf (Accessed: 16 March 2021).

Parker-Rees, R., Leeson, C., Willan, J. and Savage, J. (eds.) (2010) *Early Childhood Studies*. Exeter: Learning Matters Ltd.

Pescott, C. (2017) What we can learn from UK curricula. In Thomas, A. and McInnes, K. (eds.) *Teaching Early Years: Theory and Practice*. London: Sage, pp. 9–28.

Plows, V. and Whitburn, B. (2017) *Inclusive Education: Making Sense of Everyday Practice*. Rotterdam: Sense Publishers.

Selbie, P. and Wickett, K. (2010) *Early Childhood Studies*. 3rd edn. Exeter: Learning Matters Ltd.

Sellers, M. (2013) *Young Children Becoming Curriculum: Deleuze, Te Whariki and Curricular Understandings*. Abingdon: Routledge.

Siraj, C., Wilmes, D. and Havis, J. (2016) Examining children's agency with participatory structures in primary science investigations, *Learning, Culture and Social Interaction*, 10: 4–16.

Swift, T. (2017) *Learning through Movement and Active Play in the Early Years*. London: Jessica Kingsley Publishers.

Thomas, A. and Lewis, A. (2016) *An Introduction to the Foundation Phase*. London: Bloomsbury.

Thomas, V. (2016) *Winnie and Wilbur: The Amazing Pumpkin*. Oxford: Oxford University Press.

Trevor, G., Ince, A. and Ang, L. (2020) Towards a child-centred education. In Moss, P. and Cameron, C. (eds.) *Transforming Early Childhood in England: Towards a Democratic Education*. London: UCL Press, pp. 100–118.

UNICEF (1989). *United Nations Convention on the Rights of the Child*. Available at: https://www.unicef.org.uk/wp-content/uploads/2010/05/UNCRC_united_nations_convention_on_the_rights_of_the_child.pdf (Accessed: 18 March 2021).

Welsh Government (2015) *Curriculum for Wales: Foundation Phase Framework*. Available at: https://gov.wales/sites/default/files/publications/2018-02/foundation-phase-framework-revised-2015.pdf (Accessed: 10 March 2021).

Welsh Government (2018) *Professional for Teaching And Leadership: National Approach to Professional Learning*. Available at: https://hwb.gov.wales/professional-development/national-approach-to-professional-learning/professional-teaching-and-leadership-standards-national-approach-to-professional-learning/ (Accessed: 16 March 2021).

Welsh Government (2020) *Curriculum for Wales Guidance*. Available at: https://hwb.gov.wales/api/storage/afca43eb-5c50-4846-9c2d-0d56fbffba09/curriculum-for-wales-guidance-120320.pdf (Accessed: 13 March 2020).

Wood, E. (2013) *Play and Learning and the Early Childhood Curriculum*. 3rd edn. London: Sage.

Wood, E. (2014) Free choice and free play in early childhood education: troubling the discourse, *International Journal of Early Years Education*, 22 (1): 4–18.

Wood, E. and Hedges, H. (2016) Curriculum in early childhood education: critical questions about content, coherence and control, *Curriculum Journal*, 27 (3): 387–405.

Woods, A. (ed.) (2017) *Child-initiated Play and Learning: Planning for Possibilities in the Early Years*. London: Routledge.

Part II
Using research to develop inclusive pedagogies

5 Socialising a pedagogy of care in a New Zealand early childhood refugee centre

Amanda Bateman and Linda Mitchell

The New Zealand early childhood education context

Aotearoa New Zealand's history offers a basis for understanding early childhood education and the curriculum in New Zealand. New Zealand is a small island country in the South Pacific Ocean. The population is just over five million and can be described as ethnically and linguistically super-diverse. Māori are the indigenous people, first migrating in canoe groups from Eastern Polynesia in the 13th century AD or earlier (King 2003). It was not until 1769 that Europeans came to Aotearoa New Zealand and started settling here. Te Tiriti o Waitangi, signed in 1840, was meant to be a partnership between Māori and the British Crown, ensuring tino rangatiratanga (absolute sovereign authority) for Māori over their lands, villages and all their taonga (everything that they value), and all the rights and privileges of British subjects. But, in the following century and more, rapid immigration, processes of colonisation, the New Zealand wars, land confiscations, and assimilationist policies and practices occurred. Nevertheless, Te Tiriti was to provide the foundation for a country with three official languages, Māori, English and New Zealand sign, with a vision of a bicultural society. A key education challenge currently is revitalising language and culture, and moving away from an ethnocentric, monocultural education system.

Early childhood education in New Zealand is characterised by a diversity of provision (May 2013). Education and care centres (childcare centres) cater for the largest number of children and offer full day, sessional or half day provision. Home-based services (family daycare) provide an educator to work with children in the educator's home or the child's home at hours to suit parents. A large percentage of both these service types are for-profit, owned and managed by private companies or business owners. All other services are not-for-profit, usually community-based. Kindergartens mainly operate a school day or sessional provision and cater for children two to five years, with all children moving to primary school on their fifth birthday. The Correspondence School is a distance education service, and is directly provided by the state. Kōhanga reo (Māori immersion language nests) were established in 1982 and have been described as 'the most

DOI: 10.4324/9781003163206-8

vigorous and innovative educational movement in this country (dare I say in the world)' by Reedy (2013, 65). They offer total immersion in Māori, and foster Māori cultural identity and self-determination. Pacific Early Childhood Groups are total immersion or bilingual in their home Pacific language. In sessional playcentres, parents are the educators, manage and administer the playcentre, and are trained through their national or regional organisation. Sessional playgroups are also run by parents, but playgroup parents require no training.

The early childhood curriculum, *Te Whāriki* (Ministry of Education [MoE] 1996/2017), is a bicultural curriculum that is intended to recognise Te Tiriti o Waitangi rights and obligations. It has a focus on equity and respect for children's rights and responsibilities, together with the aim of supporting children growing up in a democracy in which they will make a contribution. The curriculum is founded on aspirations for children: 'To grow up as competent and confident learners and communicators, healthy in mind, body and spirit, secure in their sense of belonging and in the knowledge that they make a valued contribution to society' (MoE 1996/2017, 5).

Te Whāriki begins with four curriculum principles: Empowerment–Whakamana; Holistic development–Kotahitanga; Family and community–Whānau tangata; and Relationships–Ngā hononga. The aspirations are also elaborated in five strands or forms of mana (a Māori concept meaning prestige or power) to embody areas of learning and development within early childhood. These are Belonging–Mana whenua; Wellbeing–Mana atua, Exploration–Mana aoturoa; Communication–Mana reo; and Contribution–Mana tangata. In the research for this chapter, we focus on one strand: Belonging–Mana whenua. Belonging–Mana whenua relates to authority over land, and the sense of identity and belonging traditionally associated with connections to people, past, present and future, to the spiritual world and to the universe (Barlow 1991; Mead 2003).

The refugee context in Aotearoa New Zealand

The global refugee crisis is affecting many young children. In 2020, around half of the nearly 26 million refugees who had been forcibly displaced from their homes were under the age of 18 years (UNHCR 2020). Aotearoa New Zealand takes part in the UN regular refugee resettlement programme, taking an annual quota of refugees, which from July 2020 was 1500 per year (this quota was not met in 2020 because of COVID-19). UN quota refugees first come to the Mangere Refugee Resettlement Centre in Auckland, where they live on site for five to six weeks. The Resettlement Centre is managed by Immigration New Zealand which works in partnership with other government agencies and non-government organisations to run a six-week reception programme. The programme aims to prepare refugees for their lives in Aotearoa New Zealand. Its key focus areas are:

- health and mental health assessments, initial treatment and health promotion.
- settlement planning, including orientation to working and living in Aotearoa New Zealand and an employment assessment for working age refugees.
- education, including English language, schooling and early childhood education (Immigration New Zealand 2021).

Following their participation in the programme, refugees are settled in one of eight regions in Aotearoa New Zealand, where some support is provided for up to 12 months. Refugee families and children have highly complex needs that have resulted from the refugee experience, which the New Zealand Ministry of Health describes as 'the physical, psychological and social experiences of refugees as they flee conflict and persecution and seek safety' (Ministry of Health 2001, 3). Challenges include dealing with extreme trauma, severe health and mental health issues, loss of support networks and family, coming to live in a new country with different languages, patterns of childrearing, gender roles, and social values (Deng and Marlowe 2013; McMillan and Gray 2009; Ministry of Health 2001). All of these issues directly affect the degree to which refugee children and family feel a sense of inclusion in Aotearoa New Zealand.

The research project

To investigate how refugee children and families were supported in their sense of belonging and inclusion in New Zealand, a research project *Refugee families in early childhood education: Constructing pathways to belonging* (Mitchell et al. 2018) was initiated and funded by the Royal Society Marsden Fund. The project aims to develop evidence-based policy and practice theories that illustrate how early childhood education can enable refugee families and children to retain important cultural capital from their home country–thereby adding cultural capital to their new country–and construct positive outcomes for belonging and participating in Aotearoa New Zealand. The project uses design-based implementation research (Penuel 2014) involving cycles of data gathering, theory building, critical analysis and evaluation, and adaptation of design, carried out in participation with children, teachers and families in five early childhood settings that have a total or high proportion of refugee families. This chapter draws on findings from this research project.

For the purpose of this chapter, we focus on the research question: 'How can the people, places and practices in early childhood education strengthen belonging for refugee children?' Specifically, we explore the interactions taking place in an early childhood centre between two toddlers, both from Afghanistan. The chapter draws on data from research carried out in the first cycle of data gathering from one of the settings, the Carol White Family Centre, which caters for refugee children and families. In this section, we provide details of the Carol White Family Centre, and outline the research methods and analytic approach.

The Carol White Family Centre

The Carol White Family Centre has a largely refugee community and is located in the grounds of a secondary school, Selwyn College. Most of the centre children have parents attending Selwyn College's Refugee Education for Adults and Families (REAF) programme, which operates in buildings adjacent to the centre. The REAF programme offers English language, literacy and numeracy programmes, resettlement and advocacy support, community education projects, including IELTS (International English Language Testing System) preparation, gardening and patchwork, and makes connections with community and government agencies, such as Work and Income New Zealand and Housing New Zealand. The two organisations are closely connected with parents being called to come over from their language class if a child is upset or needs them, and always coming together at morning teatime.

The Centre employs bilingual support staff to assist teachers in working with children and families. Often these support staff started there as parents and helped in a voluntary capacity. The principle, 'Family and community– Whānau tangata', and the focus on 'mana' in the curriculum, *Te Whāriki* (MoE 1996/2017), is a powerful guide. In describing the Centre philosophy and values in a recorded presentation at the beginning of the research project, Robyn Gerrity, the director, portrayed the Centre as opening up opportunities for 'a fairer world through education' and that 'the Centre is for all'. She conveyed an empathetic understanding of trauma experienced by refugee families and their need for support networks. At the heart of her practice is a concept of the 'child as citizen' and insistence on 'dignity and social justice for all'. Democracy in education is a core value.

> As a refugee family centre, the only one of its kind in New Zealand, our programme is enhanced by a knowledge and awareness of the refugee experience and the United Nations Convention on the rights of the child. There must be dignity and justice for us all. We pay special attention to supporting and enhancing children's languages and cultures enabling children and their families to develop a strong, rich identity which we believe bridges the past and the present and the future learning of us all.
>
> (Gerrity 2018, 14 March)

Participants

Research participants, whose data is discussed in this chapter, were the director of the Carol White Family Centre Robyn Gerrity, two toddlers who attend the Centre, Zaineb and Zaynab, and Shazia, the mother of Zaineb.

Robyn Gerrity, the director, is a highly experienced registered early childhood teacher, who has been teaching for over 30 years and has worked with refugee families for 20 years. The two toddlers are named Zaineb and Zaynab. Zaineb was born in New Zealand and is the youngest child in a family of three. When the data was gathered for the research, she was two years two months old. She started attending the Carol White Family Centre at the age of six months, which her siblings had also attended. Zaineb lives with her mother, Shazia, father and siblings in a house with another family also from Afghanistan. Shazia (Zaineb's mother) came to New Zealand as a refugee from Afghanistan. She attended the REAF programme and was a volunteer at the Centre when the data was collected. We did not interview Zaynab's mother and the family has now left Aotearoa New Zealand. However, Zaynab's mother gave consent for Zaynab's video-recording to be collected, analysed and used in publication. Zaynab was also two years two months when the data was gathered.

Methods

The data discussed in this article is derived from the following sources:

- A presentation by the director of the Carol White Family Centre about the Centre philosophy, understandings and ideas about belonging, and teaching and learning strategies the Centre used.
- Video-recordings of children where they were engaging in curriculum events as they occur naturally and where children were using communication tools of their own and other cultures.
- An interview with Zaineb's mother (Shazia), who viewed Zaineb's video episode and discussed connections with home and Centre experiences.
- An interview with the director of the Carol White Family Centre on her perspectives of the video-recording.

The Faculty of Education University of Waikato Research Ethics Committee gave ethical approval. Particular care was taken to explain issues of confidentiality and anonymity for this group of participants to enable them to make a thoroughly informed decision on whether to use their real names or pseudonyms. The director and other teacher participants gave signed consent for their real names to be used. Participating parents gave written consent for video-recording of their child, the gathering of documentation about their child, their own interview and for their first name to be used. Teachers explained the project to children, invited them to participate and to give their assent for video-recording. Teachers gave written consent for video-recording of teaching and learning episodes and their own interview. Parents gave written consent for their children's first names to be used.

Analysis

In this chapter we explore what pedagogic interactions were taking place between two toddlers who each came to New Zealand from Afghanistan. The analysis was placed within the context of the children's home experiences and the Carol White Family Centre.

An ethnomethodological approach to the analysis is taken. Ethnomethodology is seen as a tool for understanding people's sense-making, interpretation and reaction towards others' interactions in their everyday exchanges with one another (Garfinkel 1967). This analytical approach of studying social order affords detailed insight into *how* people co-construct their social worlds in what is considered as normal daily interactions to the people being observed (Silverman 2006). The inductive characteristic of ethnomethodology avoids preconceptions of what we *think* might be happening for the participants and instead encourages the researcher to study 'the orderliness of social life as experienced, constructed and used from within' (Pollner and Emerson 2001, 119). An inductive approach to the study of social interactions offers a unique insight that would otherwise be limited by predefined hypothesis (Benwell and Stokoe 2006). Using an ethnomethodological approach to the study of early childhood interactions affords insight into the unique moments of children's social interactions directly as they occur, in order to reveal how they make sense of their worlds through their collaborative, orderly sequences of actions. We understand that children have their own unique societies and cultures separate but still connected to adults (see Corsaro 2020 for an overview), and ethnomethodology affords insight into how children's cultures might look in their everyday co-construction.

Such an inductive approach is relevant in the context of Aotearoa New Zealand's socio-cultural approach to early childhood education where learning moments often arise in improvised ways, and kaiako (teachers) are encouraged to 'provide resources and equipment that encourage spontaneous play and the practising of skills, both individually and in small groups' (MoE 1996/2017, 50). The socio-cultural framing of the early childhood curriculum in New Zealand, *Te Whāriki* (MoE 1996/2017) supports an holistic pedagogy for infants, toddlers and young children in ways that acknowledge children's social competencies in initiating and maintaining learning interactions with others. Ethnomethodoloy provides an analytical tool to unpack how children's social interactions–including the co-construction of inclusion and exclusion–takes place through paying close attention to the details of the children's interactions.

Conversation analysis is often viewed as 'perhaps the most visible and influential form of ethnomethodological research' (Maynard and Clayman 1991, 396). Through investigating the turns of talk and action (gesture) that co-produce the immediate context, conversation analysis aligns with the inductive teaching approaches within the socio-cultural curriculum framework *Te Whāriki*. A conversation analysis approach to studying the interactions of Zaineb and Zayneb involved watching the naturalistic video-recordings of their everyday interactions with each other and others present, over and over so that their orientation to specific people, places and things became noticeable as significant to them at that time, in situ. For Zaineb and Zayneb, the significant moments within their video footage were centred around the care of baby dolls in their play through non-verbal gesture, therefore the sequential orderliness of these gestures were transcribed and analysed in detail. At one point in the baby doll play, Zaineb interacts with a teacher–this part of the interaction is transcribed in detail using conversation analysis transcription convention symbols so as to represent in as much detail as possible the interaction as it unfolded. The transcription symbols (Jefferson 2004) include pauses in tenths of a second, intonation such as emphasis on a word or words spoken softly or lengthened, as these characteristics will have significance to the participants in their use (for a list of transcription conventions used in this chapter please see the Appendix).

The interaction

Excerpt 1: 0–23 seconds

Zaineb and Zaynab are standing very closely together in one of the rooms of the Carol White Centre, surrounded by other children, parent helpers and early childhood teachers. The interaction begins with Zaineb reaching her hand towards a doll that Zaynab is currently holding close to her body. We see that Zaineb gently pulls at the doll as she takes a couple of small steps backwards whilst her hand is scooped around the back of the doll that Zaynab holds. Zaynab responds to this by stepping back slightly and then giving a high-pitched cry whilst both toddlers are locked in a gaze and close physical proximity together. Zaynab's cry prompts Zaineb to turn her gaze away and position herself slightly away from Zaynab and her doll as she looks around the room. It is difficult to hear if a teacher calls out to the children, but 11 seconds into this interaction, both children look towards the same direction out of camera shot, and a teacher quickly approaches from that direction. As the teacher approaches, she gently touches Zayneb's hair and strokes her arm in a comforting gesture. Zaineb also strokes Zayneb's arm, and then the teacher gently places her hands on Zaineb's shoulders, moving her away.

Children's cries are often met with adult approach, especially during moments of dispute where cries are recognised as legitimate requests for help that warrant adult attention (see Cekaite and Burdelski 2021). A usual adult response to a child's cry in disputes is to intervene and prevent further escalation of the dispute (Bateman 2015; Butler and Edwards 2018; Church 2009). This is often accompanied with the adult *shepherding* the child or children away from the interactional space by physically steering them in a specific direction (Cekaite 2010) in order to end the dispute, which is what occurs here. Another usual way for adults to intervene in disputes is to attribute blame, categorising children in a dichotomy of either victim or perpetrator (Bateman and Church 2008) and insisting on an apology being made by the perpetrator to the victim and telling about their feelings of upset (Kyratzis and Köymen 2020). Such approaches draw significant attention to the dispute and shape such occurrences of conflict, no matter how temporal, as worthy of receiving much attention and time within the early childhood education day. However, in the situation here between Zaineb and Zaynab, we see the teacher immediately entering into a comforting touch (Cekaite and Holm Kvist 2017) to both children, as she gently strokes Zaynab's hair and arm on her approach.

The teacher's comforting and gentle approach to the dispute prompts a parallel action from Zaineb, who shifts her touch from the doll Zaynab is holding to reach gently to stroke Zaynab's hair too, in a co-operative action (Goodwin 2018) with the teacher. Just prior to the teacher shepherding Zaineb away, Zaineb also offers another gentle caress of Zaynab's arm before she leaves. These gentle gestures demonstrate a caring approach to the crying child for all to see, instilling a compassionate approach to how members care for each other within that setting in a socialisation of empathy (Burdelski 2013). Rather than reprimand a child or both children for engaging in a possible dispute, the teacher enforces a caring approach, highlighting that this is the specific culture of the place. Each temporal moment–sometimes comprising just a few seconds as is evident here–where such a caring approach towards children is enacted works to build a wider culture of care through 'culturally rooted community routines' (Rogoff et al. 2007, 490) over time. Such caring cultural practices align with the overarching principles and strands of the New Zealand early childhood curriculum, *Te Whāriki* (MoE 1996/2017) which encourage early childhood teachers to provide culturally responsive environments to support equitable learning for the diverse range of children they care for each day in each setting.

Excerpt 2: 24–53 seconds

As Zainab is *shepherded* (Cekaite 2010) out of the participation framework she had initiated with Zaynab, a teacher shouts out her name, prompting her to first look in the teacher's direction and then walk towards the teacher, who is sitting at a nearby table with two other children. As Zaineb approaches, the teacher is leaning towards her, smiling and opening up a blanket onto her lap, patting it with both hands as she makes reference to the baby doll. Zaineb and the teacher engage in the following interaction which once again demonstrates a specific moment where a culture of care is played out during an everyday, impromptu interaction in this setting.

01	Teacher:	Zaineb?
02	Zaineb:	((*turns to face Teacher*))
03	Teacher:	Zaine::b () baby::::.. >here?<
04	Zaineb:	((*approaches Teacher*))
05	Teacher:	baby:.
06		(1.2) ((*Zaineb continues walking towards Teacher.*
07		*Teacher places a blanket on her lap*))
08	Teacher:	$yeah:: baby::.$ ((*pats blanket*)) bishy::
09	Zaineb:	[((*places baby on the blanket*))
10	Teacher:	[$aw thankyou Zaineb¿$
11		((*reaches for doll. pulls it on to the blanket*))
12	Zaineb:	((*steps backwards, watching*))
13	Teacher:	$wrap the ba:by ↑up$.

14		((places one side of the blanket over the doll))
15		(1.6)((Holds out the opposite side of the blanket
16		looking at Zaineb))
17	Teacher:	$wrap$ ((nods head looking at Zaineb))
18	Zaineb:	((nods her head))
19	Teacher:	((continues wrapping the doll))
20		$<the:re:>$ ((holds wrapped doll out towards Zaineb and
21		kisses its forehead))
22	Zaineb:	((takes hold of the wrapped doll))
23	Teacher:	nice ba:by::. ((moves hands off doll and places
24		them on Zaineb's waist))
25		((Zaineb walks away))

On leaving the prior interaction with Zaynab, Zaineb is immediately called by a nearby teacher who is sitting at a table with two older children. The call of Zaineb's name alerts her attention to the teacher, as she turns to face her direction, but remains in the same position and does not approach her. Further clarification to Zaineb that she is being invited to participate in an interaction with the teacher is then put on display, as the teacher calls her a second time, placing more emphasis on her name by speaking it in a drawn out way and suggesting that she move more closely to the teacher 'here' (line 03). Interestingly, this invitation also makes reference to the doll that Zaineb is holding, demonstrating the teacher's understanding that this is a valuable object in the current situation and orienting to it in order to initiate a successful interaction (Bateman and Church 2017). This prompts movement as Zaineb then moves more closely to the teacher. Although these turns of talk and action are very short, they work to initiate a new participation framework that includes Zaineb, demonstrating to her that she is an important member of the setting whose contribution and participation are valuable to those present (MoE 1996/ 2017).

Once Zaineb approaches the teacher she stands in front of her, clutching her doll closely and only places the doll on the blanket once prompted to by the teacher. The teacher's prompt is performed with gesture, as she pats the open blanket, and verbally with the word 'bishy' (line 08) which is spoken in Zaineb's home language of Dari, meaning to 'sit'. The teacher's actions here are performed in a recipient designed (Sacks 1992) way to maximise the potential of understanding between herself and Zaineb as she uses her home language and gesture to invite Zaineb to sit with her, engage her in an inclusive interaction positioned around the baby doll. This invitation is accepted by Zaineb in her subsequent turn as she approaches the teacher and hands her doll to her.

The next turns (lines 09–11) show a transition of the doll from Zaineb to the teacher as a co-operative action (Goodwin 2018) where Zaineb places it on the blanket and the teacher places her hands gently on the doll's head as she accepts it. These giving and receiving actions are performed with very gentle touch in what has been termed *haptic sociality* (Cekaite and Holm Kvist 2017; Goodwin

2017) which refers to the intimacy of co-operative interaction and how bodies intertwine during *affectively rich interchanges* (Goodwin 2017). The gentle haptic touch during the transitioning interchange of the doll between Zaineb and the teacher is woven with positive affect, marked by the teacher's smile talk ($ transcription symbol) as they collaboratively act in a caring way to position the doll together. This intimate interaction, initiated by the teacher, works to socialise acceptable ways of caring for others and again emphasises the cultural routines that are woven with care and respect in this place (Rogoff et al. 2007; Ochs and Schieffelin 2011).

The importance of the act as being a collaborative one between the teacher and Zaineb are demonstrated in lines 13–19 where the teacher begins the action of wrapping the doll, but pauses to wait for a confirmation from Zaineb that this is acceptable before she progresses. It is only once Zaineb gives the go ahead, communicated with gesture by a nod of her head (line 18) that the teacher continues, demonstrating that Zaineb has autonomy over what happens to the doll and that the wrapping of the baby is a co-operative action (Goodwin 2018). The teacher brings the collaborative activity of wrapping the doll to a close, communicating this activity as complete to Zaineb with 'there', as she holds out the doll towards her (line 20). Zaineb again demonstrates her skilful reading of social cues in her response where she steps forward with her arms open to receive the doll to 'reveal an appreciation of, and agreement to, the intention of closing' (Schegloff and Sacks 1973, 298) of the interaction at the appropriate time. The final turn in the interaction is taken by the teacher, who places the doll in Zaineb's arms, whilst pulling the blanket down from its face slightly and leaning forward to kiss the doll on its forehead.

These actions help build a picture of empathy socialisation where the child and teacher together build the co-operative action of caring for the doll in empathetic embodied actions (Burdelski 2013). By engaging together in the early socialisation practices through the employment of semiotic resources for socialisation (Ochs and Schieffelin 2011) in systematic and orderly ways, Zaineb and the teacher make observable their belonging to a collection of people who engage in these caretaking activities, where teaching about caring for others is initiated by following the child's interests.

Excerpt 3: 1min 22

With her wrapped baby now in her arms, Zaineb walks into the garden area of the centre towards where Zaynab is sitting on a wall, also holding her wrapped doll. Both children sit happily alongside each other with their wrapped babies for almost a minute, without any talk until Zaynab drops her doll and its blanket on to the floor. Zaineb's attention is drawn to the doll, now on the floor, as she leans to look at it and moves her finger around it in an upwards movement. Zaynab responds to Zaineb's upwards gesture by picking her baby up, again demonstrating a preferred approach to caring for the dolls in an affectionate way, and the co-operative effort taken to care for these dolls as though they were real babies. This caring approach towards the positioning of the dolls is then escalated further, as the blanket belonging to Zaynab's doll is picked up off the floor by Zaineb and handed back to her. Zaynab moves the blanket around the baby for a few seconds, before Zaineb stands up, places her doll gently on the floor, and takes the blanket back off Zaynab. In a parallel movement, Zaynab hands her doll to Zaineb, giving her the responsibility of wrapping the doll up once again.

What happens next demonstrates the knowledge exchange Zaineb has gained from the prior collaborative interaction with the teacher in excerpt 2, Zaineb mirroring the actions of the teacher by laying flat the blanket, then placing the baby gently on to it, and folding the blanket carefully around the doll. Such actions show how children can be socialised into caring routines through everyday interactions that they can collaboratively engage in with others (Ochs and Schieffelin 2011; Rogoff et al. 2007). Such daily interactional practices map out the culture of a place where each member collaboratively contributes to caring for others through recognisable actions (Sacks 1992). Children are acculturated into engaging in specific actions that are recognisable as belonging to the culture to which they belong, and engaging in these actions constructs their identity (Clift 2016) as capable and competent carers (MoE 1996/2017).

Collaborative caring and protection are highly valued in the Carol White Family Centre, embedded in its culture and visible in many practices. Collaborative caring was evident in the Centre philosophy from its opening: 'It takes a village to raise a child and since people are so far from home, we are part of their New Zealand village' (Gerrity 2018). When asked for her interpretation of the video episode, the director, Robyn, said that the children's behaviour 'was ongoing, they did it every day. They had their dolls, swaddled their babies, and off they went.' She described the children as being close to each other and spending a lot of time outside together, engaging in imaginative play and planning. The Centre is informed by the UN Convention on the Rights of the Child and the Convention Related to the Status of Refugees. Protection is a key principle of both Conventions, that is particularly relevant to the refugee experience, and that Robyn said underpins everything in the Centre. Emotional safety is a particular focus. She thought the doll play episode could be likened to protecting babies, and the adult intervention could be seen as protecting the children, during what was a very busy morning teatime.

Both Robyn and Zaineb's mother, Shazia, described Zaineb as being very caring from a young age and intensely interested in babies and mothering. 'At home she's, she's, she's very gentle with others, and respecting them a lot … She is very kind' (Shazia). Shazia thought the interest and learning that Zaineb showed came from some home experiences, and were strongly influenced by the Centre, which Zaineb attended from the age of six months. 'And then she find out interesting with baby. Because I'm working here she might saw me holding the baby … Because when she found it to be interested with baby. She really love them.'

Conclusion

The ways in which the teachers approach and engage in such caring activities with children demonstrate 'culturally rooted community routines' (Rogoff et al. 2007, 490) which are embedded in the everyday practices and experiences of the teachers and children who attend and contribute to the Carol White Centre. The co-operative actions of caring for baby dolls demonstrate the toddlers' competence in 'performing specific operations ... on materials' (Goodwin 2018, 6) to co-produce participation frameworks (Goffman 1981; Goodwin and Goodwin 2004) through their skilful use of semiotic resources. The importance of a culture of caring and providing space and opportunities for children to engage in playful interactions with each other and practise these social organisation activities offers autonomy for children to feel a sense of belonging and inclusion in their environment.

Key points

- Children as young as two years old are capable and competent to engage in compassionate caretaking activities for and with others.
- Toddlers can competently communicate social play roles to each other in multimodal ways, as they collaboratively build inclusive and shared role-play scenarios.
- Having a diverse linguistic and cultural team of teachers and parents in early childhood centres affords opportunities for children to hear and use the language of their own culture, supporting and extending a sense of belonging in their early childhood community.
- Providing opportunities for early empathic socialisation practices were a priority in this refugee centre where a culture of care was embedded and woven throughout everyday practice.

Further reading

Mitchell, L., Bateman, A., Kahuroa, R., Khoo, E. and Rameka, L. (2020) *Strengthening Belonging and Identity of Refugee and Immigrant Children Through Early Childhood Education. TLRI Final Report.* Retrieved from: http://www.tlri.org.nz/tlri-research/research-completed/ece-sector/strengthening-belonging-and-identity-refugee-and (accessed 1 July 2021).

Mitchell, L. and Bateman, A. (2018) Belonging and culturally nuanced communication in a refugee early childhood centre in Aotearoa New Zealand, *Contemporary Issues in Early Childhood*, 19 (4): 379–391. doi:10.1177/1463949118781349.

Mitchell, L. (2020) Transforming early childhood education: dreams and hope in Aotearoa New Zealand. In: M. Vandenbroeck (ed.), *Revisiting Paulo Freire's Pedagogy of the Oppressed. Issues and Challenges in Early Childhood Education*, pp. 166–186, UK: Routledge.

Rameka, L., Ham, L. and Mitchell, L. (2021) Pōwhiri–The ritual of encounter, *Contemporary Issues in Early Childhood*. doi:10.1177/1463949121995591.

Acknowledgements

The research was supported by the Marsden Fund Council from government funding, managed by Royal Society Te Apārangi.

Thanks to the Carol White Family Centre teachers, parents and children for their willingness to participate in this research study.

Thanks also go to the UCLA Co-op Lab for their insightful guidance and feedback on early analysis on the data.

References

Barlow, C. (1991) *Tikanga whakaaro: Key Concepts in Māori Culture*, Auckland New Zealand: Oxford University Press.

Bateman, A. (2015) *Conversation Analysis and Early Childhood Education: The Co-Production of Knowledge and Relationships*, Hampshire: Ashgate/Routledge.

Bateman, A. and Church, A. (2008) Prosocial behavior in preschool: the state of play, *British Journal of Educational and Child Psychology*, 25 (2): 19–28.

Bateman, A. and Church, A. (2017) Children's use of objects in an early years playground, *European Early Childhood Education Research Association Journal*, 25 (1): 55–71.

Benwell, B. and Stokoe, E. (2006) *Discourse and Identity*, Edinburgh: Edinburgh University Press.

Burdelski, M. (2013) 'I'm sorry, flower': socializing apology, relationships, and empathy in Japan, *Pragmatics and Society*, 4 (1): 54–81.

Butler, C. W. and Edwards, D. (2018) Children's whining in family interaction, *Research on Language and Social Interaction*, 51 (1): 52–66.

Cekaite, A. (2010) Shepherding the child: embodied directive sequences in parent-child interactions, *Text and Talk*, 30 (1): 1–25.

Cekaite, A. and Burdelski, M. (2021) Special Issue: Pragmatics of crying in adult-child interactions: interactional responses to distress, *Journal of Pragmatics*, 175: 358–363.

Cekaite, A. and Holm Kvist, M. (2017) The comforting touch: tactile intimacy and talk in managing children's distress, *Research on Language and Social Interaction*, 50 (2): 109–127.

Church, A. (2009) *Preference Organisation and Peer Disputes: How Young Children Resolve Conflict*, Hampshire, Ashgate/Routledge.

Clift, R. (2016) *Conversation Analysis*, Cambridge: Cambridge University Press.

Corsaro, W. (2020) Big ideas from little people: what research with children contributes to social psychology, *Social Psychology Quarterly*, 83 (1): 5–25.

Deng, S. A. and Marlowe, J. M. (2013) Refugee resettlement and parenting in a different context, *Journal of Immigrant and Refugee Studies*, 11 (4): 416–430. doi:10.1080/15562948.2013.793441.

Garfinkel, H. (1967) *Studies in Ethnomethodology*, Oxford: Prentice-Hall.

Gerrity, R. (2018) *Creating Treasures, Carol White Family Centre*. Paper presented at the Workshop on team philosophies, conceptualising belonging, and teaching strategies.

Goffman, E. (1981) *Forms of Talk*, Pennsylvania: University of Pennsylvania.

Goodwin, C. (2018) *Co-operative Action*, Cambridge: Cambridge University Press.

Goodwin, M. H. (2017) Haptic sociality: the embodied interactive constitution of intimacy through touch. In: C. Meyer, J. Streeck and J. S. Jordan (eds.), *Intercorporeality: Emerging Socialities in Interaction*, pp. 73–102, Oxford: Oxford University Press.

Goodwin, M. H. and Goodwin, C. (2004) Participation. In: A. Duranti (ed.), *A Companion to Linguistic Anthropology*, pp. 222–243, Oxford: Basil Blackwell.

Immigration New Zealand (2021) 19 February 2021, New Zealand refugee quota programme. Retrieved from: https://www.immigration.govt.nz/about-us/what-we-do/our-strategies-and-projects/supporting-refugees-and-asylum-seekers/refugee-and-protection-unit/new-zealand-refugee-quota-programme (accessed 19 February 2021).

Jefferson, G. (2004)Glossary of transcript symbols with an introduction. In: G. H. Lerner (ed), *Conversation Analysis: Studies from the First Generation*, pp. 13–31, Amsterdam: John Benjamins.

King, M. (2003) *The Penguin History of New Zealand*, New Zealand: Penguin.

Kyratzis, A. and Köymen, B. (2020) Morality-in-interaction: toddlers' recyclings of institutional discourses of feeling during peer disputes in daycare, *Text and Talk*, 40 (5): 623–642.

May, H. (2013) *The Discovery of Early Childhood*, Second edition, Wellington: Auckland University Press with Bridget Williams Books.

Maynard, D. W. and Clayman, S. E. (1991) The diversity of ethnomethodology, *Annual Review of Sociology*, 17: 385–418.

McMillan, N. and Gray, A. (2009) *Long-term Resettlement of Refugees: An Annotated Bibliography of New Zealand and International Literature*. Quota Refugees Ten Years on Series. Retrieved from: www.dol.govt.nz/research (accessed 19 February 2021).

Mead, H. (2003) *Tikanga Māori: Living by Māori Values*, Wellington New Zealand: Huia.

Ministry of Education (1996/2017) *Te Whāriki. He Whāriki mātauranga mō ngā mokopuna o Aotearoa. Early childhood curriculum*. Retrieved from: https://www.education.govt.nz/assets/Documents/Early-Childhood/ELS-Te-Whariki-Early-Childhood-Curriculum-ENG-Web.pdf (accessed 19 February 2021).

Ministry of Health (2001) *Refugee Health Care: A Handbook for Health Professionals*. Retrieved from: https://www.moh.govt.nz/notebook/nbbooks.nsf/7086510ecd1c88e1cc2573b70071599b/70bf0d88efa0ab6ccc256bc70080da82?OpenDocument (accessed 19 February 2021).

Mitchell, L., Rameka, L., Bateman, A., Atatoa Carr, P., Carr, M., Ang, L. and Khoo, E. (2018) Refugee families in early childhood education: Constructing pathways to belonging. Retrieved from: https://www.waikato.ac.nz/wmier/projects/early-years-research/refugeefamiliesinearlychildhoodeducationconstructingpathwaystobelongin (accessed 19 February 2021).

Ochs, E. and Schieffelin, B. (1989) Language has a heart, *Text*, 9 (1): 7–25.

Ochs, E. and Schieffelin, B. (2011) The theory of language socialisation. In: A. Duranti, E. Ochs and B. B. Schieffelin (eds.), *The Handbook of Language Socialisation*, pp. 1–21, New York: Blackwell.

Penuel, W. R. (2014) Emerging forms of formative intervention research in education, *Mind, Activity and Culture*, 21 (2): 97–117. doi:10.1080/10749039.2014.884137.

Pollner, M. and Emerson, R. (2001) Ethnomethodology and ethnography. In: P. Atkinson, A. Coffey, S. Delamont, J. Lofland and L. Lofland (eds.), *Handbook of Ethnography*, pp. 118–135, London: Sage.

Reedy, T. (2013) Tōku Rangatiratanga nā te Mana Mātauranga: 'Knowledge and power set me free … '. In: J. Nuttall (ed.), *Weaving Te Whāriki*, Second edition, pp. 35–49, Wellington New Zealand: NZCER Press.

Rogoff, B., Moore, L., Najafi, B., Dexter, A., Correa-Chávez, M. and Solís, J. (2007) Children's development of cultural repertoires through participation in everyday routines and practices. In: J. E. Grusec and P. D. Hastings (eds.), *Handbook of Socialization*, pp. 490–515, New York: Guilford.

Sacks, H. (1992) *Lectures on Conversation (Vol. I & Vol. II)*, Oxford: Blackwell.

Schegloff, E. A. and Sacks, H. (1973) Opening up closings, *Semiotica*, 8 (4): 289–327.

Silverman, D. (2006) *Interpreting Qualitative Data: Methods for Analyzing Talk, Text and Interaction*, Third edition, London: Sage.

UNHCR (2020) 18 June 2020, figures at a glance. Retrieved from: https://www.unhcr.org/en-au/figures-at-a-glance.html (accessed 19 February 2021).

Appendix: Conversation analysis transcription conventions

The conversation analysis symbols used to transcribe the data are adapted from Jefferson's conventions described in Sacks, Schegloff and Jefferson (1974) and Jefferson (2004).

?	raising intonation
((brackets))	unspoken actions
::	lengthening of the prior sound
(brackets)	utterance could not be deciphered
.	falling intonation
>arrows<	utterance spoken quickly
(0. 4)	the time of a pause in seconds
$	smile talk
[	the beginning of an overlap of talk
]	the end of an overlap of talk
↑	sharp rising intonation in speech
<arrows>	utterance stretched and spoken slowly
¿	intonation that rises more than a comma but less than a question mark

References

Jefferson, G. (2004) Glossary of transcript symbols with an introduction. In: G. H. Lerner (ed.), *Conversation Analysis: Studies from the First Generation*, pp. 13–31, Amsterdam: John Benjamins.

Sacks, H., Schegloff, E. A. and Jefferson, G. (1974) A simplest systematics for the organisation of turn-taking for conversation, *Language*, 50: 696–735.

6 Social embodiment in early childhood education for children with PMLD

Ben Simmons

Introduction

The extent to which every child could (and should) be educated in a mainstream school is a contentious issue, with debates taking place on a national and international level. Recent criticism of the United Kingdom's disability rights record offers a clear example of such tension. The *Conventions on The Rights of Persons with Disabilities* (CRPD) states that all children should 'access an inclusive, quality, free primary and secondary education on an equal basis with others in the communities in which they live' (United Nations 2006, Article 24). However, despite ratifying the CRPD in 2009, the United Kingdom government continues to support the view that some children are best educated in special schools, and that an education system can be considered 'inclusive' as long as children receive some form of education–regardless of whether the setting is mainstream or special (Armstrong, Armstrong and Spandagou 2010, Alliance for Inclusive Education 2021). The United Nations (2017) has expressed disapproval of this dual education system, claiming that it has led to a rise in the number of disabled children being segregated. It has also criticised insufficient teacher education in the field of inclusion, and recommended that the government take concrete steps to realise the rights of disabled children to an inclusive education (EHRC 2017).

Children with profound and multiple learning difficulties (PMLD) form part of the group for whom inclusive education is deemed unrealistic, and debates in academia mirror those taking place between nation states and intergovernmental organisations. Proponents of segregated education have argued that children with PMLD experience global developmental delay, function at the preverbal stages of representation, and require developmental pedagogy and curricula that contrast sharply to the subject-based education offered by mainstream schools (Imray and Colley 2017). By contrast, mainstream schools have been described as spaces that offer children with PMLD the opportunity to participate in the global project of 'inclusive education', with the promise that mainstream education leads to social cohesion and, ultimately, more inclusive societies (Lacey and Scull 2015).

DOI: 10.4324/9781003163206-9

Whilst there is strong sentiment on both sides of the debate, a key problem is that there is very little research evidence on which to draw, meaning that the perspectives of children, their parents/carers and teaching staff have been ignored. This leads to detached and abstract commentary where appeals are made either to human rights or common sense without any real understandings shown about what actually happens when children with PMLD attend mainstream schools. Hence, debates lack substance–they are ignorant of the concrete realities of classroom practice and associated lived experiences–and can be considered unethical from a disability rights perspective insofar as commentators and policy makers fail to listen to the voices of children with PMLD and those involved with their education and care (Oliver 1992). This leads to questions not just about the value of such debate, but whose interests are being served by the silencing.

This chapter contributes to the debate by presenting the findings of a project that examined how different educational settings (mainstream, special, nursery, primary and secondary) provide social interaction opportunities for children with PMLD. Whilst some of the findings have been described elsewhere (e.g., Simmons 2021a, 2021b), this chapter presents the first detailed analysis of data that relates to early childhood education, and is the first published study involving children with PMLD in mainstream early years settings. The study makes no pretence about its methodological nature–the aim and design of the research was researcher-led and therefore not consistent with emancipatory approaches to disability research (Oliver 1992). However, it provides a novel and concrete description about what mainstream education for children with PMLD can look like in early years settings, and involves the experiences of children with PMLD in the inclusion debate. What emerges from this description is the view that mainstream education can be consistent with special education in terms of how children are supported by staff. It also raises awareness of the importance and complexities of supporting peer interaction.

Finally, whereas the PMLD field has been heavily influenced by psychological theory when developing intervention strategies, this chapter employs an enactivist theory (Varela, Thompson and Rosch 1991) to guide analysis of how different educational milieus support the social engagement of children with PMLD. Rather than assuming that children with PMLD lack the behavioural and cognitive abilities to meaningfully engage with mainstream settings, an enactivist account holds that diverse settings are central to the enrichment of our conscious awareness and abilities. These themes are explored in more detail later in the chapter.

The next section will briefly describe the history of behaviourism and cognitivism, and the influence it has had on PMLD research. This paves the way for discussion of enactivism and its significance for the PMLD field. After describing the aims and methodology, the findings of the research will be described, and the discussion will apply the enactivist lens to help illuminate the findings in more detail. The conclusion will offer further reflection about inclusion debates in light of the presented evidence.

Traditional theory in the PMLD field: behaviourism and cognitivism

Educational research involving children with PMLD has traditionally been informed by behaviourism and cognitivism. This section will briefly outline these approaches before exploring enactivism as an alternative way of thinking.

Behaviourism, as the name suggests, is a branch of research concerned with the scientific study of behaviour. In its classical form (e.g., Watson 1913), behaviour is conceptualised as a reflex response that is caused by (or is under the control of) environmental stimuli. Rather than theorising behaviour in terms of agency (free will), behaviourists examine the relation between a stimulus and a response in order to discover laws that allow researchers and practitioners to shape or control the behaviour of others. In the PMLD field, behaviourism underpins interventions such as applied behaviour analysis (ABA) whereby researchers attempt to teach children through positive reinforcement. This involves children being 'rewarded' with access to 'preferred stimuli' (e.g., toys, food, music and film) if they behave in a manner that the researcher/practitioner would like to see repeated (Simmons and Watson 2014).

Whilst behaviourism still informs research in the PMLD field, some academics (particularly in the UK) have drawn conceptual resources from cognitivism to develop intervention strategies and assessment tools that address the emerging communication skills and social awareness of children with PMLD (see for example Goldbart and Ware 2015). The roots of cognitivism can be traced back to the 1950s 'cognitive revolution'. Inspired by technological advances such as the invention of the microprocessor, cognitive scientists began to develop a computational model of the mind that viewed cognition in terms of 'software' that runs on the 'hardware' of the brain. The computational model drew attention to the complex information processing that mediates the relationship between environmental stimulus and behavioural response (Thompson 2007) and, in doing so, began to investigate how cognition involves re-presenting the pregiven world symbolically in the mind prior to action (Varela, Thompson and Rosch 1991).

Researchers in the PMLD field who have been influenced by cognitivism draw heavily from developmental studies that examine how cognitive representations emerge from birth onwards (e.g., Piaget 1952, Schaffer 1971). This has led to a shift in focus away from experimental approaches that emphasise controlling or shaping children's behaviours, to exploring how practitioners can support the emerging cognitive representations of children who are deemed to be 'stuck' at the preverbal stages of development (the pre-symbolic stages of representation). Hence, the language of 'stimulus' and 'response' has been gradually replaced with a language of 'object permanence' (the ability to represent that objects continue to exist even when they are out of sight) and 'contingency awareness' (the ability to represent cause-effect relations) and so on (Simmons and Watson 2014).

Enactivism: a third way

Enactivism provides an alternative way of thinking about cognition and behaviour that has so far been overlooked by researchers in the PMLD field. Enactivism is a theory of cognition that emphasises its situated and embodied nature, and draws influence from a range of disciplines including cognitive science, biology, phenomenology and Buddhist philosophy. The approach was first popularised by Varela, Thompson and Rosch (1991) in their seminal text *The Embodied Mind: Cognitive Science and Human Experience*. Whilst cognitivism has been celebrated for legitimising the scientific study of mind through the introduction of computational models and associated metaphors (e.g., 'information processing') (Baars 1986), it has been criticised for downplaying the role of the body, or reducing the 'hardware' of cognition to neural processes, thus ignoring the importance of the body in its broadest sense. Furthermore, both scientists and philosophers have questioned the value of studying cognition in artificial contexts (e.g., computer simulations of cognition in laboratories) as this ignores debates about the nature of the world that is supposedly represented, and whether diverse groups experience the world in exactly the same way (Thompson 2007, de Bruin and de Haan 2012). Enactivism emerged out of the growing unrest with cognitivism's narrow focus. Instead of thinking about cognition in terms of building internal representation of a pregiven external world, enactivism examines how cognitive structures emerge through interactions with the world, how these interactions can be socially, historically and culturally contingent, and how the history of our interaction leads to the development of a perceiver-relative world:

> human cognition is not the grasping of an independent, outside world by a separate mind or self, but instead the bringing forth of or enacting of a dependent world of relevance in and through embodied action. Cognition as the enaction of a world means that cognition has no ground or foundation beyond its own history.
>
> (Thompson 2016, xvii)

Enactivist accounts of social cognition: participatory sense-making and social needful freedom

The different interpretations of 'cognition' offered by cognitivists and enactivists have implications not just for how we think about individual cognition, but also *social* cognition. Social cognition concerns 'the ability to cognize the mental states of other agents: To understand how they feel, what they think, expect or are up to' (Satne 2021, S509). Discussions of social cognition have been dominated by cognitivism and often framed in terms of 'theory of mind' (Premack and Woodruff 1978), i.e., the capacity to attribute mental states to others, which in turn allows the observer to interpret, predict and explain observed behaviour (Satne 2021). Theory of mind presupposes a passive, third-person observational stance and relies on the competency of the individual observer to impute the mental state of the other. By contrast, enactivists understand social cognition as an intercorporeal process where concrete interaction plays a constitutive role in the emergence of social awareness. Two theories help illuminate the role of interaction in social cognition: participatory sense-making (Fuchs and De Jaegher 2009) and social needful freedom (Kyselo 2014). Each will be discussed in turn.

Participatory sense-making (Fuchs and De Jaegher 2009) refers to the ways in which two people unconsciously synchronise their behaviours during social interaction. During face-to-face conversations there is a reciprocal, subtle and rhythmic coordination of micro-behaviours such as changes in posture, eye gaze, hand gestures, facial expressions, vocal intonation, etc., and this on-going exchange of gestures is said to sustain the interaction and allow one person's body to 'read' the other. The coordination is not always symmetrical, however, and there can be changes in who leads the exchange. Fuchs and De Jaegher (2009) use the terms 'coordination to' and 'coordination with' to describe this. 'Coordination to' means that the exchange is one-sided with one person following the lead of another. 'Coordination with' implies co-regulation where two people jointly influence the interaction.

Kyselo's (2014) theory of 'social needful freedom' also illuminates how interaction is at the heart of the enactivist account of social cognition. Needful freedom is a biological term that refers to how an individual organism creates an identity by negotiating an on-going and permanent tension between a need for resources from the world, and a drive to emancipate or free itself from such materials so it can exist as an independent entity (Jonas 1966). Kyselo (2014) applies this concept to help explain how the self emerges from a social context– from 'a sea of social relational, not merely bodily processes' (page 9). *Social needful freedom* describes how the self depends on social relations, but also has to resist and free itself from such relations to be an individual. Kyselo (2014) uses the term 'distinction' to capture the emancipation of the self from social relations, and 'participation' to denote the opposite side of social needful freedom: the reliance on others. Distinction means that a person experiences herself as emancipated or distinguished from social interactions and relations, leading to a sense of separation and individuality. A range of self-conscious experiences fit Kyselo's (2014) concept of distinction: practising yoga, feeling nervous when presenting in front of an audience, feeling distant from a partner, being proud of an individual achievement, not knowing anybody at a party, and also the joy of being alone after spending a day working with others. By contrast, participation refers to the experience of feeling connected and open to others, our 'readiness to affect and to be affected by the other' (Kyselo 2014) Experiential examples include the pull we feel when we are attracted to others, the feeling of letting go while dancing with a partner, being one with the crowd at a concert or sport events, etc. 'Such experiences refer to the basic structure of social autonomy as striving to remain connected and open to particular types of social interactions and relations' (page 11). The examples above describe experiences where either distinction or participation is more prominent.

However, Kyselo (2014) explains, the experience of self as separate from, or willing to engage with others, can precede or follow each other, and even overlap.

What participatory sense-making (Fuchs and De Jaegher 2009) and social needful freedom (Kyselo 2014) suggest then, is that communication and social awareness are embodied and interactive, not passive and observational, that the individual subject emerges through social interaction and as such is always dependent on others to some degree, that interactions can be understood in terms of power dynamics (i.e., who is taking the lead), and that the more diverse our opportunities to interact, the richer our sense of self and other becomes. These themes will guide discussion of research findings later in the chapter. The next section will report the research aims and findings.

The study

This chapter reports the findings of a three-year project, funded by the British Academy, which examined how different kinds of school settings (special, mainstream, nursery, primary and secondary) provide alternative social interaction opportunities for children with PMLD. The study explored how children with PMLD respond to different opportunities, and the impact of these opportunities on children's communication skills. Whilst some of the findings have been described elsewhere (e.g., Simmons 2021a, 2021b), this chapter presents the first detailed analysis of data related to early childhood education contexts.

Three children from early years settings participated in the study: Emma, Felix and Ruby. Emma attended a reception class in a special school class four days a week, and a reception class in a neighbouring primary school one day a week. There were approximately 15 students in her special school class, and 40 in her mainstream school class. Felix and Ruby attended an integrated nursery five days a week. The nursery was based in a mainstream school and consisted of two classrooms interconnected by a short corridor. One classroom was run by a team who had specialist training, expertise and resources to support a group of eight children who had special educational needs, including children with severe to profound learning difficulties. The other classroom was run by early years staff with more conventional mainstream training, and this team supported approximately 30 children. For most of the day the two classrooms functioned as one continuous space since children were free to move from one class to another, and each day there would be whole class routines, such as register, singing and lunch.

Methodology

Children with PMLD can embody unique or individualised communication repertoires which can be overlooked or misinterpreted by researchers who are unfamiliar with the children they are researching. Given this, this research design drew on participatory and interpretivist approaches in order to support the co-construction of knowledge regarding children's actions in context. This involved working closely with children and school staff whilst also seeking the wisdom of parents. This approach was developed to guide the researcher in developing interpretations of the meaning of participants' actions and involved three methods: focus groups and interviews, participatory approaches, and vignette-writing (Simmons and Watson 2015).

Before undertaking fieldwork, the research consulted significant others who knew the participants well and could inform the researcher's initial interpretive lens. This consultation took place via pre-observation focus groups where teaching staff would share insights into each child's communicative abilities, e.g., how each child expressed happiness or distress, how they demonstrated interest and possible examples of communicative intent. For example, Emma's staff described how she would 'pretend to be asleep' if she did not want to participate (she would close her eyes in order to 'opt out' of social interaction). However, staff also explained that Emma was capable of tilting her head back and opening her eyes slightly to peek at others and observe her surroundings, meaning that she was interested in others but was not ready to interact (something her parents confirmed). These subtle descriptions guided the researcher's understanding during observation.

The researcher's understanding of each child's actions was further developed through participatory observation (by supporting children in class). Participatory observation helped develop rapport with children and also led to informal discussions with staff in real time over the meaning of children's behaviours. Staff would suggest what children were thinking and feeling, and propose interaction strategies. Emma was observed 20 days in total (ten days of observation in a mainstream school and ten days of observation in a special school). Ruby and Felix were observed eight days each in the integrated nursery.

The main source of data consisted of writing live observational fieldnotes or 'vignettes'. Vignettes are prosaic fieldnotes about children's social interactions. They have a story-like structure and a chronological flow. Vignettes describe the location, time, actor(s), sequence of events and so on, and can vary from a few lines of descriptions to several paragraphs. When opportunities emerged for the participants to engage with others, the researcher wrote detailed notes of the observed opportunity as it unfolded, paying particular attention to who initiated the interaction and how, the responses, how the event developed over time, and contextual information such as location (e.g. carpet or corridor), context of the interaction (e.g. planned teaching session or outdoor play) and the materials that were involved (e.g. toys, balls, paintbrushes). The vignettes were shared or discussed with teaching staff who observed or participated in the event, allowing staff to offer their own interpretations. The vignette data was analysed using an inductive thematic approach.

Findings

Emma in the special school

Specialist interactions

Emma experienced very little peer interaction in her special school beyond the occasional greeting in the playground, or during whole class singing routines (e.g., where staff and students would sing good morning songs to each other in the morning). Emma's main communication partners were members of staff who embodied a specialist 'style' of interaction. The interaction was typically timetabled, dyadic (one-to-one), face-to-face and developmentally functional insofar as staff interacted with Emma to support her emerging social awareness and communication skills. Emma was regularly asked to make a choice between two objects (e.g., drink or food), or ask for more access to an object (e.g., more drink, more music, more time playing with a toy) by looking at the desired object (or a symbolic representation of the object), vocalising and/or reaching out to the object. Staff would begin by asking a question verbally whilst signing, present Emma with the actual objects being offered, or a symbolic representation (a picture of a yogurt, or a spoon to signify a yogurt option). If Emma did not respond as intended, staff would offer a range of prompts including verbal prompts (repeating the question, perhaps in a more dramatic tone), gestural and visual prompts (pointing at the object or showing a symbolic representation of the object), followed by a physical prompt (e.g., turning Emma's head to face the object, rubbing her arms to arouse her, or place her hand between the two objects on offer). Emma's actions were commented upon and celebrated, including unprompted responses to environmental changes (e.g., if Emma turned to see who was entering the classroom she would be praised: 'Good looking, Emma! You're being nosey and checking out who's at the door?').

Care-based interactions

A similar dyadic style was observed during care-based routines (coded as 'care-based pedagogy') whereby Emma was asked to indicate if she wanted more hugs, etc. However, not all dyadic interaction was designed to teach. Sometimes staff worked one-to-one with Emma trying to rouse her by wiggling her arms, talking loudly and shaking her wheelchair. Emma would sometimes rub her nose and pull her hair over and over, and staff would hold her arms, sing to her and put splints on her arms to stop what was perceived to be self-harming behaviour. Staff would also perform physiotherapy, stretching her legs and massaging her arms after sitting for a long time in her wheelchair, sometimes talking to her. Emma was largely passive or frustrated during these exchanges.

Emma in the mainstream school

Narrated bodily appropriation

Whilst staff embodied a specialist style of interaction towards Emma in the special school, Emma's teaching assistant (TA) adapted how she engaged with Emma when supporting her in the mainstream school. The mainstream style, referred to in terms of 'narrated bodily appropriation', still had a normative dimension. However, rather than trying to develop Emma's symbolic communication skills, the TA would move or control Emma's body according to the contextual demands of the situation. For example, during whole class phonics or numeracy, Emma would be sat upright, and the TA would turn her head so that she faced the interactive whiteboard. When the teacher asked a question (e.g., 'Who would like to do some painting before lunch?') the TA would raise Emma's hand, and the TA would help Emma write a number on a mini whiteboard using a hand-over-hand technique. This appropriation of Emma's body involved the TA making Emma mimic the actions of children around her, and was often accompanied by narration, e.g., the TA would explain to Emma why she was turning her head, what she had to write on the whiteboard and that 'Painting would be fun, so let's volunteer'.

Group-based attraction: co-presence and group affect

Emma experienced lots of peer interaction in her foundation class. Whilst interaction in her special school was dyadic in nature and adult-led, interaction between Emma and her mainstream peers was typically group-based or plural. Initially, large groups of up to 12 children would flock towards Emma during playtime, greet her (say hello, hold her hand, wave), before running away again and returning several minutes later. During these moments, Emma appeared shy and tried to disengage (e.g., by closing her eyes, turning her head away, and–according to her TA–'pretending to be asleep'). However, Emma soon began to feel more comfortable in the presence of large groups and was increasingly excited when they ran over to greet her, or when she was sat beside other children during carpet time. Emma's happiness in the presence of groups was evident in her squeals of excitement and smiles. Emma would laugh when children were told off, watch them intensely as they ran around the playground, turn to see groups of children shouting and playing, and observe as children played with toys, painted or used musical instruments. Emma's TA noticed that her ticks would reduce in intensity whilst she was observing others (e.g., her face rubbing, hair pulling and teeth grinding would slow or stop). The TA also admitted that Emma's growing interest in other children made it difficult to get her on task (e.g., Emma would not show interest in painting when other children sat near her).

Staff-supported peer interaction

Sustained direct engagement between Emma and children in her mainstream school was initially supported by Emma's TA. The TA would move Emma to spaces where groups were playing or working together (e.g., playing with musical instruments, making jigsaws, painting, playing with toys, dressing up). The TA would celebrate children's activities with Emma ('That's a lovely drawing!' 'Emma likes your costume!'), sometimes raising Emma's hands in the air and cheering when children completed a task (e.g., finished a jigsaw puzzle or finished telling a story). Children would be invited to interact with Emma, and given strategies to follow ('Tell her your name.' 'Could you roll the ball to Emma?' 'Emma likes to have her hands held.' 'Could you read her a story?'). The TA would model how to interact, and help peers 'read' Emma's body language ('She's opening her eyes! She likes that. Look, she can see what you're holding. See her smile? She likes your painting!'). The TA would also provide physical support, such as raising Emma's hand in the air so others could high-five her. The TA answered lots of questions from the children ('Why can't she talk?' 'Where does she live'? 'What's her favourite colour?'). Children who interacted with Emma received praise from the TA. Sometimes the TA would play games with Emma that attracted the attention of others, such as blowing bubbles above Emma which children tried to pop.

Independent peer interaction

As the project progressed, children began to initiate interactions themselves without the support of the TA. Whilst some children mimicked the TA whilst interacting with Emma (e.g., providing hand-on-hand support to draw a picture with a crayon), most interactions appeared to be spontaneous and playful. For example, children would choose to sit next to Emma (e.g., drink milk beside her during snack time, sit on the carpet with her during register). They would greet her without being prompted and say farewell when they moved away. They would perform for her (e.g., by singing, dancing, acting out a scene, pulling funny faces to make her laugh and dress her in fancy dress clothes, including hats, crowns and feather boas). In addition to such performances, children would interact using everyday classroom objects and toys. For example, they would show her what they had made using Lego or playdough, give her objects to play with (e.g., put a wooden figure in her hand, or a ball at her feet), show her how objects work (e.g., whoopie cushions), and give her objects of affection (daisy chains and party invitations). Children invited Emma to play with them (join them at the water table, computer or dollhouse), and were given permission by the TA to wheel Emma to where they wanted to play, or push her around the playground. During these exchanges Emma would become more awake, active and alert, and turn to look at children gathered around her and the objects on display. If Emma appeared drowsy the children would still interact with her (e.g., give her playdough to squeeze, or shake her arms). Children's interaction was sometimes intimate, and involved hugging, kissing her on the cheek, stroking her arms and hair, holding her hand, rubbing her shoulders and tucking her in with a blanket if she appeared cold. During these activities Emma would typically smile, make happy vocalisations and engage in prolonged looking.

Felix and Ruby in the integrated nursery

Whilst Emma was afforded a range of opportunities to engage with peers in her mainstream school, Felix and Ruby experienced very little peer engagement in the integrated nursery, and the majority of data describes Felix/Ruby interacting with members of staff. Interactions with staff resembled a combination of the specialist style and mainstream style described above. Staff typically embodied a dyadic and developmentally normative approach whilst also utilising narrated bodily appropriation and whole class instruction.

Specialist interactions

Felix's interactions often revolved around intimate and physical exchanges with members of staff on the classroom carpet. Felix sometimes initiated social exchanges. For example, whilst laying on his tummy he would touch staff hands and play with their fingers, climb on staff laps (with staff support) and grasp their ears and nose if he could reach. He would happily lean back on TAs and let them support his weight, and enjoyed staff whispering in his ears. Staff would hold on to Felix so he could sit upright, hug him, rock and bounce him, dance with him, pat his back and shoulders, massage his hands, mimic his actions and playfully move his limbs (e.g., holding his arms out wide like a plane, or move his arms to pretend that he was driving a car). These interactions took place several times a day (e.g., on the classroom carpet or in the multisensory room) and were joyous, with Felix smiling, vocalising, making eye contact and returning the gestures such as hugging staff back and bouncing on their laps. Through these exchanges staff attempted to develop Felix's emerging communication skills. For example, they would stop hugging or bouncing him then ask him to signal that he wanted more hugs/bounces (e.g., they asked him to vocalise, use sign language or use his arms to gesture). If Felix did not respond then staff would employ a series of prompts, such as verbally repeating a question whilst simultaneously using sign language ('Does Felix want more?') and use physical prompts (e.g., helping Felix to sign 'more' using a hand-over-hand strategy).

Whilst intimate physical exchanges were unique to Felix, staff often interacted with Ruby through the exchange of objects in order to develop her joint attention skills. To these ends, staff requested that Ruby pass objects to staff (e.g., books, switches, food, flowers), and also invited Ruby to request objects (e.g., toys, spoons, symbols) that were in her line of sight. Staff would sometimes explain why Ruby had to give an object to another person (e.g., it was another child's turn to play with a toy, or it was time to pack away). Ruby would sometimes reach for objects on the table in front of her which were slightly too far away. These actions were interpreted by staff as 'reach for signal' behaviours, and Ruby was praised by staff whilst also being encouraged to vocalise before they gave her the desired object.

In addition to intimate physical interaction and the exchanging of objects, both Felix and Ruby experienced traditional approaches to teaching symbolic communication, such as using symbol systems and switch technology. Both children were regularly asked to make a choice between two or more objects by looking at, pointing to or reaching towards a picture of what was desired (e.g., the picture of the banana or the picture of a drink). Sometimes images were attached to switches, and Ruby/Felix were asked to tap a switch to indicate a preference. Ruby would typically hit both switches or grasp all of the pictures at once, whilst Felix would bypass the symbols altogether and reach for the desired object if it was nearby. Such formal communication approaches were used during breaktime and playtime when the classroom was quiet. These kinds of strategies were similar to those used by Emma's staff in the special school.

Narrated bodily appropriation and whole class activities

Similar to Emma's experience of staff support in the mainstream school, both Felix and Ruby were involved in narrated bodily appropriation and whole class activities, often at the same time. For example, children would be encouraged to sit down on the carpet quietly while the teacher explained the day's activities. Felix and Ruby would sit on staff laps, supported to sit upright by being held by staff. During whole class singing activities, staff would help Ruby and Felix performing the actions to songs, waving their arms in the air, stomping their feet on the floor and clapping their hands together. Felix found these daily routines particularly exciting–he smiled, squealed, shook with excitement and sometimes continued to clap after the TA had let go of his hands. He was also encouraged to use switches during morning register but never pressed a switch independently so was helped hand-over-hand. Teaching staff helped Ruby write, draw, cut paper, paint and colour using hand-over-hand support (e.g., whilst making a Father's Day card or classroom decorations).

Peer interaction

Despite Felix showing interest in peers and vice versa, there is very little evidence to suggest that Felix interacted with his classmates. Felix's teacher agreed that more work was needed to help him make friends, and suggested that other children lacked the confidence and skills to interact. The lack of engagement between Felix and peers may also stem from his limited opportunities to play alongside other children. During breaktime and lunchtime Felix would remain in the classroom with the teaching staff whilst other children went out to play. By contrast, Ruby experienced some (albeit limited) peer interaction opportunities. She had more freedom to crawl around the carpet space during indoor play, and was supported by a TA each breaktime and lunchtime. Occasionally a TA would help Ruby play with others by turning her around to face children close by, and help her via hand-over-hand support (e.g., helping her to roll balls or push toy cars to other children, or sign 'hello' to others). Staff would explain the rules of play to Ruby such as the need to take turns ('It's time to pass the ball, Ruby') and asking her not to throw toys. During breaktime and lunchtime a TA would help Ruby outside, and this primarily led to Ruby watching other children run around and play. Ruby appeared to be attuned to children's emotions, smiling and laughing in excitement as children laughed, or frowning and looked concerned when other children were upset. Sometimes children mimicked staff (e.g., repeating staff praise for Ruby–'Fab painting!'). When Ruby was free from staff support other children approached her and initiated interaction by patting her on the head, sitting beside her, smiling at her, holding her hand and pressing their nose against Ruby's nose. Ruby found these moments exciting and reciprocated by smiling back, making prolonged eye contact and grasping the hands of children attempting to hold her hand. On one occasion Ruby reached out to and held the hand of one of her classmates. However, these moments were rare, brief and sometimes interrupted by a TA or cut short because the session had ended.

Discussion

Debate about inclusive education for children with PMLD has focused on the extent to which segregated education violates the human rights of children with PMLD, and whether mainstream provision (e.g. its subject-based curriculum) is appropriate for children described (by some) as functioning at the earliest stages of development. The research presented in this chapter suggests that a more nuanced understanding is required. As demonstrated in the findings, mainstream provision (such as the integrated nursery) can appear socially inclusive in the sense that children with PMLD can be observed learning alongside mainstream peers. However, in the case of Felix and Ruby, there was limited peer interaction. Felix's and Ruby's main communication partners in the integrated nursery were members of staff who engaged in a similar style to Emma's special school staff. Emma also experienced limited peer interaction in her special school, and her staff engaged with her via a specialist style defined in this chapter as being functional, developmental, dyadic and aimed to teach her how to communicate. Hence, despite the heavy presence of mainstream peers in the integrated nursery, concrete social interactions resembled the kind illuminated in the special school.

The data described in the findings section can be theorised with reference to participatory sense-making (Fuchs and De Jaegher 2009). Participatory sense-making draws attention to the implicit, intercorporeal exchanges that accompany intentional face-to-face interaction. It also highlights the ways in which interaction can be shared (actors can coordinate 'with' one another), and how one actor can take the lead whilst the other follows (one actor can coordinate 'to' the other). Emma commonly experienced teaching staff taking the lead during social interactions in the special school (coordination 'to'). Staff attempted to develop Emma's ability to coordinate 'with' others by teaching her how to interact through models of symbolic communication (e.g., choose between two photographs through prolonged looking). However, the process of teaching Emma how to coordinate 'with' others resulted in staff dominating the interaction and thus expecting Emma to coordinate 'to' staff requests. Similarly, Ruby and Felix experienced a specialist style of interaction that was dyadic and developmentally normative which can be interpreted as Ruby and Felix being asked to coordinate 'to' staff. Arguably, it was Felix's determination to engage in intercorporeal exchanges that allowed him to move away from 'coordination to' towards 'coordination with'. He initiated intercorporeal exchanges, sometimes appeared to lead them (by getting what he wanted–climbing on staff and grabbing their ears and noses), and commanding cuddles through reaching behaviour. Staff were skilled at transforming these situations into 'coordination to' contexts whereby they attempted to teach Felix how to communicate using more conventional symbolic gestures (e.g. to request 'more' through sign language). Whilst Felix did not acquire the skills that staff aimed to teach, the data can be read in terms of an oscillation between Felix and his staff's intentions for interaction (coordination 'with' and coordination 'to'), and this dialogue (or perhaps negotiation) is what allowed Felix to stand out, resist fixed regimes of PMLD communication intervention and be understood as a communicative agent with his own intentional forms of communication that should be identified and respected.

Furthermore, whilst Felix and Ruby experienced little peer interaction in the integrated nursery, Emma found her mainstream school a space that afforded a range of opportunities to make friends and engage in new forms of social interaction that were rarely observed in the special school. Arguably, her TA in the mainstream school still engaged in a normative style of interaction whereby Emma was expected to coordinate or conform to the expectations of the mainstream environment (writing, watching phonics videos, raising hands to ask questions, etc. during whole class activities). However, the TA was also radical in breaking away from such expectations and supported mainstream peers in developing confidence and awareness regarding how to interact with Emma. This eventually led to a rich social milieu with diverse forms of participatory sense-making where Emma's social agency emerged in her willingness to be open to peer interaction, her invitations to interact through eye contact, excited screaming and laughter, and her expressions of interest tracking peers. Whilst this may appear mundane and trivial to those who do not know Emma, these pro-social behaviours can be understood as her moving from 'coordination to' peer expectation, to an emerging 'coordination with'. In the field of participatory sense-making, sharing communicative intent is not simply an intellectual act underpinned by symbolic forms of communication, but an intercorporeal, affective and pre-reflective form of social participation.

The social needful freedom lens (Kyselo 2014) extends analysis further, by providing an account as to why peer interaction emerged in some contexts but not in others. Social needful freedom holds that the self emerges from a sea of social relational processes. 'Distinction' refers to the emancipation of the individual self from social relations. Without distinction the individual subject is at risk of being limited to a basic set of social interactions that are determined by others. However, without 'participation' and being open to others, the individual risks isolation. These classifications (distinction and participation) can help illuminate why Felix and Ruby experienced little peer interaction, whilst Emma experienced rich and diverse peer interaction opportunities in the mainstream. Felix rarely went outside to play during break and lunchtime and his main communication partners were members of staff. Furthermore, whilst Ruby experienced more freedom to engage with peers insofar as she was present during whole class indoor and outdoor play, she rarely interacted with peers and staff failed to be proactive in supporting peer interaction. Because of a lack of peer participation there was a lack of opportunities for Felix and Ruby to achieve 'distinction' against a peer backdrop.

By contrast, Emma experienced an abundance of participation with mainstream peers during her placement in a reception class. Through the careful guidance of Emma's TA, peers appeared to develop confidence around Emma and approached her more and initiated interaction and play. The TA's lead was central in shaping the early interaction experiences of Emma and her peers, and in doing so created contexts for Emma to not only participate (follow), but also express keenness to be with peers, an openness to their interactions and excitement in the presence of others. Through the lens of social needful freedom, Emma's peer participation was reliant upon (needful of) the support of the TA, and her distinction as a socially open and excited peer emerged through this interaction. Furthermore, Emma's mainstream peers did not simply learn interaction strategies from the TA, but also experimented with and deployed a diverse range of alternative communication strategies, defined in terms of plurality, intercorporeality, play, object-sharing or gift-giving, showing off and performing for Emma. These strategies emerged over time and correlated with Emma appearing to come out of her shell and show increasing interest in peers, e. g., demonstrating anticipation such as laughing and squealing with excitement when children approached her, as well as tracking peers in the playground, locating the sound of familiar peer voices, and what the TA felt was a reduction of her ticks (her teeth grinding, hair pulling and nose rubbing) and avoidance behaviours (pretending to be asleep). Extending analysis of social needful freedom, it could be argued that the peer group itself moved away from participating in the received wisdom of the TA in order to develop a distinct peer group identity in terms of interaction strategies, which in turn provided a backdrop for Emma to further emerge as a distinct individual.

Key points

- This chapter presents the first study that examined the experiences of children with PMLD who attended mainstream early childhood education settings. In doing so, it moves beyond abstract discussion by grounding the inclusion debate in the concrete realities of day-to-day mainstream practice.
- To date, the inclusion debate has been polemic–it revolves around a binary whereby mainstream schools and specials schools are seen as polar opposites that afford alternative kinds of support and resources. The research presented in this chapter suggests that mainstream schools and special schools are not always distinct in terms of the opportunities they provide for children with PMLD.
- If there can be congruence in practice between mainstream and segregated settings then debates about which setting is most appropriate seems misplaced. As this chapter has highlighted, children with PMLD can be at risk of being socially isolated from peers in both mainstream schools and special schools.
- Researchers must highlight the extent to which such isolation takes place, and suggest strategies to support practitioners so they are not just aware that isolation takes place, but have the skills and resources to tackle this.
- Whilst this chapter does not aim to create a user-guide to inclusion it does suggest that TAs can play a central role by giving children confidence, advice and strategies, as well as creating opportunities for groups to come together and learn from each other. This is difficult to achieve in spaces where adults dominate the interaction, and where children are afforded little chance to interact with one another.

Further reading

Nind, M. and Strnadová, I. (Eds.) (2020) *Belonging for People with Profound Intellectual and Multiple Disabilities: Pushing the Boundaries of Inclusion*. Abingdon: Routledge.

Simmons, B. and Watson, D. (2014) *The PMLD Ambiguity: Articulating the Life-worlds of Children with Profound and Multiple Learning Disabilities*. Abingdon: Routledge.

References

Alliance for Inclusive Education (2021) *Article 24: The UN and the Human Right to Inclusive Education*. Available at: https://www.allfie.org.uk/campaigns/article-24/ (accessed 28 June 2021).

Armstrong, A., Armstrong, D. and Spandagou, I. (2010) *Inclusive Education: International Policy and Practice*. London: Sage.

Baars, B. (1986) *The Cognitive Revolution in Psychology*. New York: The Guildford Press.

de Bruin, L. and de Haan, S. (2012) Enactivism and social cognition: in search of the whole story, *Journal of Cognitive Semiotics*, 4 (1): 225–250.

Equality and Human Rights Commission (ENRC) (2017) *Disability Rights in the UK: UK Independent Mechanism Updated Submission to the CRPD Committee*. London: EHRC.

Fuchs, T. and De Jaegher, H. (2009) Enactive intersubjectivity: participatory sense-making and mutual incorporation, *Phenomenology and the Cognitive Sciences*, 8 (4): 465–486.

Goldbart, J. and Ware, J. (2015) *Communication*. In: Lacey, P., Ashdown, R., Jones, P., Lawson, H. and Pipe, M. (Eds.) *The Routledge Companion to Severe, Profound and Multiple Learning Difficulties*, pp. 258–270. Abingdon: Routledge.

Imray, P. and Colley, A. (2017) *Inclusion Is Dead: Long Live Inclusion*. Abingdon: Routledge.

Jonas, H. (1966) *The Phenomenon of Life: Toward a Philosophical Biology*. Chicago: University of Chicago Press.

Kyselo, M. (2014) The body social: an enactive approach to the self, *Frontiers in Psychology*. 5 (986): 1–16.

Lacey, P. and Scull, J. (2015) Inclusive education for learners with severe, profound, and multiple learning difficulties in England. In: Forlin, C. and West, E. (Eds.) *Including Learners with Low-incidence Disabilities*, pp. 241–260. Bingley: Emerald Publishing.

Oliver, M. (1992) Changing the social relations of research production? *Disability, Handicap & Society*, 7 (2): 101–114.

Piaget, J. (1952) *The Origins of Intelligence in Humans*. New York: International Universities Press.

Premack, D. and Woodruff, G. (1978) Does the chimpanzee have a theory of mind? *Behavioral and Brain Sciences*, 1 (4): 515–526.

Satne, G. (2021) Understanding others by doing things together: an enactive account, *Synthese*, 198: 507–528.

Schaffer, H. (1971) *The Growth of Sociability*. Harmondsworth: Penguin.

Simmons, B. (2021a) The production of social spaces for children with profound and multiple learning difficulties: a Lefebvrian analysis. *British Journal of Sociology of Education*, 42 (5–6): 828–844.

Simmons, B. (2021b) From living to lived and being-with: exploring the interaction styles of children and staff towards a child with profound and multiple learning disabilities, *International Journal of Inclusive Education*, 25 (6): 657–670.

Simmons, B. and Watson, D. (2014) *The PMLD Ambiguity: Articulating the Life-worlds of Children with Profound and Multiple Learning Disabilities*. Abingdon: Routledge.

Simmons, B. and Watson, D. (2015) From individualism to co-construction and back again: rethinking research methodology for children with profound and multiple learning disabilities, *Child Care in Practice*, 21 (1): 50–66.

Thompson, E. (2007) *Mind in Life: Biology, Phenomenology and the Sciences of Mind*. London: The Belknap Press of Harvard University Press.

Thompson, E. (2016) Introduction to the revised edition. In: Varela, F., Thompson, E. and Rosch, E. (Eds.) *The Embodied Mind: Cognitive Science and Human Experience*, pp. xvii–xxxiii. London: MIT Press.

United Nations (2006) *Convention on the Rights of Persons with Disabilities Optional Protocol*. New York: United Nations.

United Nations (2017) *Convention on the Rights of Persons with Disabilities: Concluding Observations on the Initial Report of the United Kingdom of Great Britain and Northern Ireland*. New York: United Nations.

Varela, F., Thompson, E. and Rosch, E. (1991) *The Embodied Mind: Cognitive Science and Human Experience*. Cambridge Massachusetts: The MIT Press.

Watson, J. (1913) Psychology as the behaviorist views it, *Psychology Review*, 20: 158–177.

7 Foundation Phase teachers' understandings and enactment of participation in school settings in Wales

Alison Murphy, Jacky Tyrie, Jane Waters-Davies, Sarah Chicken and Jennifer Clement

Introduction

Given the rhetoric about children's rights in Wales and the emancipatory purposes of the New Welsh Curriculum (Donaldson 2015), as signposted in Chapter 1, we sought to explore how young children's participation rights are understood and enacted in the school context from the perspective of the teacher. We hope that our study contributes to the empirical evidence-base, which is currently minimal, and provides a basis upon which research and practice development can build. The chapter considers the results of a qualitative study which investigated teachers' perceptions of children's participation rights within Foundation Phase settings in Wales, focusing on Article 12 of the UN Convention on the Rights of the Child (UNCRC). Teachers were also asked to consider what these rights look like when translated into practice. The survey provided data, therefore, about teachers' *understanding* and *enactment* of Article 12. This chapter builds on the previous literature-based research undertaken by some of the authors that established the paucity of the empirical evidence-base about the enactment of children's rights in educational settings in Wales (Lewis et al. 2017).

The Welsh policy context

As Chapter 1 detailed, within the Welsh context there has been a consistent commitment to a rights-based agenda as demonstrated by a range of progressive policies that support the participation rights of children (Williams 2013; Lewis et al. 2017; Tyrie and Beauchamp 2018). The wider policy environment in Wales has produced a 'children first' approach in the first decade of devolved government as summarised in the Seven Core Aims (Welsh Government 2019). These aims were created to inform decision making on priorities and objectives locally and nationally around policy and practice with children. In 2011, the National Assembly for Wales passed a law requiring Welsh Ministers, whenever they exercise their functions, to have due regard to the UNCRC (Rights of Children and Young Persons (Wales) Measure 2011). Three years later, a further law was passed imposing a similar legal duty on persons and bodies having social services and well-being functions (Williams 2013). As a result of the Measure, a number of policies have been developed to support children's rights in Wales, including the Children and Young People's National Participation Standards. The Standards supported by the UNCRC, and the Well-being of Future Generations (Wales) Act 2015, put the involvement of children at the centre of improving well-being at a national level.

Alongside prominent policy rhetoric, the Welsh Government has made efforts to undertake training for early years professionals around children's rights, with 150 individuals attending training to date, though it is clear further support and resources are required (Welton et al. 2019). Cited within the Welsh Government's overarching commitment to the Seven Core Aims (emanating from the UNCRC), the Foundation Phase Framework for 3–7-year-olds in Wales was introduced in 2008 and updated further in 2015 (Welsh Government 2008, 2015). This play-based curriculum is based on experiential learning which is characterised by a combination of adult- and child-led activities. Sitting within an overarching emancipatory vision for children (Waters 2016), the Foundation Phase Framework, with personal development and well-being of the child centrally placed, was intended to further support children's enactment of their rights. These policy directives and others are indicative of an explicit sustained strategy to embed children's rights within policy in Wales, particularly within educational contexts.

However, despite the emphasis upon children's rights at the level of policy rhetoric, there is a paucity of research which focuses upon *how* children's rights are enacted within settings and this is particularly neglected for children below the age of seven who would be in Foundation Phase classes (Lewis et al. 2017). What follows is an overview of relevant and available literature pertaining to the issues central to this chapter.

Children's participation within early education in Wales

There is limited literature pertaining to the enactment of children's participation rights within Foundation Phase settings in Wales. However, some research has been undertaken, as outlined below, which addresses issues connected to children's participation rights in Welsh Foundation Phase classrooms.

Research from Maynard and Chicken (2010) found that whilst Foundation Phase teachers may claim to value a child's right to navigate the direction of their own learning (and thus recognised a child's right to do so), they also felt duty bound to prioritise pedagogy driven by pre-specified external targets which often run counter to a children's rights agenda. In doing so, this study surfaced a tension between an outcome driven focus, in which children have to achieve pre-specified targets, and a focus upon UNCRC principles, which highlight the voice and agency of the child.

Related to this, Maynard et al. (2013a) found that teachers recognised a need to develop child-initiated learning opportunities for the under-sevens, but that this was more likely to take place in the outdoor environments. These findings suggest that there was acknowledgement by teachers of a child's right to have personal interests valued within the Foundation Phase provision, but that this was shaped by differing expectations in different spaces.

More recently, the study by Clement (2019) can be viewed as more explicitly associated with a children's rights agenda. This study explored the use of spatially democratic pedagogy arguing that the design and co-creation of space by children and educators can be utilised as a pedagogical practice which supports young children's authentic participation in early years classrooms. Clement argues that when children are not completely involved with the process of classroom design, their involvement tends to be tokenistic.

Lyle (2014) considered the enactment of children's rights in Welsh primary classrooms and suggested that teachers' varied constructions of childhood shape how they respond to the UNCRC principles and how they attempt to enact these within their practice. Findings suggest that teachers held a range of different constructions of children, such as 'the innocent child', 'the child as a blank slate' and 'the developing and immature child'. Some of the participants as noted by Lyle (2014) felt that the implementation of UNCRC principles was a 'threat' to how they viewed their role as teachers, erasing some of their power and agency, and this belief was more likely for practitioners who favoured an authoritarian teaching style. Teachers who held a socially competent view of the child were more likely to embrace UNCRC principles, particularly Article 12 which refers to a child's right to have their voice recognised within the curriculum. Whilst this study was related to teachers working with children over 7 years of age, it is relevant to the current study since it suggests that the constructions that teachers hold of children, and their associated views of their roles as teachers, shape their understanding and enactment of UNCRC principles within their practice.

Children's participation within early education in the UK

The paucity of studies in this area supports the views of Lewis et al. (2017) that there is a gap between the policy rhetoric of a children's rights agenda within Wales and the practical application within educational settings. Although there has been limited research focus within Wales on the enactment of children's participation rights within early childhood education, there has been some research undertaken within the UK which provides some useful insights. Within the Scottish context, Konstantoni (2013) reflects on the processes of children's active participation and argues that practitioners interpret participation too selectively in practice. Konstantoni (2013) argues that children's right to non-discrimination was not effectively implemented, exemplifying the 'selective' nature of children's participation. The articles discussing children's participation across English settings (Daniels 2014; Murray 2016; Helavaara Robertson et al. 2015; Waller 2006) frame participation in a number of ways. The remit and boundaries of participation as a concept range from broad understandings of children's participation as a way of supporting general approaches to teaching and learning, to focused consideration of how children's gender, ethnicity, disability and friendship groups mediate children's experiences of participation.

Waller (2006) highlights children's experiences of a regularly attended outdoor project and discusses how young children can develop their own learning paths in this environment. Daniels (2014) considers the collaborative (participatory) creation of written texts as a way to support children to bring their experiences to their setting. Daniels critiques the policy in England at the time, which focused on individual and predefined skills to be acquired by children, as undervaluing the experiences that children bring to early educational settings. In a similar vein, Helavaara Robertson et al. (2015) considered data from English, Finnish and Estonian settings and focused on the co-construction of learning experiences and child-initiated pedagogy. The paper concludes that, 'when given an opportunity, the children are skilful in sharing the responsibility of control with peers and adults' (page 1825). This paper provides an empirical example of children in early childhood education enacting participation in their classroom. Murray (2016) also considers young children's decision making as a vehicle for their participation.

Taking the concept of social justice Luff et al. (2016) argue that children in early education and care should be afforded a 'pedagogy of citizenship' within their settings to ensure a democratic approach. The six key ways they suggest this can be delivered are as follows:

- Seeing and valuing the whole person and encouraging appreciation of diversity.
- Upholding individual and collective rights and enabling participation.
- Encouraging critical and creative thinking.
- Promoting equity and social justice.
- Fostering peace and conflict resolution.
- Challenging consumerism and encourage in action or sustainability.

(Luff et al. 2016, 197)

It is possible that this 'pedagogy of citizenship' is a method that affords the enactment of the participation by children in early educational settings. However, this has not been empirically explored by the authors.

Participatory pedagogies

As stated by Dunphy (2012), children's participation rights in early childhood education and care can only be realised in terms of pedagogy if educators facilitate a change in their own knowledge and status in the classroom. Participatory pedagogies foreground the co-construction of educational processes *with* children (Formosinho and Formosinho 2016). This shaping of meaning and learning through active participation can be understood as a pedagogical approach that does not, in advance, fully define an activity, process or outcome. Indeed, participatory pedagogies, in valuing the multiple voices and perspectives of all children, provide space for all voices to create shared understandings between and across different pedagogical relationships (Sousa et al. 2019). In this construction, children and other stakeholders are active learners (Dewey 1916).

Gaining insight into participation through pedagogic practice, Lyndon et al. (2019) focus on the development of participatory pedagogy through pedagogic mediation. Whilst the focus is on practitioners, pedagogic mediation is considered to provide an effective and participatory mechanism through which listening practices can be extended and embedded. In an interesting exploration of what matters to children, Meehan (2016) utilised pedagogical documentation to explore the 'voice' of children using visual research methods to explore children's understanding of what matters in their lives.

In enacting participatory pedagogies, the pre-schools of Reggio Emilia equally position children as co-constructors of learning through an interdependent relationship with adults, families and their communities (Malaguzzi 1998). Their participatory pedagogies do not see children as educationally passive, and instead view them as becoming participants in the creation of an emergent curriculum: the *progettazione* (Rinaldi 1998). Knowledge in pre-schools is seen to be created through the process of self and social construction, and it is the relationships, communications and interactions children have with their parents, other children and teachers that are at the heart of the teaching and learning process (Rinaldi 1998). It is interesting to note that, during the development of the Foundation Phase in Wales, 'explicit and implicit references' (Maynard et al. 2013b, 14) were made to the practices of pre-schools in Reggio Emilia.

Participatory pedagogies in the Foundation Phase in Wales

In terms of pedagogy, the Foundation Phase is play-based (Welsh Government 2015), bolstered by a developmental approach and including detailed statutory curriculum guidance as stated by Murphy and Waters-Davies in Chapter 1. The pedagogical approach taken by this curriculum advocates that well-being is central and that the participation of the child is implicit.

Across the Foundation Phase documentation, pedagogical participation alludes to a broad understanding of the term participation. Linked to the sociocultural approaches introduced in the Foundation Phase Framework (Welsh Government 2008, 2015), children are expected to play an active role in decision making (Maynard et al. 2013b), practitioners are to provide a balance of practitioner-led and child-initiated activities (Maynard et al. 2013b) and curriculum content should 'focus more on children's interests ... rather than ... pre-determined outcomes' (Welsh Government 2008, 28). However, a large scale, government funded evaluation of the Foundation Phase by Taylor et al. (2015) reported children's participation as their ability to spontaneously initiate and direct their own learning. Specifically, Taylor et al. (2015, 136) identify children's ability to 'spontaneously direct the learning, e.g. making mud cakes for the café'. This participation, according to Taylor et al., 'spans a variety of learning zones and includes the addition of enhanced challenges in various parts of the classroom, e.g. following a challenge on creating a nest in the creative area' (page 143). We note here that such an interpretation of children's participation is limited to their freedom to make decisions within specific and bounded learning activities; it does not extend to their participation in decisions regarding pedagogy, the environment or the *ways of being* within the setting.

As outlined in Chapter 1, from 2022 the Foundation Phase Framework will be replaced in Wales by the Curriculum for Wales (Donaldson 2015). This requires that learners contribute to the design of the curriculum and identifies a number of pedagogical principles, including that children are 'exercising choice, participating, being involved, initiating and directing their own learning over a period of time' (Welsh Government 2016, 8). Also noted in Chapter 1, the Children's Commissioner for Wales (CCW) has called for the new curriculum to be strengthened by a commitment to children's rights and for the children's workforce to become 'rights-informed, rights-aware and rights-based' (CCW 2018, 9). For the latter to be realised, participatory pedagogies will need to be adopted in order to fully position children as co-constructors of their learning.

Methodology

This chapter draws on a research study which had the aim of investigating the following question: 'How do Foundation Phase teachers understand and enact the notion of participation as it relates to the children they teach?' To address the primary research question, empirical data was collected via a qualitative online survey. The research draws upon a sociocultural approach (Rogoff 2003) and is underpinned by a critical realistic epistemology (Bryman 2016), alongside the conceptual framework of agency (Prout and James 1997). This theoretical framework is employed to explore how children's participation rights are understood and shaped by the adults who structure the educative spaces in which children participate.

Data was collected during the Covid-19 pandemic of 2020/21, so an online method was used thus enabling the researchers to gather responses easily from participants around Wales. The focus of the qualitative survey was what Foundation Phase teachers understood by the term 'participation' and how they perceived children's participation to be enacted within their classrooms and schools. The survey was bilingual, available in Welsh and English, reflecting the bilingual nature of Wales' education system, and responses were received in both languages. Twenty-six participants, all of whom were early childhood educators working with 3–7-year-olds, gave detailed responses to the questions. Interestingly, of the 26 responses completed, five respondents did not attempt the questions related to enactment despite offering their understanding of participation. This may be indicative of the difficulty that participants might find in conceptualising enactment of participation within settings at a practical level.

The findings are presented according to three themes which relate to the aim of the research, which was to explore how young children's participation rights are understood and enacted in the school context from the perspective of the teacher. The three themes are as follows: understanding participation, that is, teachers' perceptions of children's participation rights; enactment of participation, that is, what these rights look like when translated into practice; and barriers and enabling factors for participation, that is, what factors are reported to influence teachers' enactment of children's participation.

Findings

Understanding participation

Across the data set, participation was described by respondents using though a similar set of words: 'active', 'engagement', 'ownership', 'voice' and 'choice.' In most cases participation was viewed broadly in relation to taking part, engaging and choosing. When asked the question 'What does children's participation mean to you as a teacher?', responses were often linked to specific themes, including children's involvement in curriculum, their dispositions in learning, and spatial aspects of the learning environment. The noted exception was a participant who linked understanding explicitly to the Rights Respecting Schools Award, which is centred around schools' commitment to embedding UNCRC principles in planning, policies, practice and ethos (UNICEF 2021) (for further details see Chapter 1). This participant noted the following:

> As a level 2 Rights Respecting school, we believe that children should have a clear voice in their education.
>
> (P11, age 4–5)

> Class charter completed by the children with association rewards and sanctions. This is based on the UNCRC statements.
>
> (P11, age 4–5)

One respondent drew attention to a child's right 'not to participate'. This was the only example in the data which acknowledged this perspective and the challenges that this posed when teachers are under pressure to address curriculum outcomes and developmental milestones: 'To a degree I think children have the right to not participate in activities, but this draws in difficulty with meeting the required needs of the curriculum and child development.'

(P25, age 6–7)

Children's involvement in the curriculum

When explaining participation, respondents drew attention to children's ownership over and involvement in planning of their learning through the recognition and support for 'pupil voice'. One respondent stated, 'it means pupil voice, children's engagement, joining in, exploration of activities and opinions' (P9, age 4–5). Another commented:

> The aim should be to fully immerse the child in the provision. They should be given a voice, to have some ownership of the task. They should be challenged and supported to reach their full potential.
>
> (P12, age 4–5)

Pupil voice was cited as enabling teachers to support children's interests and plan learning opportunities that would build upon children's ideas. One respondent expressed it this way:

> Pupil voice is essential and leads to improved learning experiences as children have been involved in their own learning and taken ownership of what they would like to learn.
>
> (P18, age 5–7)

By the time the children are 6–7 years old, understanding about participation seems to be related to children having some input and ownership of the content of the curriculum (rather than just specific activities, as with the younger age), either as individuals or as part of a group activity. One respondent defined it as 'active engagement in learning, Pupil Voice in shaping and determining how we teach and choice' (P22, age 6–7), whilst another described it as:

> Participating in planning their own learning and reflecting and evaluating. Learning from their mistakes and trying things in a different way.
>
> (P23, age 6–7)

Across all age ranges, responses indicated children's participation in these curriculum endeavours were often bounded within class frameworks/structures, for example:

> Planning involves children's input into curriculum around a broad theme and set of Big Books (literacy)–this involves activities outside–leading to a set of questions to be answered during the topic.
>
> (P21, age 6–7)

> Firstly, curriculum-wise, we integrate pupil-led learning, having input in what is taught and how. For instance, we share ideas at beginning of topic and plan for these learning opportunities. On a weekly basis we use the

children's ideas for enhanced areas, e.g., building the giant's castle in the block play area together and uploading photo to seesaw. We also consider topic themes and whether these are linked to the children's interests.

(P4, age 3–5)

The definition of participation as described below is linked to parts of the continuous or enhanced provision as seen in Foundation Phase curriculum documentation (Welsh Government 2015):

Engaging in 'independent challenges' in the classroom whereby pupils access continuous or enhanced provision and apply or practice skills taught.

(P24, age 6–7)

This participant linked participation to the curriculum as well as viewing it as a teacher-led, time-bound activity which is timetabled as a fortnightly event, rather than participation being an integral part of everyday practice:

Participating in 'Pupil Voice' sessions which include pupils discussing things they would like to learn about, skills they would like to practise, activities they enjoy and want to do again, and engaging in collaborative discussion about how to enhance the classroom on a fortnightly basis to enhance the learning but equally continuing to stimulate interest and engagement.

(P24, age 6–7)

Alongside definitions of participation linked to ownership and involvement in curriculum planning, it appears that participation, for this age range in particular, is bounded by particular activities, for example, 'actively engaged in designing role play …' (P20, 6–7). Similarly, in the example below, children are able to set their own challenges but there are identifiable boundaries, in this instance, the class topic:

The children are encouraged to share their ideas and views, ask questions and have a voice to express themselves. They plan their own learning challenges related to class topics and enjoy doing so.

(P26, year 1)

This does raise questions regarding the level of agency afforded to children in terms of the boundaries of participation that are established by the teacher.

Dispositions in learning

Participation for the youngest learners (3–4 years) was understood to be children being able and willing to access what might be considered as standard high quality early childhood education and care, for example a rich and varied environment for learning, and practitioners who observe and respond to children's interest in order to plan effectively for future provision (Welsh Government 2008). Children were identified to be participating if they could be seen to be joining in and this participation was often connected to learning behaviours and dispositions. For example:

> Coming to school, listening, asking questions, giving opinions, trying their best even if it doesn't interest them fully.
>
> (P3, age 3–4)

> Being part of creating and looking after the learning environment. Finding out through real experiences cause and effect.
>
> (P4, age 3–4)

> Being curious, to observe, explore, experiment. To be present in the moment and to be able to express and share thought feelings and emotions.
>
> (P5, age 3–4)

Similarly, teachers of children from 4 years onwards were also more likely to comment on participation being akin to children engaging in particular learning activities and 'taking part'. One respondent noted that 'it means that they are engaged and interested in the task or activity and want to learn' (P17, age 5–6), whilst another commented:

> Children's participation means allowing pupils to engage within lessons through discussions and to have a voice within the classroom setting.
>
> (P20, age 5–7)

These notions of 'taking part' were viewed broadly, usually outside of the UNCRC framework. However, in some instances participants did make links to more formal participatory structures, grounded in the UNCRC. For example:

> It is all about listening to children's views. It is ensuring children understand that they have a right to a voice and to be listened to. In order to do this, it is important to make links to the UNCRC articles as much as possible during teaching and learning. It is allowing children to get involved with planning and leading their learning.
>
> (P5, age 3–5)

> Teachers fostering ideas from the pupils and using them to plan more meaningful activities for learning that engage learners. Being guided by pupil's interests and current stimuli and including these to create more personalised learning within a topic/theme.
>
> (P24, age 6–7)

The term participation at this age range was also understood as children's enjoyment of their time in school. One participant listed the following: 'enjoyment, sparking their imagination, whether through language or physical movement' (P3, age 3–4).

Spatial aspects of the learning environment

For some participants, participation was linked to the learning environment, in particular to the outdoors. One respondent noted:

> Pupil Voice on what activities are accessible outside (During the Autumn Term they requested a pirate ship with a treasure chest and maps.... during Summer Term we are looking to revamp our mud kitchen.)
> (P11 aged 4–5)

The notion of participation is governed by the location of the learning activity, for example, one respondent stated:

> Outdoors–engaged in task, being creative, working co-operatively with others, problem solving and resilience when faced with problems
> (P22, aged 6–7)

Again, we see that responses offer a vision of a highly bounded and contextualised understanding of participation.

Enactment of participation

Several themes emerged from the data about enactment of participation, that is, what it 'looks' like and how it is 'seen' in classrooms, outdoor spaces and teaching activities. These themes include provision of spaces with choices, children's engagement with and ownership over their learning and involvement in planning processes, children's self-expression and independence and their engagement in formal democratic participation processes. It should be noted that listening to children was only mentioned twice and this was in relation to older children (6–7 years). Some of the key themes around how teachers 'see' participation are outlined below with exemplars from respondents provided.

Provision of spaces with choices

For those who taught young children (3–5 years), there was a clear focus on the importance of the environment as a site for enactment of participation. Both indoor and outdoor spaces were deemed as important to facilitate the enactment of participation through the learning environment allowing children to play, connect and learn with others as well as the resources available to them. The role of the adult in adapting the environment in response to the children's interests is also evident in this response:

> Class spaces and outside are areas of exploration and wonder as children explore and make new connections, solve problems, work with and alongside others … The environment is carefully created and adapted as learners demonstrate learning styles, needs and express their interests.
>
> (P3, age 3–4)

Enactment of participation was seen by some teachers as children being able to have access to and choose their own resources/play, for example, one participant stated, 'children can access all resources and can use them in their play without boundaries' (P14, age 4–6).

Alongside the environment as a space for participation to be enacted, some participants highlighted the important role that adults play in supporting and scaffolding participation, for example, by providing 'engaging hooks' (P3, age 3–4) for learners.

Ownership of spaces

Another way that teachers saw participation enacted was in children feeling an ownership of spaces, particularly outdoor spaces. In the following example, reference is made to independent exploration of spaces and play, particularly outside:

> The children are encouraged to take ownership of the classroom and the outdoor areas. Learners are able to move resources, e.g., wooden planks, boxes, and use as they wish … Encourage balanced risk-taking with trees to climb, balance beams etc.
>
> (P4, age 3–5)

Children's engagement with and ownership over their learning

In the older age range (5–7 years), there was more emphasis on participation being 'seen' in children's engagement and ownership of *learning* rather than ownership over the spaces alone. This engagement in/with activities was seen as a 'sign' of participation in classrooms; including getting the tools for learning, taking an active role in the classroom and their learning and deciding how to record this learning. Participation was also seen to be enacted in children engaging socially, for example making eye contact and talking (although choosing to work alone was also acknowledged). This is demonstrated by one response which suggested that children who are not engaging in communication or activities are not participating: 'a small number need a lot of encouraging to take part, e.g. responding to questioning' (P19, age 5–6).

Involvement in planning processes

Children's participation was perceived as being seen or enacted through involvement of children in the planning of learning, in particular where activities were planned in response to child-initiated topics or ideas. Children being able to make (or 'being allowed' to make) decisions or contribute to planning was noted as enactment of participation. Sometimes this was reported as being seen through teachers' observation of children's interests, and at other times as discussions with children about topics of interests. It was also suggested that listening to children formed part of this process of involving them in planning. Some examples of how children are involved in planning are provided below:

> As part of their topic lessons, pupils identify at the beginning of each term what they would like to learn and this is then used by myself to plan lessons.
>
> (P20, age 5–7)

> Once the children's ideas have been gleaned at the planning stage, the activities are planned so that they are in charge of their own learning. This is done through open ended questioning and asking for their thoughts, ideas and opinions.
>
> (P11, age 4–5)

While one teacher reports 'using children's ideas' to plan topic and trying to 'follow ideas that arise spontaneously' from the children (P6, age 3–5), they also identify competence as a barrier to this form of participation:

> At the earliest age, children need guidance to be able to formulate suggestions, and all need training to be able to make realistic workable contributions.
>
> (P6, age 3–5)

This suggests a view whereby only children who are deemed competent can participate and those who are lacking in competence need to be taught how to be competent in order to participate.

Children's self-expression and independence

For children aged 3 to 5 years, teachers described enactment of participation as choice, self-expression and independence, and emphasised the importance of self-directed play. When asked how participation was 'seen' in their classroom one respondent stated:

> Children are given opportunities to express what they would like to explore and learn. They discuss opinion, likes and dislikes. They give their

own views on what they want to learn. Children have a right to their own opinions … Children are given opportunities to provide ideas of what they would like to explore, learn or actively engage in. They decide what they would like to see/do for focused activities or enhanced provision. Children can decide where they would like to learn!

(P9, age 4–5)

There was a sense that participation was seen as children engaging, expressing likes and dislikes and giving their own views. The enactment of participation is expressed by children being competent and confident learners; for example, one respondent stated:

The children are independent and confident in their learning and have given their ideas in the areas of provision provided which enables them to access the learning they are enthused to do.

(P10, age 4–5)

Teachers who worked with older children, that is, those aged 6–7 years old, also cited sharing ideas, asking questions and communicating in the classroom, such as in class discussion, games and through circle time, as a way that participation was 'seen' in their classrooms:

The children are encouraged to share their ideas and views, ask questions and have a voice to express themselves. They plan their own learning challenges related to class topics and enjoy doing so.

(P26, age 5–6)

Whole class participation on the carpet–asking/answering questions, offering ideas, opinions, questioning why. Also means listening to others and responding to others

(P22, age 6–7)

Teachers stated that children undertaking activities independently (rather than being directed) was one way that participation was seen in the classroom. Children choosing activities at certain times of day was also viewed as a way that participation was enacted in classrooms, such as the challenge areas, or role play topic. One respondent described it as 'free access to relevant equipment and resources to allow pupils to participate fully, at any level, in their work' (P22, age 6–7).

Formal democratic participation processes

A small number of participants felt that pupil voice groups were how participation was evident in their classroom, for example:

All children are also members of a pupil voice group. We have 9 groups which have pupils from each year group. This gives them a voice not only within our classroom but also across the wider school.

(P11, age 4–5)

This mechanism was also, for some, connected to classroom planning processes.

Enablers and barriers to participation

Very few participants (6 out of the 19 responses to this question) described enablers for participation in their schools or classrooms. Again, we conjecture this might illustrate difficulties teachers may have in articulating their views around enactment of participation. The main enabler discussed was 'allowing' or 'valuing' pupil voice, the comment below providing an example of this:

Allow pupils to have a voice and to feel their opinions have been valued and listened to will encourage them to have the confidence to participate.

(P18, age 5–7)

Following on from the discussion above about understandings and enactment of participation, the learning environment was seen as being a significant enabler as described below:

Learning environment which is resourced with open ended resources. Enhancing to follow individual needs and interests. Adapting spaces when needed.

(P3, age 3–4)

Alongside the learning environment, participants also raised the need for differentiation as an enabler and the necessity of meeting individual needs. For example, one respondent emphasised 'differentiation so that all pupils have opportunities to participate at their own level of input' (P24, age 6–7).

Other enablers were described in terms of solutions to the barriers, for example, the use of technology to overcome the barriers caused by the Covid-19 pandemic and the use of other pedagogical tools to improve language skills. The following two responses provide examples of this:

I use a lot of P4C [Philosophy for Children] to help the children develop speaking and listening skills. This will help them develop their voice and ability to share what they want.

(P5, age 3–5)

You can overcome this barrier (Covid-19) with technology.

(P9, age 4–5)

Participants seemed much more willing and able to describe barriers for participation in their schools and classrooms. Key themes emerging from this part of the data include the need for staff to be trained to support participatory approaches, class size coupled with the need for support staff, children with additional learning needs, children's maturity, and children's willingness or confidence. The Covid-19 pandemic was also reported to be a barrier to participation.

Staff training was reported to be a significant barrier, not just for teachers, but also in terms of support staff. Attitudes and dispositions of staff members was seen as problematic by some participants, one of whom commented that 'motivation to change is needed in the part of staff to enable meaningful participation' (P4, age 3–5).

However, a barrier to participation was also reported to be class sizes. One teacher reported that they could not offer one-to-one time for each child and that consequently some children were not included. Commenting on barriers to participation, this participant wrote:

> Class sizes. I can't reach all the children's interests/needs. Support–mainstream are asked to be fully inclusive but I feel more adult support is needed to achieve this. Sometimes I feel we just make it through a day and some children that are happy to keep themselves occupied don't get any 1:1 attention.
>
> (P3, age 3–4)

This suggests that participation is understood to be tied to engagement with the teacher–children who are 'happy to keep themselves occupied' seem to be deemed to be at some disadvantage or lacking in participation.

The remaining barriers expressed by practitioners concerned children with additional learning needs (ALN), the maturity of the children, and children's willingness or confidence to participate. This suggests that understanding of participation was limited by judgements about competence and capability of individual children to take part in prescribed mechanisms. Children with ALN were identified as needing additional support in order to contribute to these mechanisms, with comments below providing a flavour of this view:

> Children that have additional needs that don't have the adult support they need to help them participate.
>
> (P24, age 6–7)

> ALN–lack of support/ expertise from outside agencies to support adults and children. Not enough staff in certain year groups to provide interventions.
>
> (P18, age 6–7)

It is interesting to note that confidence and willingness to participate is perceived as a barrier created by children themselves:

> Barriers–lack of confidence, not yet resilient or willing to persevere.
>
> (P18, age 6–7)

> Confidence and willingness on behalf of the children.
>
> (P28, age 5–6)

> Barriers–pupils lack of confidence could prevent them from participating and voicing their opinions
>
> (P20, age 6–7)

The issues raised here indicate that the enactment of participation is established within specific mechanisms and, should these not be suited to some children, then they are deemed lacking rather than the mechanism being at fault.

As stated above, solutions to overcoming barriers include use of technology to overcome the barriers that have developed as a result of the Covid-19 pandemic and other mechanisms to support speaking and language skills, the latter arguably suggesting deficits in children's language skills prevent them from participating. There were other solutions implied as indicated below:

> However, most barriers can be overcome or nurtured by ensuring inclusion, nurture and sometimes bespoke intervention.
>
> (P24, age 6–7)

In terms of the Covid-19 pandemic, this was reported as a barrier by teachers of children primarily between the ages of 3–5 years, though applicable across the school setting. One respondent stated, 'C19 was a barrier to participation across a whole school' (P9, age 4–5), while another commented:

> Currently in the pandemic there are lots of barriers in terms of what resources and activities we are allowed to do.
>
> (P5, age 3–5)

Discussion

Findings from our study indicate that teachers' understandings of participation in the classroom are varied. Primarily they focus on *taking part* or *joining in* despite using key terms from the UNCRC such as pupil voice. This indicates a selective interpretation of participation which is also reflected in Konstantoni's (2013) study. Participation seems to be seen as the responsibility of the child–to join in and take part–as opposed to the responsibility of the adults to listen and employ practices to ensure they hear the voice of the child.

Even though notions of competency are not explicitly mentioned, there are examples where teachers acknowledge that children's ability to articulate their views can be challenging, for example:

> At FP [Foundation Phase], the children sometimes find it difficult to articulate what they would like to learn/find out, but they can articulate what interests them and what enhanced and continuous provision they would like to access.
>
> (P11, age 4–5)

Helavaara Robertson et al. (2015) emphasise that children are skilful in the co-construction of their own learning experiences, but this competent view of the child was not always evidenced in the participants' responses in this study.

There appears to be age-related differences in the responses, with participation for younger children (aged 3–4 years) focusing on what could be described as a high quality early childhood education in the form of rich and varied learning environments and practitioners who observe and respond to children's interests (Welsh Government 2008). This is also seen in the review of the Foundation Phase (Taylor et al. 2015) where participation was characterised as what could be conceived as high quality early childhood education and care, that is, children initiating their own learning.

Teachers' understandings of participation, particularly with the older age range (6–7 years), were characterised by a range of boundaries based on when, where and how participation occurs. This is coupled with a concern for meeting curriculum objectives and developmental goals. Within the Welsh context, Welsh Government guidance (2008) indicates that curriculum content should focus on children's interests rather than pre-determined outcomes. Some of the participants in this study appeared to be more focused on the latter, revealing tensions between participatory approaches and the translation of policy expectations. Similarly, Daniels (2014), reflecting on the educational context in England, expressed concern that a skills-based policy agenda could undervalue the experiences that children bring to early educational settings. Similar notions are evident in this current study too. The teacher-led discourse that is evident does not seem to account for the agentic child in early childhood education and suggests that notions of participation are not all encompassing, integral and inclusive, but rather managed and staged to meet school and curriculum requirements.

The key themes which emerge from the data in relation to how teachers viewed the enactment of children's participation as children's engagement and ownership of classroom spaces, children 'talking' to teachers about their preferences of topic or provision, children being able to 'voice' their likes and dislikes, and engagement from children in the democratic processes of participation. This raises some interesting questions about the way in which participation is enacted by educators.

There was a clear focus on the importance of the environment as a site for enactment of participation. Both indoor and outdoor spaces were deemed as important to facilitate the enactment of participation, with the learning environment allowing children to play, connect and learn with others as well as the resources available to them. This finding supports the work of Waller (2006) who focused on the role of the outdoor environment. In terms of indoor spaces, Clement (2019) explored the use of spatially democratic pedagogy to design and co-create space with children and teachers. She found that this can be utilised as a pedagogical practice which supports young children's authentic participation in early years classrooms. Similarly, both Robertson et al. (2015) and Malaguzzi (1998) argue that, during co-construction of learning, children can be skilful in sharing the responsibility of control with peers and adults. However, we saw limited evidence of teachers utilising co-creation of space or learning. Rather, many respondents tended to refer to participation being enacted through children being involved in more simplistic decision making, for example, expressing their interests as regular or one-off 'conversations' when teachers 'consulted' children about their interest in 'topics' or the use of space. This finding is in line with Murray (2016) who suggests that young children's decision making is a vehicle for their participation. Data presented here also reflects the findings of Maynard et al. (2013b) which, in evaluating the Foundation Phase, suggest that participation is a combination of practitioner-led and child-initiated activities and therefore, essentially, the taking of a 'lead' on interests from children. Similarly, Taylor et al. (2015) suggest participation should involve focusing on child-led interests and providing enhanced challenges in response to need.

At times the enactment of participation was expressed as simple choices about provision and resources, although some teachers expressed a more nuanced understanding of the complexities involved in the enactment of participation in their classrooms. For example, Participant 3 explained that participation looked like 'areas of exploration and wonder as children explore and make new connections, solve problems, work with and alongside other' (P3, working with children aged 3–4).

A further point of discussion is how enactment of participation was viewed very differently amongst respondents, which in turn may impact their understanding of the enactment of participation. Dunphy (2012) argues that participation rights can only be realised if educators facilitate a change in their own knowledge and status in the classroom. However, Lyle (2014) suggests that rather than all educators 'changing', there should be a consideration of the constructions of childhood that educators hold since these influence how educators respond to the enactment of rights in practice. Lyle argues that where a social competency model of the child is held, teachers are more likely to embrace a child's participation rights. In line with this message, it has been suggested by Sousa et al. (2019) that in order to enact children's participation in the classroom, the adults in this space must be able to value the multiple voices and perspectives of all children, providing space for all voices to create shared understandings between and across different pedagogical relationships (Sousa et al. 2019) and to view children as active learners (Dewey 1916).

Teachers reported a number of barriers to participation but seemed reluctant to comment on the enablers. Less than a third of the overall sample were able to provide this information. Covid-19 featured heavily in responses which is expected considering the severity of the current health crisis in the UK and around the world for educational settings. A recent study by Bowyer-Crane et al. (2021) confirmed that schools felt that those that children who started school in Autumn 2020 needed more support than children in previous cohorts due to the effects of the pandemic.

Class size was cited as a significant barrier which prevented the enactment of participation in the classroom. Teachers perceived additional learning needs as a barrier to participation as well as the child's confidence or willingness to engage. There was a distinct lack of reflection on practices that could be used to develop engagement for these children. Participation is seen, it seems, to be the responsibility of the child–to join in and take part–as opposed to the responsibility of the adults to listen and create mechanisms to ensure they hear the voice of the child. As discussed by Waller (2014), staff in early childhood education require sufficient time for reflection on pedagogy and practice, which has implications for the ways in which settings are managed. Although the current study did not explore teacher reflection, training was identified as a means to overcome attitudinal and motivational concerns (particularly in relation to support staff). This is despite the training offered by Welsh Government for early years professionals around children's rights (Welton et al. 2019). There is a need for further initiatives to support teachers and support staff in delivering a participatory pedagogy to support the curriculum which is centred around well-being and underpinned by the Welsh Government's 'child first' ethos.

Conclusions

As discussed, the Welsh Government's 'child first' commitment to children's rights is evident but this does not necessarily guarantee that it will then translate into practice. This issue was also recognised by Bae (2010) in the Norwegian context, who noted that 'being high on the educational policy agenda is … no guarantee for the realization of participatory rights' (2010, 214).

The findings suggest that practitioners' perceptions of participation are varied and context-specific. The rights-based terminology utilised in this study asked practitioners to reflect on their understanding and enactment of participation. The findings indicate that some teachers were unaware of where participation was part of their pedagogy and others were acutely aware and reflective about the role of participation in their daily pedagogical decision making. However, perceptions of participation both in terms of knowledge and practices were bounded in some instances by notions about the competency and agency of young children. For some respondents, participation is enacted within specific activities rather than being an overarching participatory pedagogy.

There is a need for further professional learning to ensure an early years workforce which is not only informed and aware of children's rights, but also able to translate this knowledge and understanding into participatory pedagogies. These pedagogies would allow children to be viewed as agentic and capable of active involvement in their own learning journeys. Coupled with this requirement, there is also a need for further qualitative co-constructed research to fully understand the enactment of participation in classrooms. This would allow for a better understanding of the lived, seen and experienced reality of participation for children and teachers.

Key points

- Young children's participation rights are a central feature of early childhood education, particularly in the context of Wales where this research took place.
- There is limited research into the enactment of children's participation rights in the classroom, though the research that exists suggests a gap between the policy rhetoric on children's participation rights and the application of this within educational settings.
- The study presented in this chapter draws from a qualitative survey aimed at exploring how teachers in early childhood education in Wales understand and enact children's participation.
- Responses suggest that practitioners' perceptions of participation are varied and context-specific. Findings indicate that some teachers were unaware of participation as part of their pedagogical approach, whilst others were acutely aware of the need to view children's participation as an important practice in their setting.
- We conclude that Welsh Government's 'child first' commitment to children's rights is evident but this does not necessarily guarantee that it will then translate into practice.

Further reading

Clement, J. (2019) Spatially democratic pedagogy: children's design and co-creation of classroom space, *International Journal of Early Childhood*, 51(3): 373–387.

Lewis, A., Sarwar, S., Tyrie, J., Waters, J. and Williams, J. (2017) Exploring the extent of enactment of young children's rights in the education system in Wales, *Wales Journal of Education*, 42(2): 27–50.

References

Bae, B. (2010) Realizing children's right to participation in early childhood settings: some critical issues in a Norwegian context, *Early Years*, 30(3): 205–218, doi:10.1080/09575146.2010.506598.

Bowyer-Crane, C., Bonetti, S., Compton, S., Nielsen, D., D'Apice, K. and Tracey, L. (2021) The impact of Covid-19 on school starters: interim briefing 1 parent and school concerns about children starting school. Available at: https://educationendowmentfoundation.org.uk/public/files/Impact_of_Covid19_on_School_Starters_-_Interim_Briefing_1_-_April_2021_-_Final.pdf [Accessed 1 June 2021].

Bryman, A. (2016) *Social Research Methods*, 5th ed., Oxford: Oxford University Press.

Children's Commissioner for Wales (CCW) (2018) Human rights education in the new curriculum: position paper of the Children's Commissioner for Wales. Available at: https://www.childcomwales.org.uk/wp-content/uploads/2018/11/CCFW-Children-Rights-and-Curriculum-Reform-Position-Paper-2018.pdf [Accessed 1 June 2021].

Clement, J. (2019) Spatially democratic pedagogy: children's design and cocreation of classroom space, *International Journal of Early Childhood*, 51: 373–387.

Daniels, K. (2014) Cultural agents creating texts: a collaborative space adventure, *Literacy*, 48(2): 103–111.

Dewey, J. (1916) *Democracy and Education: An Introduction to the Philosophy of Education*, New York: MacMillan.

Donaldson, G. (2015) *Successful Futures: Independent Review of Curriculum and Assessment Arrangements in Wales*, Cardiff: Welsh Government.

Dunphy, E. (2012) Children's participation rights in early childhood education and care: the case of early literacy learning and pedagogy, *International Journal of Early Years Education*, 20(3): 290–299, doi:10.1080/09669760.2012.716700.

Formosinho, J. and Formoshino, J. (2016) Pedagogy-in-participation, the search for holistic practice. In: Formosinho, J. and Pascall, C. (eds.), *Assessment and Evaluation for Transformation in Early Childhood*, pp. 26–57, London: Routledge.

Helavaara Robertson, L., Kinos, J., Barbour, N., Pukk, M. and Rosqvist, L. (2015) Child-initiated pedagogies in Finland, Estonia and England: exploring young children's views on decisions, *Early Child Development and Care*, 185: 11–12, 1815–1827, doi:10.1080/03004430.2015.1028392.

Konstantoni, K. (2013) Children's rights-based approaches: the challenges of listening to taboo/discriminatory issues and moving beyond children's participation, *International Journal of Early Years Education*, 21(4): 362–374, doi:10.1080/09669760.2013.867169.

Lewis, A., Sanwar, S., Tyrie, J., Waters, J. and Williams, J. (2017) Exploring the extent of enactment of young children's rights in the education system in Wales, *Wales Journal of Education*, 42(2): 27–50.

Luff, P., Kanyal, M., Shehu, M. and Brewis, N. (2016) Educating the youngest citizens– possibilities for early childhood education and care, in England, *The Journal for Critical Education Policy Studies*, 14: 197–219.

Lyle, S. (2014) Embracing the UNCRC in Wales (UK): policy, pedagogy and prejudices, *Education Studies*, 40(2): 215–232.

Lyndon, H., Bertram, T., Brown, Z., and Pascal, C. (2019) Pedagogically mediated listening practices; the development of pedagogy through the development of trust, *European Early Childhood Education Research Journal*, 27(3): 360–370, doi:10.1080/1350293X.2019.1600806.

Malaguzzi, L. (1998) History, ideas and basic philosophy. In: Edwards, C., Gandini, L. and Forman, G. (eds.), *The Hundred Languages of Children*, pp. 49–90, Norwood, NJ: Ablex.

Maynard, T. and Chicken, S. (2010) Through a different lens: exploring Reggio Emilia in a Welsh context. *Early Years: An International Journal of Research and Development*, 30(1): 29–39, doi:10.1080/09575140903443000.

Maynard, T., Waters, J. and Clement, J. (2013a) Exploring Reggio outside: further explorations of child-led learning in a Welsh context, *Education 3–13*, doi:10.1080/03004279.2011.578750.

Maynard, T., Taylor, C., Waldron, S., Rhys, M., Smith, R., Power, S. and Clement, J. (2013) *Evaluating the Foundation Phase: Policy Logic Model and Programme Theory*, Social Research No. 37/2012. Cardiff: Welsh Government.

Meehan, C. (2016) Every child mattered in England: but what matters to children? *Early Child Development and Care*, 186(3): 382–402, doi:10.1080/03004430.2015.1032957.

Murray, J. (2016) Young children are researchers: children aged four to eight years engage in important research behaviour when they base decisions on evidence, *European Early Childhood Education Research Journal*, 24(5): 705–720, doi:10.1080/1350293X.2016.1213565.

Prout, A. and James, A. (1997) *Constructing and Reconstructing Childhood: Contemporary Issues in the Sociological Study of Childhood*, London: Routledge Falmer.

Rinaldi, C. (1998) Projected curriculum constructed through documentation–Progettazione: an interview with Lella Gandini. In: Edwards, C., Gandini, L. and Forman, G. (eds.), *The Hundred Languages of Children*, pp. 113–126, Norwood, NJ: Ablex.

Rogoff, B. (2003). *The Cultural Nature of Human Development*, New York: Oxford University Press.

Sousa, J., Loizou, E. and Fochi, P. (2019) Participatory pedagogies–instituting children's rights in day to day pedagogic development, *European Early Childhood Education Research Journal* 27: 299–304.

Taylor, C., Rhys, M., Waldron, S., Davies, R., Power, S., Maynard, T., Moore, L., Blackaby, D. and Plewis, I. (2015) *Evaluating the Foundation Phase: Final Report*, Cardiff: Welsh Government.

The Rights of the Child and Young Persons (Wales) Measure (2011) Available at: https://www.legislation.gov.uk/mwa/2011/2/contents [Accessed 25 June 2021].

Tyrie, J. and Beauchamp, G. (2018). children's perceptions of their access to rights in Wales: the relevance of gender and age, *The International Journal of Children's Rights*, 26(4), 781–807.

UNICEF (2021) *Rights Respecting Schools Award*. Available at https://www.unicef.org.uk/rights-respecting-schools/ [Accessed 25 June 2021]

Waller, T. (2006) 'Don't come too close to my octopus tree': recording and evaluating young children's perspectives on outdoor learning. *Children, Youth and Environments*, 16(2): 75–104.

Waller, T. (2014) Voices in the park: researching the participation of young children in outdoor play in early years settings, *Management in Education*, 28(4): 161–166. doi:10.1177/0892020614547488.

Waters, J. (2016) The Foundation Phase in Wales–time to grow up? *Wales Journal of Education*, 18(1): 179–198.

Welsh Assembly Government (2008) *Foundation Phase Framework for Children's Learning for 3–7 years olds in Wales*, Cardiff: Welsh Assembly Government.

Welsh Government (2015) *Foundation Phase Framework (Revised 2015)*, Cardiff: Welsh Government.

Welsh Government (2016) *Foundation Phase Action Plan*, Cardiff: Welsh Government.

Welsh Government (2019) *Programme for Children and Young People*. Available at: https://gov.wales/sites/default/files/publications/2019-06/seven core-aims-for-children-and-young-people.pdf [Accessed 25 June 2021]

Welton, N., Tinney, G., and Saer, S. (2019). Enabling children's rights in Wales with early years professionals: Policy and practice. In: Murray, J., Blue Swadener, B. and Smith, K. (eds.), *The Routledge International Handbook of Young Children's Rights*, pp. 260–275, Abingdon: Routledge.

Williams, J. (2013) *The United Nations Convention on the Rights of the Child in Wales*, Cardiff: University of Wales Press.

8 Using an environmental affordance perspective to consider children's 'challenging behaviour' in the classroom and at Forest School

Angela Rekers

Introduction

There is a tension in whether the values, expectations and demands of early childhood settings, which relate to measurable learning outcomes and meeting the needs of children so that they realise their potential as future participating members of society, also provide space for children to be valued in the moment. In light of our expectations, do we recognise all children as already competent, active learners transitioning between home and school or other institutions? Are we able to consider children's development in terms of the ways in which they meet, appropriate, negotiate and challenge the multiple demands encountered as they move between settings? Perhaps we are impatient or perhaps we feel under pressure as educators for the children in our care to 'be' a certain way and to 'become' someone who has particular skills and competencies so that they 'fit in' with certain collective practices. Hedegaard (2010) observes that:

> in the field of early childhood education, one is presented with a dilemma—whether to guide and educate young children in relation to already established [institutional] values or whether to give children room to become people in their own right.
>
> (page vii)

Such 'already established values' may present an homogenised ideal that creates challenges for children of all ages as they struggle to meet expectations and demands. Noticeably, children for whom this is difficult may be targeted for behavioural support or labelled as 'challenging'. The aim of this chapter is to assert that viewing children's behaviour through an environmental affordance lens enables the practitioner to consider institutional practices from the child's perspective, thus providing an opportunity to better support the child. Furthermore, an understanding of Hedegaard's (2012) concept of *motive orientation* in activity settings allows the practitioner (or parent/carer) to view moments of conflict or crisis and see what drives the child in the moment. In doing so, the practitioner is better able to guide the child, but also to reflect upon pedagogical practices from the child's perspective.

DOI: 10.4324/9781003163206-11

Children in transition, whether transitioning 'vertically' between year levels at school, for instance, or 'horizontally', between home and school, are navigating complex cultural demands (Hedegaard 2014). Perceptions of competence are based upon the child's engagement and motive orientation aligning with those of the institution as they navigate these expectations. The framing of 'competence' from multiple perspectives, for example, that of the teacher, the parent or the child, enables us to look at children's behaviours and goal-oriented activity as a dialectical unfolding as the child meets and transitions between the values and expectations of multiple institutions. According to Hedegaard (2020), it is this point of contact between the child and the demands of the institutional practice that creates a dynamic social situation of development.

Learning to participate in ways that align with institutional demands requires the development of particular competencies. Part of becoming a valued member of institutions, whether a family or a classroom, is learning what Dreier (2003, 2) calls 'species specific forms of activity [that] involves a learned modifiability of cognitive, emotional and motivational processes as well as of their functional links in life activities'. It is worth reflecting on types of participation, therefore, that may be considered oppositional or negative in respect of institutional objectives and the tension that exists between individual agency and participation in collective activity. These tensions can highlight how the child is participating as motive development in alignment–or not–with the motive orientation of the institution. Indeed, the competencies being developed and learned in one institution may not be valued competencies in another, or there may be generational differences in what is valued and expected. Children may be navigating conflict demands between adult and peer culture or between home and school. Societies in general consist of many cultures that are in a state of continuous development in terms of 'values, beliefs, activities, and practices that continue from generation to generation', and so are identified by their diversity (Tudge et al. 1999, 68). Government education policy, on the other hand, tends to be based upon the values, beliefs, activities and practices of the dominant culture in an attempt to unify a diverse population (Hedegaard 2012). Also, policy is based upon adult agendas. This not only influences adult perceptions of children's competencies (see Mahn and John-Steiner 2002), but significantly affects equitable practices with children for whom these are most essential (Wood 2009).

Perceptions of competencies are an important consideration when studying the interactions within institutional settings, especially if we consider Whitebread's (1996) argument that '[c]hildren's views about themselves develop as a reflection of the views transmitted to them by others in social interaction' (page 7). Perceptions of children as lacking the 'right' or 'essential' skills when they start school impact upon how classroom practice is shaped. Yet, from a 'whole child' perspective, cognitive performance is in itself related to the child's experience of participating in everyday activities within and across multiple institutions, which may promote values and practices in conflict with each other (Hedegaard 2012). Therefore, in order to address issues of equity and inclusion, understandings of diversity need to include conceptualisations of participation that consider differing institutional practices from the perspective of the individual child and their agency in negotiating everyday activities. Indeed, a children's rights perspective views the child as 'both engaged and self-initiating, while at the same time as part of a collective cultural tradition' (Hedegaard 2010, vii).

Importantly, it is critical that children feel valued and are guided toward a sense of belonging within education and care institutions, so that all children see themselves as competent learners throughout the school years and beyond. Egan (2018, 240) writes: 'The possibility that students at any point in their learning journey become disengaged, are excluded or lack self-esteem and self-efficacy can all impact on their learning and achieving their potential.' By seeing things from the child's perspective, it may be clearer how to appreciate their individual 'take' on the world in order to support their development.

The research project

Hedegaard and Fleer's (2008) dialectical-interactive approach to research builds upon the reflexivity of interpretive ethnography by articulating the interactive means of gathering data and the interpretive aspect of analysis. The study that is the focus of this chapter sought to gather information about multiple interactions in early childhood settings in order to capture the experiences of a group of linguistically and culturally diverse 4- and 5-year-olds in an urban reception year classroom and at Forest School (Rekers-Power 2020). In this doctoral study, the Forest School sessions were delivered one day a week by a charity that specialises in Forest School and outdoor learning practice, thus differentiating itself from the classroom as an institution, based upon Zittoun's (2016) definition. The study aimed to conceptualise the child's participation in sociomaterial activity settings from the child's perspective, using Hedegaard and Fleer's (2008) dialectical-interactive approach to research. By making visible the social and material affordances of learning spaces, analysis of children's dialectical reciprocity with institutional values and practices was undertaken using an environmental affordance perspective, based upon the work of Bang (2008). The analytical framework is grounded in both cultural-historical activity theory and affordance theory.

For the study, observations and audio-visual recordings were made of whole group activity over a period of 20 days, with a particular focus on a small group of six children. Following this, visual-stimulated (VS) interviews were carried out, with the audio-visual recordings used to support discussion with children, staff and parents. These data were categorised according to *activity setting*—common institutional practices, such as 'circle time' and 'free play'—and episodes of conflict were chosen for VS interviews and analysis. Using the concept of *conflict* to interpret children's motive orientations is based upon the work of Hedegaard (2008).

The study drew upon the cultural-historical tradition of making visible the 'dynamic layering' (Vianna and Stetsenko 2006, 82) of sociocultural practices and individual participation that shapes the child's experience in relation to their environment. Hedegaard and Fleer (2008, 3) argue that, only by exploring the perspectives and practices of both the teacher/adult and the child, are we able to understand the 'child's social situation of development'. Therefore, a theoretical- and rights-informed study of children's participation needs to take into account the experience of the child, conceptualised as the *child's perspective*, as an individual actively engaging in collective practices across institutions. To begin to interpret the child's perspective, Hedegaard (2012) argues that we need to consider the child's *motive orientation*, defined as that to which the child orients themselves whilst engaging in *activity settings*, or the everyday activities and routines that consist of both perceptual affordances and mediated cultural demands. Institutional activity settings are intended to shape children's development by directing them toward the skills and competencies valued by the institution as essential for future success (Hedegaard 2008; Rogoff et al. 1993).

Socialisation is understood, therefore, to be a process of acquiring competencies, which demonstrate an alignment of the individual's motive orientation and that of the institution (Hedegaard 2012). Children's participation needs to be considered, then, in relation to the dialectical reciprocity between the individual and the socio-material environment (Figure 8.1).

The child's developing motive orientations may be observed in the ways in which they participate in pedagogical practices with specific motive orientations and expectations, mediated by the availability and use of natural/cultural objects (artefacts), tools and social others. A conceptualisation of mediated activity was applied by Bang (2008) to the notion of behaviour settings (Barker and Wright 1951), in which children's behaviour is viewed in light of their social and material encounters in everyday activities. Such activities create

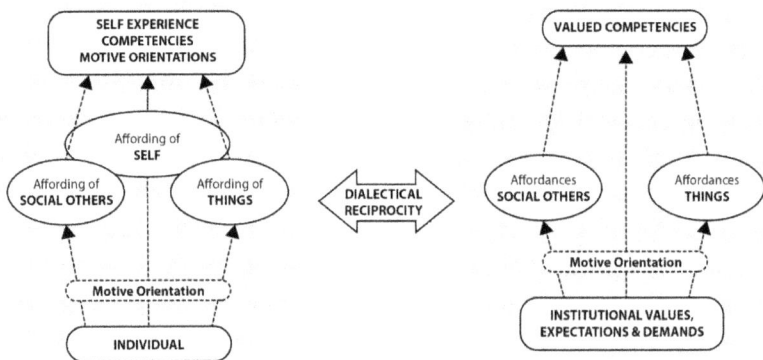

Figure 8.1 A model of environmental affordance perspective. (Rekers-Power 2020)

patterns described as a psychological/physiological habitat or ecological niche. In his ecological perceptual affordance theory, Gibson (1979/2015, 120) describes 'a niche [as] a set of affordances.' He writes, 'The medium, substances, surfaces, objects, places, and other animals have affordances for a given animal. They offer benefit or injury, life or death. This is why they need to be perceived' (page 134). Gibson proposed that rather than the environment simply stimulating the animal into responsive action, the animal actively orients itself toward or away from what there is in the environment. Importantly, affordances relate to both the properties of objects, tools, surfaces and so on, the intentions of others and self, and the capabilities of the perceiver.

Affordance theory then shifts our descriptive focus from *forms* (for example, a tree) in the environment to *function* (for example, a tree that is climb-able) in an attempt 'to describe environmental features in terms of their functional significance for an individual' (Heft 1988, 29). These functions may be multiple in a way that form-based descriptions are not: a tree is always a tree, but its functions are multiple in relation to the perceiver. For example, it provides shade, shelter, climbing, and so on. Thus, affordances are not only perceptual but also relational between the individual and the environment. For example, depending upon individual capabilities, a tree may not afford climbing for every child in a group. In order to be perceived as *climbable*, it needs to have branches a child can reach (*reachable*) and grasp (*graspable*) as tools to help them accomplish their goal of climbing, if the child's intention is *to climb*. If a tree does not have these properties, the child, or an adult or more capable peer, may mediate such affordances by dragging a log closer to the tree so the child can reach a branch. Or, climbing trees may not be allowed, so no help is given or the child is told to stop.

Institutional intentions, as well as the child's intentions, are important for the researcher to surface so that the perspective of the child is considered alongside the perspective of the settings within which the child participates. This consideration of intentionality is critical for understanding why and how a child takes up an affordance. Heft (1989) asserts that 'the affordances of an object are realized in relation to some intentional act in the individual's behavior repertoire' (page 21). This 'behavior repertoire' is reflective of the individual being a 'creature of his or her situation' (Gibson 1979/2015, 135), or 'keeping-in-touch with the world' as a self-experience of perception (page 228). Yet, such self-directed intentions may be mediated by institutional practices.

In order to make visible the range of affordances provided by institutional practices and the patterns of behaviour children exhibit by acting upon them, Bang (2008) articulates an environmental affordance framework. This framework may be used to interpret the affordances of *things* (features, surfaces and artefacts) and *social others* that are taken up by the child. Then, one may consider how these relate to the child's experience of self as an active participant, as these 'affordings' (Bang 2008) align with institutional values, demands and expectations. For example, at Forest School, a tree may afford *climbing*, a peer standing nearby may afford *watching*; therefore, upon climbing the tree, the child experiences themselves as *climbing-able* and *watching-able*. Affordances of social others are considered to be 'the first functionally meaningful features that are noticed in infancy, and they remain a lifelong preoccupation for all of us. To varying degrees, we receive information about the efficacy of our actions through social sources' (Chawla and Heft 2002, 210). If affordances are supported and valued by the institution, the child may also experience self as one who is capable and competent from the perspective of the institution, as well as self and peers.

However, there may be a conflict between the motive orientation of the child and the institution. If the affordance of the tree for climbing is constrained by the teacher, but the child places high value on *climbing/climb-able–being watched/ watchable*, whether that value is based upon previous motive alignments with self, from peers or from home, there may be a conflict. The child may be presented with a crisis in which they have to decide whether to align with the demands of the institution or peers, or self, or even tree. In a Forest School or adventure education institution, these may all be aligned. However, in some settings, there may be divergence. In this case, if the adult understands the child's motive orientation, they can utilise the child's goal-oriented behaviour toward *being watched-able* or *climbing-able* to consider an alternative activity that enables the child to engage in activity that provides alignment between their own values and those of the institution. At the time, and over time, the child experiences self as capable, as one whose competencies are valued from the institutional perspective even as new competencies as being encouraged, and as one who is both valued as an individual and a member of the community. Thus, mediated activity in relation to the functional properties of a tree, along with the child's capabilities and motivated behaviour, shapes participation and possibilities in the moment, as well as in the future.

Findings and discussion: using 'conflict' as a condition for analysis

In the doctoral study, moments of conflict were used as a basis for choosing which observed events to analyse. Transitions, crises and conflict are all considered pivotal to the social situation of development as the individual participates in collective activities (Hedegaard 2009; Vygotsky 1998). Vygotsky (1998) argued that conflicts between the individual and the social environment in which the individual is participating can trigger changes within the individual as they meet new demands. Over time, the individual develops new motive orientations by participating in activities and accepting, appropriating, negotiating or challenging those expectations which characterise the institutional practice. For this reason, Hedegaard (2008) suggests viewing episodes of conflict as an opportunity to observe children's motive orientation. Furthermore, Hedegaard (2008, 23) argues that conflicts 'do not need to be seen as negative', since they can be used to indicate the ways in which a child is developing, as well as an opportunity for the adult to support the child's developing competencies.

The child's experience of affordances in the classroom and at Forest School

For the children in the study, the socio-material environment in the classroom held affordances for *being a student, being creative, being a friend, being a helper* and so on. These were similar to the affordances of the Forest School setting. A primary difference between the two institutions was that in the outdoors, there were additional affordances in relation to artefacts and features both actualised by the child and accepted by the adults, which were more likely to be constrained in the indoor space. These included such affordances such as *being one who can hide* and *one who can explore*. Perhaps more interestingly, however, was the affording in the outdoors of *being a 'real' worker*, that is, one who can make real, functional bridges, not just those made from Lego bricks. In this respect, work was not differentiated from play the way it was in the classroom, where 'work' tended to be at desks and 'play' happened everywhere in the classroom, but during certain blocks of time.

Additionally, in relation to the concept of children as *real workers*, the demands of Forest School created conditions for autonomy. For instance, children were not asked to complete their task or play to 'tidy up' before having a snack, but could take a break from their work to have a drink or snack. Because more time was allocated to children's chosen play activity in the outdoor setting–and there was a lack of formalised assessment, which in the classroom shaped the schedule and activity considerably–the children were able to complete their self-directed tasks within a session or resume them the following week. For children who found it difficult to shift from one activity to another once they were absorbed in play, the Forest School setting lessened conflict between adults and children. The classroom teacher herself commented that, due to the demands upon her in the classroom, which conflicted with her own beliefs about how the Foundation Phase was intended to be implemented, she found Forest School more aligned to an early years commitment to play.

The affordances of peers in both the classroom and at Forest School held possibilities for *watching/being watched; helping/being helped; showing/being shown*, and so on. However, the outdoor space provided opportunities for more boisterous physical activity, which allowed the acting upon of affordances for physical contact, for example, *bumping/bumping into* and *touching/being touched*, and expanded this range into affordances for *fighting with/being fought* and *pushing/being pushed*, which were not necessarily constrained by Forest School practice. There was space, both physically and pedagogically, for the adults to accept these affordances of risky play and observe what direction they took. At some point, risky play might be constrained, but pedagogues from both settings watched first before acting. Within the classroom by contrast, it appeared necessary to act more quickly, before something escalated. By having the space to explore these affordances, the children had an opportunity to work out risky scenarios in a supportive environment, which may contribute to greater risk management skills when away from adult gaze (Sandseter and Kennair 2011). If a child did not want to *be push-able*, they could run away, seek help or fight back.

Observing how the children interacted with each other in a more spacious environment supported a recognition of some of the children's developing motive orientations toward *being fighters* and *being brave*. Much of the play fighting seemed to reflect their fascination for fantasy play figures, such as Transformers, or films, such as *The Avengers* or *The Karate Kid*. To be seen as brave and a good fighter may have been valued at home and in peer culture. Some of those who had been labelled 'challenging' were already facing a tension between the motive orientation of wanting to be held in high esteem by their peers or held in high esteem by the adults. Certainly, to be funny and make classmates laugh (often labelled 'silly') or to be the centre of attention or a good fighter (often labelled 'naughty') is not usually in alignment with the demands of the classroom as an institution and may be considered disruptive (Barnett 2018). However, these behaviours were more likely to be met with acceptance from adults in the outdoor setting where there was space, both physically and pedagogically, to work through conflict situations.

By way of illustration of this point, presented here are notes from the research journal that was kept during the data collection phase of the study:

> One of the study's participants, aged five years and four months, was frequently 'in trouble' at school for impulsive behaviour. One day we had an interview following an incident in which he had touched a baby chick who was in the classroom incubator and lied about doing so to the teaching staff when confronted. Both actions were against the rules for classroom behaviour. As a consequence, he was prohibited from play time and sent to do writing work in another class. Additionally, he was punished at home by not being allowed to go to karate class. However, from my environmental affordance perspective for analysis, it seemed his driving motive orientation patterns suggested he was driven to please both adults–lying as a way to stay in favour with them–and peers by being seen to be brave in petting the chick. Additionally, I had observed that he consistently chose to play games that involved 'super-hero' play. In our interview, when telling me what had happened, he said 'I was bad', then leaped up and wanted to show me his karate moves that were like the Karate Kid's. It would seem that by tapping into his developing motive orientation to be a 'super-hero', to please adults, and to appear brave in front of his friends, guiding him to consider the self-regulatory aspects of martial arts, rather than be excluded from activities would be a useful way to support his self-regulation. In doing so, the dichotomy between 'being bad/being good' could be addressed from a super-hero perspective to ensure he could see himself as having valued competencies in alignment with both peer and adult culture.
>
> (Research Fieldwork journal note: 4 July 2017)

For the children in the study, it seemed crucial to be in a good relationship with the adults. However, the peer group becomes increasingly important as children begin to negotiate social structures (Corsaro 2005). Within the school situation, the value positions of adults and those of peers may not always align with each other, particularly as children get older and gain independence. It is worth considering how children may begin to shift toward peer groups or institutions that more readily enable them to feel competent as they are. Making visible the motive orientations of both institutions and children is essential in order to address issues of achievement and ongoing engagement in educational practices.

Other ways of being and becoming were also surfaced in the study. In particular, children's motive orientation toward *being a leader* were often construed by adults as *being bossy* and considered challenging by adults. It seemed that one explanation for this was the constraint on space. In the outdoor setting, if children were *leading/being bossy* in a way that may have created conflict indoors, children who did not wish to be *bossed around-able* could use the affordances of the space to run away, to hide, to fight and to transform the activity using multiple loose parts and natural features at their disposal. Because of such spaciousness, the adults were able to observe how events unfolded and consider the children's developing motive orientation in their peer groups.

During video-stimulated interviews, episodes in which adult participants labelled children's participation as 'being bossy' or 'wanting it their own way', the children saw themselves as *being like adults*. In analysing the affordances of social others, children's affordances with peers often reflected the values of adult communication and the institutional values toward them, such as *instructing, praising, controlling*. This demonstrates the connection between children's behaviour and its reflection of adult positioning. Equally, the material environment was shown to provide an unintentional affordance for the children's growing awareness of social order, demonstrating how artefacts or *things* and their affordances also shape social affordances. In the classroom, there was a birthday and age chart on the wall organised into two columns marked '4' and '5' with photos of each child in the class organised by their age. When it was a child's birthday, their photograph was switched from the '4' column to the '5'. Some children gave this as a reason to exclude or tease others, indicating they felt the chart validated being older as better: 'Five is better; he's not old enough,' said one boy, who was trying to exclude another child, not yet five, from a play activity, pointing to the chart for institutional confirmation of his claim. Whether we see this as an appropriation or a manipulation of institutional values, it can be considered a developing competency. Either way, the child's motive orientation may be brought into alignment with institutional intentions by acknowledging their observation. By considering practice from the child's perspective, we may begin to notice the often paradoxical nature of institutional practices as well. Although such behaviour, from an institutional perspective, may be considered challenging, such motive orientation could be guided toward developing leadership skills in ways that support all children.

The present and the future entwined

Recognising children's existing competencies and those they need to develop in order to achieve social and academic success is critical to supporting children's learning, development and continued engagement. As the classroom teacher in the doctoral study asserted:

> In a school like ours, you've got to make the children feel they are amazing, regardless of where they are on that developmental continuum. It's your job as a teacher to make those children feel skilled in what they're doing and then say, 'Now you've got those skills, here's what we can do next!' And make them feel like they can achieve it! You've got to be highly skilled to teach in a school like this–because you have to forget outside expectations and judgements and get to know each child and what they need to accomplish and follow what children need.
>
> And, people don't realise how important that is in the early years–getting kids on board and engaged and feeling good about school and themselves … If you don't get it right now, it will impact them for life. If they think, 'I'm no good at anything' or 'I can't learn anything' or that kind of self-identity, then they do act out and push people's boundaries … it can be self-perpetuating.
>
> (Classroom teacher, interview, 4 July 2017)

This awareness of the relationship between the child's experience in the early years and their engagement with education in terms of life trajectories echoes the emphasis Hedegaard (2008) places upon supporting children's identification with institutional values. However, Hedegaard's theorising does not go far enough to consider that institutional values, expectations and demands could be more permeable to include the full range of children's existing competencies and motive orientations. Gibson (1979/2015) states that not all affordances are necessarily perceived as positive by all perceivers. Thus, the affordances of surfaces and activities toward self-regulation goals, such as *sitting still/sitting still-able*, may be available. However, when a child is un*able* to do this, they may become upset because they cannot do what is valued, or conversely, they may not care because they do not value it nor seek the approval of the adults who do. Indeed, over time children's motive orientations may find alignment elsewhere where, different capabilities are valued. Critically, a desire to align with the standards of the institution may begin to lose its allure as children discover their goal-directed behaviour continually perceived as out of alignment with institutional practice, particularly if the child finds approval from a different institution more forthcoming. Applying an environmental affordance perspective to our practice, therefore, allows us to open up our understanding of what is actually possible and look critically at whether our expectations are aligned with our values as educators.

The importance of understanding children's motive orientation in relation to institutional practices provides a new way of framing participation that considers children's activity in relation to their social and material environments as they transition between institutions, such as the home and school, or reception year and primary school, and so on. In doing so, we can better regard children's social situation of development, or the 'system of relations between the child of a given age and social reality' (Vygotsky 1998, 199) and ensure that children are valued for who they are in the present moment, as well as for who they are becoming.

Key points

- Hedegaard (2020) asserts that a 'wholeness approach' allows us to see how the child is developing in relationship with and across institutional practices. Such an approach means that we consider societal perspectives, institutional perspectives and the child's perspective in relation to children's engagement with the social and material environments of everyday activities.
- The concept of 'self-experience' is used by Bang (2008) in an environmental affordance perspective to consider how the child might experience *being* a participant in everyday activities. It is this concept of being a participant and how the child experiences that subjectively, which contributes to the child's developing competencies and orientations toward institutional practice as a positive or negative experience. This experience, made up of the child's exploration and appropriation of *things*/artefacts and cultural tools, social interactions, and the child's sense of self in relationship with others, institutional practice and activities, contributes to the child's emerging abilities, dominating motives and developmental possibilities.
- Conflict between institutional demands and the ways in which children appropriate, negotiate and challenge expectations contributes to how adults frame children's participation and how children experience their participation. Certain behaviours might be considered competent in certain situations that children find themselves in, but not in others. Learning how to navigate institutional systems with multiple demands whilst retaining a sense of self is a life skill.
- This understanding provides the premise for re-considering children's behaviour, especially that experienced as 'challenging' by practitioners, in a way that highlights the child's developing motive orientation(s) in and across cultural practices. An environmental affordance perspective, articulating the available and mediated affordances of the socio-material, draws attention to how our practice supports children in both *being* and *becoming*.

Further reading

Cavada-Hrepich P. (2017) Children's resistance in the emergence of learning as leading activity: playfulness in the transformation of spaces of participation. In Chaudhary, N.,

Hviid, P., Marsico, G. and Villadsen, J. (Eds.) *Resistance in Everyday Life*, pp. 203–222. Springer, Singapore.

Cavada-Hrepich argues here that children's resistance to school practices are often conceptualised as poor behaviour and as a consequence of the pupil's own deficiency, but need to be explored more deeply and seen as a result of a dialectical relationship between social structures and unequal power relations.

Edwards, A., Fleer, M. and Bøttcher, L. (Eds.) (2019) *Cultural-Historical Approaches to Studying Learning and Development: Societal, Institutional and Personal Perspectives*. Singapore: Springer.

The papers in this volume focus on Hedegaard's approach to understanding how learning and development take place within a 'prism of the interplay of society, institution and person'. The chapters present empirical examples from the authors' studies in a range of settings and work with families, adults, student teachers, children and young people, with chapters that focus on disability studies.

Hedegaard, M., Edwards, A. and Fleer, M. (Eds.) (2012) *Motives in Children's Development*. Cultural-Historical Approaches. Cambridge: Cambridge University Press.

This edited volume is centred upon the analytical exploration of the relationships between development, emotions, motives and identities and the social conditions and positioning within which children's learning occurs.

References

Bang, J. (2008) Conceptualising the environment of the child in a cultural-historical approach. In Hedegaard, M. and Fleer, M. (Eds.) *Studying Children: A Cultural-Historical Approach*, pp. 118–138. Maidenhead: Open University Press/McGraw-Hill Education.

Barker, R. G. and Wright, H. F. (1951) *One Boy's Day*. New York: Harper and Row.

Barnett, L.A. (2018) The education of playful boys: class clowns in the classroom, *Frontiers in Psychology*, 9: 232.

Chawla, L. and Heft, H. (2002) Children's competence and the ecology of communities: a functional approach to the evaluation of participation, *Journal of Environmental Psychology*, 22(1–2):201–216.

Corsaro, W. A. (2005) *The Sociology of Childhood*. Second edition. Thousand Oaks, CA: Pine Forge Press.

Dreier, O. (2003) Learning in personal trajectories of participation. In Stephenson, N., Radtke, H. L., Jorna, R. J. and Stam, H. J. (Eds.) *Theoretical Psychology. Critical Contributions*, pp. 20–29. Concord, Canada: Captus University Publications.

Egan, D. (2018) Shifting paradigms: can education compensate for society? In Gannon, S., Hattam, R. and Sawyer, W. (Eds.) *Resisting Educational Inequality: Reframing Policy and Practice in Schools Serving Vulnerable Communities*, pp. 236–245. London and New York: Routledge.

Gibson, J.J. (1979/2015) *The Ecological Approach to Visual Perception* (Classic edition). New York and London: Psychology Press.

Hedegaard, M. (2008) A cultural-historical theory of children's development. In Hedegaard, M. and Fleer, M. (Eds.) *Studying Children: A Cultural-Historical Approach*, pp. 10–29. Maidenhead: Open University Press.

Hedegaard, M. (2009) Children's development from a cultural-historical approach: children's activity in everyday local settings as foundation for their development, *Mind, Culture, and Activity*, 16 (1): 64–81.

Hedegaard, M. (2010) Forward. In Fleer, M. (Ed.) *Early Learning and Development: Cultural-Historical Concepts in Play*, pp. vii–x. Melbourne, AUS: Cambridge University Press.

Hedegaard, M. (2012) The dynamic aspects in children's learning and development. In Hedegaard, M., Edwards, A. and Fleer, M. (Eds.) *Motives in Children's Development: Cultural-Historical Approaches*, pp. 9–27. New York: Cambridge University Press.

Hedegaard, M. (2014) The significance of demands and motives across practices in children's learning and development: an analysis of learning in home and school, *Learning, Culture and Social Interaction*, 3(3): 188–194.

Hedegaard, M. (2020) Children's perspectives and institutional practices as keys in a wholeness approach to children's social situations of development, *Learning, Culture and Social Interaction*, 26, Article 100229.

Hedegaard, M. and Fleer, M. (Eds.) (2008) *Studying Children: A Cultural-Historical Approach*. Maidenhead: Open University Press.

Heft, H. (1988) Affordances of children's environments: a functional approach to environmental description, *Children's Environments Quarterly*, 5 (3): 29–37.

Heft, H. (1989) Affordances and the body: an intentional analysis of Gibson's ecological approach to visual perception, *Journal for the Theory of Social Behaviour*, 19 (1): 1–30.

Mahn, H. and John-Steiner, V. (2002) The gift of confidence: a Vygotskian view of emotions. In Wells, G. and Claxton, G. (Eds.) *Learning for Life in the 21st Century*, pp. 46–58. Oxford: Blackwell Publishing.

Rekers-Power, A. (2020) *Exploring young children's participation and motive orientation in the reception year classroom and at Forest School*. PhD thesis. University of Wales Trinity Saint David.

Rogoff, B., Mistry, J., Göncü, A. and Mosier, C. (1993) Guided participation in cultural activity by toddlers and caregivers, *Monographs of the Society for Research in Child Development*, 58(8): 1–174.

Sandseter, E.B.H. and Kennair, L.E.O. (2011) Children's risky play from an evolutionary perspective: the anti-phobic effects of thrilling experiences, *Evolutionary Psychology*, 9(2), 257–284.

Tudge, J., et al. (1999) Cultural heterogeneity: parental values and beliefs and their preschoolers' activities in the United States, South Korea, Russia and Estonia. In Göncü, A. (Ed.) *Children's Engagement in the World: Sociocultural Perspectives*, pp. 62–96. Cambridge: Cambridge University Press.

Vianna, E. and Stetsenko, A. (2006) Embracing history through transforming it: contrasting Piagetian versus Vygotskian (activity) theories of learning and development to expand constructivism within a dialectical view of history, *Theory and Psychology*, 16(1): 81–108.

Vygotsky, L. S. (1998) The problem of age. In Rieber, R.W. (Ed.) *The Collected Works of L. S. Vygotsky*. Vol. 5. *Child Psychology*, pp. 187–205. New York: Plenum Press.

Welsh Government (2020) *Curriculum for Wales Overview*. Available at: https://gov.wales/curriculum-wales-overview (3 November 2021).

Whitebread, D. (Ed.) (1996) *Teaching and Learning in the Early Years*. London: Routledge.

Wood, E. (2009) Developing a pedagogy of play. In Anning, A., Cullen, J. and Fleer, M. (Eds.) *Early Childhood Education: Society and Culture*, pp. 27–38. Second edition. London: Sage.

Zittoun, T. (2016) Living creatively, in and through institutions, *Europe's Journal of Psychology*, 12(1): 1–11.

9 Inclusion, participation and interaction

Challenging the discourse of in-class ability groupings in early childhood education

Eleri John

Introduction

If the pandemic has taught us anything it is that the socio-economic, ethnic, health and educational disadvantage has worsened during the last year (Anderson et al. 2020; Rose et al. 2021). In an already deeply divided country, young children's school lives have been significantly disrupted. Given these changed conditions, it is timely that the policy and practice of in-class ability grouping in the early years be re-appraised, in part because numerous studies have highlighted the disproportionality of students from poorer backgrounds in lower ability groups. This suggests that placing young children in ability groups further reinforces the cycle of poverty, and social and ethnic disadvantage (Bradbury and Roberts-Holmes 2017; Hallam and Parson 2013; Jackson and Povey 2016; Muijs and Dunne 2010; Social Mobility Commission 2017).

However, despite the challenges of the pandemic and the rhetoric of inclusion and 'levelling-up', the concept of ability remains deeply embedded in the discourse and practice of education (Bradbury 2018; Bradbury and Roberts-Holmes 2017; Hallam and Parsons 2013; Marks 2016). This practice not only raises questions about the way ability is measured, perceived and implemented, but also about the ways in which such approaches become normalised in school settings. In addition, children of all ages have their understandings too, many of which interact with their learning experiences within the classroom. This chapter takes the latter as its starting point and examines ability grouping in early years settings from the perspective of the child. In so doing, it challenges the over-deterministic view of children's intelligence often reflected in what Foucault called 'dividing practices' (Ball 1990), and which finds its expression in Bernstein's (1996) pedagogic codes and modalities. Put simply, if the 'sorting machine' (Delany 1991) metaphor is to be contested, and 'if the culture of the teacher is to become part of the consciousness of the child, then the culture of the child must first be in the consciousness of the teacher' (Bernstein 1971, 61).

The chapter is based on the findings from a qualitative research study which explored the young children's perceptions of in-class grouping and how it affected their emerging self-concept. The context and various definitions of

DOI: 10.4324/9781003163206-12

ability groupings will be examined with reference to relevant developments in the UK, where the research took place. Findings from the small-scale research project with young children will be shared, finishing with implications and recommendations that might begin to shape the outlines of a more inclusive pedagogy.

Definitional issues

Educational terminologies used to describe and define ability grouping in all its forms have been in use for more than a century. Much of this was based on rudimentary intelligence testing and the completion of specific educational stages. For ease of use, however, a more recognisable lexicon will be deployed: streaming, setting, banding and in-class grouping. I will draw upon the definitions used by Sukhnandan and Lee (1998) in their review of the literature which splits the various uses into two categories: homogenous and heterogenous. The first includes streaming which assigns pupils to groups on the basis of general ability. This tends to be by class and often stays throughout the child's school career. It is in part ordinal and is usually consistent for all subjects. Hallam and Parsons (2013) used the Millennium Study data and estimated that over 16 per cent of schools in the state sector used streaming by ability. Setting is the practice of assigning to groups by ability according to a particular subject. Setting is sometimes imposed on a whole year group especially in secondary schools. Banding, on the other hand, entails dividing a year group using bands differentiated by ability; each band, for example, can vary according to ability or size. Within-class grouping is the most prevalent practice in primary schools and usually involves grouping by ability for particular subjects, for example, maths and literacy. The heterogenous category involves classes being taught with a full mix of ability and without any grouping or streamed approach. According to recent research (Bradbury and Roberts-Holmes 2017), the majority of primary schools use a hybrid mode of curriculum setting which combines some subject setting with mixed ability teaching; however there is a clear reliance on ability groupings from as early as nursery onwards (Bradbury 2018).

Ability grouping–past and present

The term ability continues to be pervasive in our vocabularies, but its definition remains difficult. Sometimes referred to as natural cognitive power, it is often linked to certain capabilities in defined areas of learning. This view of ability is one that has developed over centuries and in its modern form stemmed from what Sir Cyril Burt called 'Intelligence Testing' (Hearnshaw 1979). The experiments used to underpin intelligence testing were 'the measuring rod for assessing mental abilities' and tests aimed at discovering 'what ratio of intelligence nature has given to each individual child at birth, then to provide him with the appropriate education' (Hearnshaw 1979, 206). Such sentiments, despite their Victorian language, carried weight for decades in education policy

(Kynaston 2007). Much of this was based on the belief that children's aptitude for learning or 'ability' was innate and often inherited. As a result of these views, the learning capabilities of children were viewed with an upper limit or ceiling and resulted in a deterministic view of the capabilities of a child.

As the 20th century progressed, intelligence testing came under increasing scrutiny. In the UK, Philip Vernon, a professor at the Institute of Education in the 1950s, published a scathing attack in *The Times Educational Supplement* in 1952 (Vernon 1952). His work claimed that intelligence testing was heavily influenced by coaching and that social class was a major factor in success. This was supported by Brian Simon (1991) at the University of Leicester who declared that parental background was a significant factor in the success at 'intelligence tests', like the 11+ exam that was historically used in schools in the UK to determined secondary school placement. In reality, the system brought children into schools governed by ability and attainment where their educational journey would be mapped out for them. J.W.B. Douglas (1969), in his groundbreaking book *The Home and School,* further claimed that concentrating on children's attainment in specific tests led to a generation of lost talent. In terms of primary education, much was made of the fact that the curriculum and teaching was often structured to take into account the looming 11+ exam. As a result, in-class and across the school ability grouping was standard until the Plowden Report (1967) and the coming of comprehensive schools challenged its verities.

In the years prior to the Plowden Report (1967), education did witness a move towards a more child-centred learning, focusing on the development of the 'whole child'. The impact of the report in 1967 and other reforms meant that by the early 1990s, streaming had almost disappeared in primary schools in the UK (Lee and Croll 1995). Such a move was supported by an array of research evidence that suggested that ability grouping within the primary classrooms damaged underachievers (Gamoran 1989; Persell 1977; Rosenbaum 1976). Other studies showed that ability grouping at a young age, coupled with lower expectations and poor behaviour, had a demoralising effect on pupils (Campbell 2013; Scherer 2016). In addition, various studies drew attention to the fact that ability grouping did little to raise standards (Ireson and Hallam 2001; Whitburn 2001; Wiliam and Bartholemew 2004). There was also evidence that such an approach had a negative effect on a child's social and emotional development (Hallam et al. 2003; Ireson and Hallam 2001) which resulted in negative feelings about school.

Nevertheless, an Ofsted report (1998) on the use of ability grouping within primary schools showed 60 per cent of junior schools used setting for at least one subject, while over a third of infant schools, and around one half of combined infant and junior schools were similarly structured (Davies et al. 2003). The coming to power of the New Labour government in 1997 saw an increased emphasis on raising standards in education. and with this came a return to the discourse of ability setting, with the labels 'more able', 'less able' and 'gifted and talented' entering common usage, and all of this despite more nuanced definitions of intelligence (Gardner 1983) becoming mainstream.

By the first decade of the new century, the use of ability grouping had once again become ingrained in primary school structures and pedagogies. This was in part a reaction to new national assessment methods at various key stages; judgements supported by Ofsted inspections and various national strategies such as the 'phonics check' introduced by Michael Gove for Year 1 pupils. This, in turn, reinforced the need for schools to categorise and organise their classrooms along particular lines to satisfy those judging their quality.

In recent years, the debate on the benefits of ability setting has continued alongside a renewed focus on inclusion, equality and social mobility. Bradbury and Roberts-Holmes (2017) used these concepts and rhetorical claims behind them to frame their study of the effects of grouping in the early years in primary schools. They found that there remained an over-reliance on ability grouping based on setting for literacy, maths, reading and phonics (Bradbury 2018). They also claimed that setting and its apparent fluidity did not mediate its negative effects, neither did it stem the loss of self-esteem, nor did it narrow the attainment gap; in fact they claim it does the opposite and exacerbates age and ability differentials (Bradbury and Roberts-Holmes 2017, 5). Marks (2016) described similar findings in her longitudinal study of ability grouping in three primary schools. Drawing on the voices of the children she challenges the ability laden theories of both policy makers and school structures claiming it leads to restrictive and anti-inclusive practices which do little to overcome entrenched educational disadvantage.

Labelling

The process of labelling children in schools according to perceived abilities in curriculum subjects is both damaging and detrimental to the development of children's self-concepts. This, in turn, prevents teachers from upholding their commitment to supporting children's learning; as Hart et al. (2004) point out, blaming the differences in children's achievement on their 'inherent ability' is both 'unjust and untenable'. Despite this critique, the labelling of children remains a common occurrence, not only in a formal sense but also as low-level understanding of what children are capable of, that is, which children can do x and which children can do y. Labelling is therefore something that is carried out on a daily basis, especially at the beginning of the school year (Swann et al. 2012).

However, its ubiquity brings with it negative connotations where young children are too quickly categorised as high, middle or low ability, a practice that is underpinned by the 'conviction that it is helpful … for teachers to compare, categorise and group young people by ability in order to provide appropriate and challenging teaching for all' (Hart et al. 2004, 8). The use of such labelling during planning for differentiation is integral to current pedagogical practice and many teachers support it, often uncritically. The categorisation and labelling of children as less able results very quickly in a sense of failure which inhibits their potential, impairs their self-efficacy and self-belief, and can exacerbate disruptive behaviour (Hargreaves 1982; Scherer 2016). Labelling children by ability strips them of 'their sense of being worthy, competent, creative, inventive, critical human beings' (Hargreaves 1982, 62) and increases the attainment gap in classrooms (Parsons and Hallam 2014). The labelling and grouping of children as early as nursery is particularly concerning, as these groups are often driven by the children's socio-economic background resulting in a significant impact on potential social mobility (Bradbury 2018; Social Mobility Commission 2017).

Despite these outcomes, the use of ability groupings is still commonplace in UK classrooms, from as early as nursery. Grouping by ability or attainment was recently found to be the most common pedagogical tool utilised in early childhood education in England, a practice that is reinforced by senior leadership teams in schools focusing on children's academic outcomes (Bradbury 2018). This approach is further reinforced by education and school inspectorates that outline in their criteria about judging and evaluating pupils' standards in relation to their 'abilities'. Teaching is judged by ESTYN (Education and Training Inspectorate for Wales) by how teachers engage and stimulate the 'most and least able,' reinforcing the use of such terminologies in classrooms (ESTYN 2019). This only further exacerbates the issue of labelling and arguably drives the categorisation and organisation of primary classrooms along these lines to satisfy those assessing their quality. However, it is important to note that, just because teachers or practitioners choose to use ability labelling, it certainly does not necessarily assume that their idea of intelligence is one that is fixed or inherent or that teachers are on board with such approaches. In fact, utilising labels in class can often be used to categorise children in specific learning areas and instead be used to satisfy performative measures imposed on teachers and schools (Bradbury 2018). To sum up, as Benn (2011) claims, educational labelling can be damaging, can last a lifetime and risks reinforcing a 'rigid, know your place society of limiting hierarchies' (page 7).

The research study

The study reported in this chapter set out to explore the issues raised above by focusing on the voice of those who experience setting–the children themselves. In particular, the ways in which ability grouping in literacy and numeracy in the Foundation Phase of a Welsh primary school were perceived by the children themselves was of interest, including how those perceptions shaped their emerging understanding of their learning in those two domains. Little research exists on the perceptions of the pupils themselves to grouping practices, particularly very young children, and how their stories of ability setting are internalised by them within classroom settings.

The interviewing of young children, however, can be challenging, sitting as it does at the interface of the adult's and child's world (Shaw et al. 2011). Eliciting their understandings and representing them so that the child's agency is recognised is complex. Nevertheless, Alderson and Morrow (2004) have shown that, when taken seriously, children are competent social actors capable of making decisions under their own volition. In addition, the emphasis placed on children's rights and in particular their right to express their feelings on matters that affect them (Article 12, UNCRC 1989) has given young children the opportunity to speak out on issues of concern whilst recognising that they still inhabit a world dominated by adults (Danby et al. 2011; Folque 2020).

In order to address these issues, I followed Danby et al. (2011) who recommend making the child feel comfortable and getting to know them well. This can improve the 'culture of communication' (Christensen 2004, 246). The use of appropriate stimulus material and artefacts to develop the conversation is a further recommendation. These concrete resources can enhance more conventional interactions and allow elaborations and depth. Recognising the child's agency and seeing them from the outset as competent verbal and non-verbal actors in the process is emphasised by Theobald (2008). Avoiding over-analysis so as not to lose context, experience and voice is thought to be another important consideration.

Twenty-four children aged between five and six years were interviewed using a purposive sampling technique (Miles and Huberman 1984). The children were chosen according to age, gender and relative ability levels using current school reports and early attainment levels in literacy and numeracy. A range of stimulus questions and materials were used to provoke a response and to encourage engagement including pictures, interactive material, various props and role plays. These included model classrooms as well as figures that children could use to represent themselves and other children or practitioners. In addition, children were given opportunities to role play as teacher and child in order to support their expression of how groupings were used and their feelings regarding this classroom practice. Children were questioned during this process and questions varied between semi-structured and open-ended interviews alongside those with a specific stimulus. The interviews, by their very nature, were informal and supported by oral recordings. Notes were taken to describe the gestures and non-verbal communications.

The interviews were transcribed and the analysis involved combing the transcripts was early themes relating to the concepts outlined in the literature review. This process was underpinned by conversational analysis techniques (Baker 1995; Sacks 1995) where a fine-grained approach to the transcripts helped reveal their essential features. Included in the analysis were the pauses, the silences, the laughter and other modes of expression. To avoid over-hypothesising from an adult perspective, I retained a focus on the child's voice and was constantly aware of the need to maintain authenticity (Burman 2008).

Throughout the 'interpretive interface' (Bernstein 1996, 136) it was evident that the children in the study, to a greater or lesser extent, expressed what I term 'experienced-derived understandings' of setting and ability grouping as it related to their classroom and classmates. These experiences were articulated along three main dimensions: inclusion, participation and interaction. Each will be discussed in turn with relevant evidence in the form of verbatim quotes taken from transcripts.

Children's perspectives on inclusion

Most of the children understood the processes by which setting was established and why it was used (Marks 2011). Much of this was expressed through an emotional investment in each other's progress–a sense of the collective which proved to be more prevalent than the social divisions that setting created. Underpinning this investment was a clear sense of optimism which, at this age, had perhaps not been adversely affected by the grouping strategies used in the classroom and the school. In fact, the setting did not really impinge on the positive view the children had of each other which was often expressed in supportive terms and underpinned by an inclusive belief that everyone could achieve–if they were given time and help.

Many of the children expressed their concerns about the way ability grouping marginalised individuals because of their perceived weaknesses. For instance, 'they might not be good at writing but they can learn if we work together' was one common refrain, while one child stated their belief that it would be good to:

> swap around so some who are good at literacy can work with some who are not so good then we can work as a team. Like sometimes we help each other and stuff and like if we are by a tricky bit then someone helps you.

This is a sophisticated articulation of how group work can be advantageous to all abilities thus negating the necessity for ability setting (Kutnick et al. 2005). Another child commented that separating into ability groups can lead to emotional upset:

> Cos some people are like good and some people are like bad and then when you put them into groups like that then they might be sad if they are in the bad group cos they would think they are not very good at their work and stuff like that.

Another child felt that sets or ability groups meant they could not help their peers:

> My friends are in another group and I like helping them and playing and talking. I help Suzie with her writing cos she can't write long like I can and I show her how to do things like Mrs May does.

The above shows that young children wish to engage in more mutual, inclusive learning where an 'expert/novice' approach to classroom interaction might be productive (Kutnick et al. 2005). According to Kutnick et al., for this to happen 'children have to be able to communicate effectively and also have mutual trust' (page 48).

Children's perspectives on participation

The second theme relates to participation which was underpinned by a strong sense of altruism, and was in part driven by an 'inequality aversion' (Fehr et al.

2008, 1079). This is where the children appeared to prefer classroom organisation that was fully participatory with reduced inequalities between them and their classmates. Throughout, however, the children were fully aware of the ability setting process and why it was used. One child commented:

> We go into different groups to do our jobs (*work*) and some are quite easy, some are hard and some are really hard. But we all get split up to do them and I don't like that cos we help each other.

Another child opined:

> Yeah we get split up I go into the top group after the test but I can do it anyway so I'd rather stay with my friend …

Children further expressed their understandings in linear terms using lines and ladders to describe their learning. This was best exemplified in their reaction to the classroom tests they had to take. One which kept recurring in their narratives was the summative '17 test' in mathematics which was a weekly maths test that tested children's mental arithmetic and challenged children to beat their best score. They also referred to the regular literacy tasks that defined their competence. For instance, one child commented:

> the people that are on the '17 test' are in the hard one [group] so then the ones that have just moved up are in the next hard group; and the easy ones, for the people that are on the first test … They are the best ones (*pointing to high ability group*) because they do all the writing and reading and Esther is on level 21 for her reading and I am only on level 8. But I can get better because Esther said we are all good.

These results were then made public (often unintentionally) with all the children knowing what order they came in the maths test and who could or could not do what in literacy. Above all, the children were fully aware that the setting process according to ability was ingrained in the fabric of the school, but all felt able to empathise through their attachments to their friends. As a result of this, setting according to ability often results in feelings of sadness and loneliness for many. This short interaction with a child in a 'low ability' group is self-explanatory:

Q: How do you feel in your group?
A: Sad, 'cos sometimes I'm not very good at the work. And then I feel a little bit sad.
Q: Why?
A: Because I like working with Zadie and we do things together.

Often directed at those who were perceived to be struggling, the interviews were littered with comments about the effects of grouping on their friends' emotional state and how they would prefer to contribute together. Many also expressed their concerns about the unfairness that emerged from the way the groups were established, a process that led to disparities in both levels of participation and support. The following extracts illustrate this:

> I would rather stay with Philip then I can help him … he's just a bit slower not stupid or anything … he can get better quicker then.
> I don't really like the groups because I like miss and she seems to spend more time with Steven and Lydia and I want her to spend time with us cos I like her and it's fair.
> We all work together and I don't think we should be selfish.

This was often linked to a set of beliefs about fairness in terms of outcome. Many were content with the marks they were given especially in the '17 test' as long as they were perceived to be fair and that no one was given unfair help.

These altruistic 'frames of reference' (Muijus and Reynolds 2010) were often conditioned by those around them. This was not helped by the public nature of setting where even the attempt at softening with colours (green group, red group, orange group) did not hide the stark reality. This is in direct contrast to the holistic nature of the Welsh Foundation Phase, for example, which puts children's feelings of 'self-worth and self-esteem' and wellbeing at its core (Welsh Government 2015).

Children express a preference for groupings based on interaction and friendship

The centrality of interaction within the classroom underpinned a shared vision for children of groups made up of friends and classmates. Virtually all the children in the study expressed a preference for some form of friendship grouping over setting by ability. This shared view of the classroom and its structures is in contra-distinction to the policy of the school and was underpinned by a belief that such a configuration would be fairer and more cohesive. Here the children's sense of mutuality and collaboration comes to the fore reinforced by their idea that all could achieve given the right time and support. One female pupil put it thus:

> Cos there's a good group and they could make fun of the bad group and that's not very good … But even if you're not friends with the bad group you still don't have to laugh at them because they're not very good … It isn't very nice really … It isn't nice to say they're not good at maths or writing.

Underpinning this sense of reciprocity was the idea that the children were willing to help and support their friends and those who had not yet caught up with the others, for example one girl opined when asked if a 'low ability' child could join her 'high ability' group:

Well Sally isn't as good as us in my group so she might find it tricky. It would be hard for her because she would need lots of help because we write lots of pages when we do stories and Sally doesn't do lots of pages and we can spell words and Sally might find that tricky. We could help her to I guess, cos we could be her teacher *(laughs)*. Yeah, I can be the teacher! … we could all work together to do our work really good.

Many felt that all the class could succeed if they were given time and support and for some it was a developmental process where age was a factor. This sense of young children as 'experts in their learning' (Muller et al. 2015) shows them to have a sophisticated idea of interaction where they were willing to help others and exchange benefits. This idea of the 'co-construction' of learning is maybe in its very early stages, but it 'recognises and values the child as a powerful agent in their own learning' (Jordan 2009, 5).

Discussion and implications for practice

The research undertaken, despite its limitations, indicates that young children can be viewed as 'experts in themselves' (Muller et al. 2015, 271), with sophisticated belief systems about their social world that transcend the structures of the school and classroom. Often the children stated a clear preference for mixed, friendship groups to avoid emotional labelling. These beliefs were characterised by an altruistic enthusiasm to help others, supported by a belief in the idea that all can achieve given time and encouragement. Praise was viewed as important as was a desire to be included and not separated, especially if they had put effort into their work. Sometimes the open nature of praise was deemed important and it gave many the confidence to interact and participate in the whole class question and answer sessions.

This correlates with earlier work in this area. Mercer (2011), Marsh and Yeung (2001) and Marks (2011) found that children's ability-related concepts were distinctive and often differentiated. Furthermore, Wigfield and Eccles (2000, 72) discovered that within specific subject areas, children's ability beliefs and participation were distinctive and linked to what they were perceived to 'be good at', and how they 'valued themselves'. However, in early childhood education, these traits and values appear less differentiated (Marks 2011; Marks 2016; Singal and Swann 2011) and, as other research indicates, interaction with the teacher therefore becomes more important at a young age in order to help children evaluate the feedback they receive from the teacher and other significant adults. Ability grouping, in this sense, could be viewed as a reinforcing 'negative capability' and beginning the 'self-fulfilling prophecy' cycle (Bradbury and Roberts-Holmes 2017, 26) where the label eventually becomes the person.

Most of the children in the study knew grouping was taking place because the social and classroom structures were so visible. The testing environment further encouraged a form of early competition which seemed to go against the more altruistic grain of the children. For some this meant lowering their expectations, but for many it meant having to speed up their learning by getting more help from the teachers. Much of this was expressed through an emotional investment in each other's progress: a sense of the collective inclusivity which proved to be more prevalent than the social divisions that setting created. Underpinning this was a clear sense of optimism which at their age had not been tarnished by the effects of the grouping strategies. In fact, the setting did not really impinge on the positive view the children had of each other, which was often expressed in supportive terms and underpinned by an inclusive belief that everyone could achieve, if they were given time and help.

All of the children acknowledged that the make-up of the groups was based to a greater or lesser extent on ability in both maths and literacy. In terms of the former, they knew that selection is related to their ordinal score on the '17 test' (which assesses cognitive speed and agility through mental arithmetic). Each child knew their ranking in comparison to others. In literacy, the assessment was based on the content of stories, the quality of grammar and punctuation, the neatness of handwriting and the volume of output. They judge themselves and each other using simple distinctions: good and bad; hard and easy; simple and difficult; high and low. In terms of mathematics many felt they were good at it because they could do it or because it was easy. In relation to literacy, judgements were based more on time and effort expended alongside relevant support and practice.

The children's perceptions of the ability groups, however, were transcended by the almost universal preference for some form of friendship grouping. This inclusive view of the classroom and its structures seemed to stem from their altruistic and participatory view of their learning experience. For instance, many felt that all the class could succeed if they were given time and support and, for some, it was a developmental process where age was a factor. This sense of young children as 'experts in their learning' (Muller et al. 2015) shows them to have a sophisticated idea of reciprocity where they are willing to help others alongside the teachers. This idea of the 'co-construction' of learning may be in its very early stages, but is an area ripe for further investigation in the early years of primary school.

Setting according to ability, whilst accepted as part of the ritual and routine of the classroom, sometimes resulted in feelings of sadness and loneliness for many. Often directed at those who were perceived to be struggling, the interviews provided numerous comments about the effects of grouping on their friends' emotional state. These 'frames of reference' (Muijus and Reynolds 2010) were often conditioned by those around them. This was not helped by the public nature of ability setting where even the attempt at softening the effect with colours (green group, red group, orange group) failed to hide the reality. Despite this, all the children exhibited subtle forms of adaptation to the system where they improvised and balanced their understandings about their own and other's ability.

Conclusion and recommendations

Unsurprisingly, the word 'ability' has given rise to a kind of Orwellian (1949) 'double-think', where policy makers over many decades have subscribed to a belief that greater educational equality is possible alongside some form of ability grouping. A further sticky problem remains–educational labelling–which, Benn (2011, 7) claims, 'can be damaging and can last a lifetime'. We sometimes forget that labelling is something that is carried out on a daily basis and continues throughout the school year (Swann et al. 2012).

This in turn prevents teachers from upholding their commitment to supporting children's learning in a fair and dispassionate way, not attributing differences in children's achievement on their perceived 'inherent ability' (Hart et al. 2004). Despite being softened with colours and neutral names, ability setting at such an early age can result in the emergence of a negative self-concept for many children. This of course is in direct contrast to key government messages of social inclusion and equality.

Perhaps through a greater emphasis on the 'co-construction' of learning, where each child can use their own particular knowledge, skills and abilities to develop their self-image and esteem, labelling might be challenged and a new, more inclusive pedagogy may emerge. Children see through the camouflage of ability groupings so that they need to be removed and replaced with individual work patterns that involve the whole class with appropriate pedagogic support. Schools and teachers need to balance the 'hidden subsidy' (Bernstein 1996) some children receive from their home environment, rather than reinforce it through ability grouping.

In light of the above, recommendations set out below would help to establish a more inclusive pedagogy:

- Ability grouping needs to be challenged at the school level because it labels children very early on and can result in a negative self-concept. In addition, groupings disguised with colours (and other approaches) need to be removed as the children see through the camouflage, and replaced with individual work patterns that involve all the whole class with appropriate pedagogic support.
- Schools need to recognise young children as 'experts in the making' and build on their understandings and ideas to work towards a greater 'co-construction' of learning where each child can use their own particular skills, knowledge and abilities.
- Schools and teachers need to balance the 'hidden subsidy' (Bernstein 1996) that some children receive from their home environment as it de-incentivises the need to change ability setting patterns.

Given the likely long-term effects of the pandemic and the comments made in the opening of this chapter, it is perhaps only fitting that the study should end with the flowing supplication:

This is learning that is free from the needless constraints imposed by ability-focused practices, free from the indignity of being labelled top, middle or bottom, fast or slow, free from the wounding consciousness of being treated as someone who can aspire at best to only limited achievements.

(Hart et al. 2004, 4)

Key points

- Though research indicates that ability grouping practices reproduce inequalities within society, nevertheless such practices remain deeply embedded in the discourse and practice of education, even for young children.
- This chapter reports on a research study that sought children's views on grouping practices within their primary school setting.
- Children were acutely aware of grouping practices in their setting and expressed a strong sense of the collective, showing concern that grouping practices result in marginalisation and difficult feelings for some children.
- Children showed a strong preference for the formation of groups based on friendship and viewed children helping each other as an important practice within groups.

Further reading

Bradbury, A. (2021) *Ability, Inequality and Post-Pandemic Schools: Rethinking Contemporary Myths of Meritocracy*. Bristol: Policy Press.

Francis, B., Taylor, B. and Tereshchenko, A. (2020) *Reassessing 'Ability' Grouping: Improving Practice for Equity and Attainment*. London: Routledge.

Marks, R. (2016) *Ability-Grouping in Primary Schools: Case Studies and Critical Debates*. Northwich: Critical Publishing.

References

Alderson, P. and Morrow, V. (2004) *Ethics, Social Research and Consulting with Children and Young People*. Ilford: Barnardos.

Anderson, G., Frank, J., Naylor, C., Wadchis, W. and Feng, P. (2020) Using socio-economics to counter health disparities arising from the Covid-19 pandemic, *British Medical Journal*, 8 (369): m2149.

Baker, P. (1995) *Deconstruction and the Ethical Turn*. Gainesville, FL: University Press of Florida.

Ball, S. (1990) *Foucault and Education: Disciplines and Knowledge*. London: Routledge.

Benn, M. (2011) Streaming primary school pupils labels them for life, *The Guardian*. Available at: http://www.theguardian.com/education/2011/aug/08/streaming-pupils-limits-aspirations [accessed 10 February 2021].

Bernstein, B. (1971) *Class Codes and Control, Volume 1: Towards a Sociology of Language*. London: Routledge.

Bernstein, B. (1996) *Pedagogy, Symbolic Control and Identity: Theory, Research and Critique*. London: Rowman and Littlefield Publishers.

Bradbury, A. (2018) The impact of the Phonics Screening Check on grouping by ability: a 'necessary evil' amid the policy storm, *British Educational Research Journal*, 44 (4): 539–556.
Bradbury, A. and Robert-Holmes, G. (2017) *Grouping in Early Years and Key Stage 1: A necessary evil?* London: National Education Union.
Burman, E. (2008) *Developments: Child, Image, Nation.* New York: Routledge.
Campbell, T. (2013) *In-School Ability Grouping and the Month of Birth Effect. Preliminary evidence from the Millennium Cohort Study.* London: Centre for Longitudinal Studies.
Christensen, P. (2004). Children's participation in ethnographic research: issues of power and representation, *Children and Society*, 18 (2): 165–176.
Danby, S., Ewing, L. and Thorpe, K. (2011) The novice researcher: interviewing young children, *Qualitative Inquiry*, 17 (1): 74–84.
Davies, J., Hallam, S. and Ireson, J. (2003) Ability groupings in the primary school: issues arising from practice, *Research Papers in Education*, 18 (1): 45–60.
Delany, B. (1991) Allocation, choice, and stratification within high schools: how the sorting machine copes, *American Journal of Education*, 99 (2): 181–207.
Douglas, J. W. B. (1969) *The Home and the School; a Study of Ability and Attainment in the Primary School.* London: MacGibbon and Key.
ESTYN (2019) *Guidance Handbook for the Inspection of Primary School.* Cardiff: ESTYN.
Fehr, E., Bernhard, H. and Rockenbach, B. (2008) Egalitarianism in young children, *Nature*, 454 (7208): 1079–1084.
Folque, M. A. (2020) Interviewing young children. In: Naughton, M. G., Rolfe, S. and Siraj-Blatchford, I. (Eds.), *Doing Early Childhood Research: International Perspectives on Theory and Practice*, pp. 239–260. Second edition. Buckingham: Open University Press.
Gamoran, A. (1989) Rank, performance and mobility in elementary school grouping, *The Sociological Quarterly*, 30 (1): 109–123.
Gardner, H. (1983) *Frames of Mind: The Theory of Multiple Intelligences.* New York: Basic Books.
Hallam, S. and Parsons, S. (2013) The incidence and make up of ability grouped sets in the UK primary school, *Research Papers in Education*, 28 (4): 393–420.
Hallam, S., Ireson, J., Lister, V. and Chaudhury, I. (2003) Ability grouping practices in the primary school: a survey, *Educational Studies*, 29 (1): 69–83.
Hamilton, L. and O'Hara, P. (2011) The tyranny of setting (ability grouping): challenges to inclusion in Scottish primary schools, *Teaching and Teacher Education*, 27 (4): 712–721.
Hargreaves, D. H. (1982) *The Challenge for the Comprehensive School.* London: Routledge.
Hart, S., Dixon, A., Drummond, M. J. and McIntyre, D. (2004) *Learning Without Limits.* Maidenhead: Open University Press.
Hearnshaw, L. (1979) *Cyril Burt: Psychologist.* London: Hodder.
Ireson, J. and Hallam, S. (2001) *Ability Grouping in Education.* London: Sage
Jackson, C. and Povey, H. (2016) 'No, it just didn't work': a teacher's reflections on all attainment teaching. CREME 10: 10th Congress for European Research in Mathematics Education. Dublin.
Jordan, B. (2009) Scaffolding learning and co-constructing understanding. In: Anning, A., Cullen, J. and Fleer, M. (Eds.), *Early Childhood Education, Society and Culture*, pp. 39–52. Second edition. Los Angeles, London, New Delhi, Singapore, Washington DC: Sage.
Kutnick, P., Sebba, J., Blatchford, P., Galton, M. and Thorp, J. (2005) *The Effects of Pupil Grouping.* Brighton: DfE.
Kynaston, D. (2007) *Austerity Britain: 1945–1951.* London: Bloomsbury.
Lee, J. and Croll, P. (1995) Streaming and subject specialism at Key Stage 2: a survey in two local authorities, *Educational Studies*, 21 (2): 155–165.

Marks, R. (2011) 'Ability' in primary mathematics education: patterns and implications, *Research in Mathematics Education*, 13 (3): 305–306.

Marks, R. (2016) *Ability-grouping in Primary Schools: Case Studies and Critical Debates*. Northwich: Critical Publishing.

Marsh, H. and Yeung, A. (2001) An extension of the internal/external frame of reference model: a response to Bong, *Multivariate Behavioural Research*, 36 (3): 389–420.

Mercer, S. (2011) Language learner self-concept: complexity, continuity and change, *System*, 39 (3): 335–346.

Miles, M. and Huberman, A. (1984) *Qualitative Data Analysis: A Sourcebook of New Methods*. Newbury Park: Sage.

Muijs, D. and Dunne, M. (2010) Setting by ability–or is it? A quantitative study of determinants of set placement in English secondary schools, *Educational Research*, 52 (4): 391–407.

Muijus, D. and Reynolds, D. (2010) *Effective Teaching: Evidence and Practice*. London: Sage.

Muller, E., Wustmann-Seiler, C., Perren, S., and Simoni, H. (2015) Young children's self-perceived ability: development, factor structure and initial validation of a self-report instrument for pre-schoolers, *Journal of Psychopathology and Behavioural Assessment*, 37 (2): 256–273.

Office for Standards in Education (1998) *Setting in Primary Schools: A Report from the Office of Her Majesty's Chief Inspector of Schools*. London: Her Majesty's Stationery Office.

Orwell, G. (1949) *Nineteen Eighty-Four*. New York: Penguin.

Parsons, S. and Hallam, S. (2014) The impact of streaming on attainment at age seven: evidence from the Millennium Cohort Study, *Oxford Review of Education*, 40 (5): 567–589.

Persell, C. (1977) *Education and Inequality: The Roots and Results of Stratification in American Schools*. New York: Free Press.

Plowden Report. Great Britain. Department of Education and Science. Central Advisory Council for Education (England) (1967) *Children and Their Primary Schools*. London: Her Majesty's Stationery Office.

Rose, S., Twist, L., Lord, P., Rutt, S., Badr, K., Hope, C. and Styles, B. (2021) *Impact of School Closures and Subsequent Support Strategies on Attainment and Socio-emotional Wellbeing in Key Stage 1: Interim Paper 1*. Berkshire: National Foundation for Educational Research.

Rosenbaum, J. (1976) *Making Inequality: The Hidden Curriculum of High School Tracking*. New York: John Wiley.

Sacks, H. (1995) *Lectures on Conversation: Language Arts & Disciplines*. London: Wiley.

Scherer, L. (2016) 'I am not clever, they are cleverer than us': children reading in the primary school, *British Journal of Sociology of Education*, 37 (3): 389–407.

Schutz, A. (1972) *The Phenomenology of the Social World*. London: Heinemann Educational Books.

Shaw, C., Brady, L. M. and Davey, C. (2011) *Guidelines for Research with Children and Young People*. London: National Children's Bureau.

Simon, B. (1991) *Education and the Social Order*. London: Lawrence & Wishart.

Singal, N. and Swann, M. (2011) Children's perceptions of themselves as learner inside and outside school, *Research Papers in Education*, 26 (4): 469–484.

Social Mobility Commission (2017) *Low income pupils' progress at secondary school*. London: Social Mobility Commission.

Sukhnandan, L. and Lee, B. (1998) *Streaming, Setting and Grouping by Ability: A Review of the Literature*. Berkshire: National Foundation for Educational Research.

Swann, M., Peacock, A., Hart, S. and Drummond, M. J. (2012) *Creating Learning Without Limits*. Maidenhead: Open University Press.

Theobald, M., (2008) *Methodological issues arising from video-stimulated recall with young children*. Paper presented at the Australian Association of Research in Education (AARE) Conference, Brisbane, Australia.

United Nations Convention on the Rights of the Child (1989) Available at: https://www.unicef.org.uk/what-we-do/un-convention-child-rights/ [accessed 4 April 2021].

Vernon, P. (1952) Intelligence testing, *The Times Educational Supplement*, 25 January. Available at: https://books.google.co.uk/books?id=-SuBAAAAQBAJ&pge=PA56&lpg=PA56&dq=vernon+intelligence+testing+1952&source=bl&ots=7gFhBTmfI_&sig=zrJ7C3wP3BtrDgp7yFdnGIvlLo0&hl=en&sa=X&ved=0CD0Q6AEwBmoVChMIpvXVys26xwIVsgjbCh2dRgIE#v=onepage&q=vernon%20intelligence%20testing%201952&f=false [accessed 18 March 2021].

Welsh Government (2015) *The Foundation Phase Framework*. Available at: https://hwb.gov.wales/api/storage/d5d8e39c-b534-40cb-a3f5-7e2e126d8077/foundation-phase-framework.pdf [accessed 23 January 2021].

Whitburn, J. (2001) Effective classroom organisation in primary schools: mathematics, *Oxford Review of Education*, 27 (3): 411.

Wigfield, A. and Eccles, J. (2000) Expectancy–value theory of achievement motivation, *Contemporary Educational Psychology*, 25 (1): 68–81.

Wiliam, D. and Bartholomew, H. (2004) It's not which school but which set you're in that matters: the influence of ability grouping practices on student progress in mathematics, *British Educational Research Journal*, 30 (2): 279–293.

10 The capable child as a threshold concept for inclusive early childhood education and care

Jane Waters-Davies and Natalie Macdonald

Introduction

This chapter reports on one aspect of the findings from a study that adopted a rating scale as a tool for driving professional learning for a group of pre-school staff working in targeted early childhood education and care (ECEC) provision across an area in Wales identified as socio-economically deprived. As background to what follows therefore, we provide here an overview of the programme of professional learning in question.

The national context for the study is important and we return to it in our discussion. Wales has the highest rate of child poverty in the UK with one in three children living in poverty (JRF 2018). We worked within one local authority, through the advisory team responsible for the 16 Flying Start childcare settings within the authority. Flying Start is the flagship early intervention programme supporting children, aged 0–4, and their families in areas of disadvantage (Welsh Government 2014), as defined by the Welsh Index of Multiple Deprivation. The initiative includes a comprehensive package of parenting support, additional health visiting services, Early Language Development Team support and 42 weeks of sessional childcare for children aged 2–3. A key element of Flying Start sessional provision is the qualified status of the early years workforce. Social Care Wales set out a minimum level of qualifications for Flying Start practitioners and managers which is above the minimum qualifications set out for those working in day care, childminders and sessional care. There is a commitment within the Flying Start service to ongoing professional learning for staff and it is within this context that the study reported here took place.

The development of the professional learning programme

The advisory staff for Flying Start in this authority wanted to develop the pedagogic skills of their practitioner team. In order to identify the content of the professional learning (PL) programme a rating scale was employed across all settings as a measure of children's day-to-day learning experiences in Flying Start provision. The content of the professional learning intervention was

DOI: 10.4324/9781003163206-13

targeted towards the identified areas of weaker performance indicated by this measure. The measure adopted was the Sustained Shared Thinking and Emotional Well-being (SSTEW) scale for 2–5-year-old provision (Siraj, Kingston, and Melhuish 2015). This scale has been developed from an extensive body of research that focusses on early educational practices that support children's 'task focus, problem-solving and imagination … well-being, self-regulation, and the kind of thinking in children that is supported through sensitive interaction with others' (Sylva et al. 2014, 5). This scale therefore targets practice that supports the kinds of development in children that the Flying Start programme seeks to promote. Within the rationale for the SSTEW scale the authors note:

> In terms of the adult role, what becomes essential is the sensitive, child-centred intervention of the adult when supporting the child's learning and development … the practitioner requires a clear understanding of their [the child's] current development, cultural heritage and achievement, and their feelings, behaviours and responses to learning.
> (Siraj, Kingston, and Melhuish 2015, 7)

The SSTEW scale focuses strongly on interaction and intentional responsive pedagogy, arguably 'previously overlooked interactional aspects of process quality' that have been positively associated with children's development (Howard et al. 2020, 12). The outcomes from the rating scale indicated that across all settings there was weaker provision relating to *supporting curiosity and problem solving* and *supporting concept development and higher order thinking*. The PL programme was designed by university-based staff from the Early Childhood Studies department, alongside the advisors, to address pedagogical practice related to these two particular aspects. We sought therefore to enhance the *pedagogical offer* the staff were providing for the children in their settings.

The PL programme was provided for all staff from each of the 16 Flying Start settings, who attended together during setting closure days. The PL programme involved two experiential sessions, including immersion in exploratory science play and talk that prompts curiosity and models metacognition. The content of the PL programme reflected the understanding that 'science' learning in the early years is supported by enquiry-oriented pedagogic behaviour (Andersson and Gulberg 2014) and directed towards concept development (Cremin et al. 2015) and higher order thinking. Throughout the programme, we also explicitly referred to the capable child, able to explore, reason and think, especially when supported by responsive adults. The sessions took place off site approximately three weeks apart with a series of directed pedagogic activities and reflection prompts to be undertaken by the staff between sessions. Detail about the PL programme is reported in Gealy et al. (2020). Of importance here is that between 6–12 months after the PL programme was undertaken the Flying Start staff were invited to evaluate the impact it had on their practice and pedagogical thinking via a text-based questionnaire. In addition, the advisory staff were interviewed about the same issue.

The evaluation responses

In summary, the responses from the Flying Start staff, the advisory team as well as from a further audit of provision using the SSTEW scale indicated an improvement in practice that supports curiosity and problem solving, and concept development and higher order thinking (see Waters and Macdonald 2020). However, for the purposes of this chapter we want to focus upon a few questionnaire responses that troubled us, and have caused us to discuss and reflect. We are therefore attending to the voices of the small minority of respondents who maintained persistent deficit views about the capability of the children in their care to think conceptually. We note that this was despite the PL programme demonstrating the ability of very young children to explore and develop working theories and early concepts through playful engagement with adults who are responsive to their exploration and thinking.

In the evaluative questionnaire, participants were invited to provide text-based responses and describe the impact of the PL programme on their understanding and their practice. About 10% of the responses were framed within deficit views of the capabilities of children that are specific to those who attend Flying Start provision. That is, a few respondents indicated that *because* the children have some form of developmental delay, they are not capable of curiosity, higher order thinking or problem solving.

Here are examples of the text-based responses, sections of which have been emboldened to be discussed further below. These examples typify the 10% of responses that we classified as inferring deficit models of certain children. They reflect, however, a discourse that is not uncommon; a discourse that requires our intellectual attention in order that its consequences do not go unchallenged.

> It reminded me of certain things that can be done with children to extend their learning **if appropriate to their level of need**.
>
> (Response 34502591)

> I felt the programme helped us to think differently how science can be taught through everyday objects we take for granted. However, **putting this in place for our children can be challenging as some who attend find it difficult to understand and communicate**.
>
> (Response 35475309)

> It has helped us to add commenting and questioning alongside activities to enhance children's learning **when they are at a stage where they are ready**.
>
> (Response 34502591)

> I feel that our **children are very young for this process** and although it will introduce new experiences we have to remember that **the majority of children in our care have some sort of delay**.
>
> (Response 33704488)

I do feel it's important **to remember the age of the children and take in to consideration the that they are from deprived areas and may have speech and language delays** and therefore I feel some content is hard to use day to day.

(Response 33763833)

This training is **useful for those typically developing children** within Flying Start and other childcare providers, however a large percentage of the children we have accessing our setting have other areas of development that I feel are more of a priority to invest time in **to get them to a stage where they are curious and able to understand and play**.

(Response 34502591)

Although it is hard with some of our children as **they are not as developmentally ready as others**—so more challenging, but we keep trying.

(Response 35475105)

The issue

When we analysed the data from the questionnaire we thought about these responses. Clearly these are children who, against normative measures, are not demonstrating expected outcomes for their age. The Flying Start provision is explicitly targeted towards families who are living in circumstances that are not considered to be optimal for children's long-term positive outcomes, and which may fall into periods of short–or long-term crisis. Children in areas of multiple deprivation have been identified as having lower levels of development than their peers with higher incidence of developmental delay, particularly speech and language (Welsh Government 2019). Interventions such as Flying Start are targeted in these areas in an attempt to address the imbalance increased by poverty. It is glib to suggest to the practitioners working with children, who at 2 and 3 years of age may be pre-lingual and highly dependent on others for personal care, that these children should be viewed as 'active, competent and capable agents' (e.g. Prout and James 1997), even when we may firmly hold this view ourselves. However, the PL programme demonstrated the capability of very young children, including those who may have developmental delays, to explore and develop working theories and early concepts through playful engagement with adults who are responsive to their exploration and thinking. We intended that the PL programme would challenge deficit constructions of children by both offering a model of the competent, active child and by the experience of the practitioners with the children in their settings. The responses from most of the respondents to the survey explained that the programme had been successful in this regard. For example, the significant majority (90%) of participants' responses resonated strongly with the following:

> the training was really informative and increased my understanding as to how, by changing my vocabulary and allowing the children to lead/discover, [this] has improved the learning experience.
>
> (Response 33546581)

> The training also helped me to think carefully about how to encourage problem solving and critical thinking through the way I interact with children and I feel this has improved my practice.
>
> (Response 34466399)

> When interacting with the children I find myself monitoring my communication to ensure I'm providing the children with opportunities to explore and extend their own learning and apply their own knowledge. Using terms such as 'I wonder' 'what would happen if'.
>
> (Response 33546581)

We note, however, from the persistence of deficit views in a small number of respondents that the PL programme did not challenge these particular individuals to think about the children in their care as competent and capable.

The issue, then, reflects what Cook reports in her first editorial for the journal *Childhood* when she comments upon her undergraduate students holding a 'default conceptual position' (2009, 6) of the 'innocent, manipulable child'. Cook recognises that:

> to inhabit the analytic space of 'childhood studies' [is] a privileged intellectual position like any other. The extent to which the writings and research of the last quarter century have now built up into something resembling a canon nevertheless reflect and embody an orientation to children and childhood which is not found often in everyday life.
>
> (Cook 2009, 9)

This is the issue we recognised, that there remains a default conceptual position of the *in*capable child and her development, visible in a minority of voices in our survey, but reflective of some wider practices within ECEC. This conceptual position is that of the un-knowing, innocent, deficit child, in need of protection, and adult-structured manipulation to reach a less deficient status. This conceptual position, the construction of the child, is central to practice. As such, this concept underpins our activity, attitude and approach to practice; it shapes the way we respond to theoretical ideas and practical policies. The construction of the child is a concept that requires, indeed demands, overt exploration if we are to meet the challenges of genuine inclusion as discussed in the introductory chapter.

In our discussions we thought about the deep-seated nature of professional beliefs and agreed that, once a practitioner constructs a child as capable, this threshold concept (Meyer and Land 2003) forms the basis of praxis. The responses indicated above were not from individuals who hold such a model of the developing child in mind. We might conceive that they, instead, hold a model of the young child that is centred around her innocence and incapacity, her need of nurture and protection. In such a model the adult has responsibility to orchestrate what is made available to the child, and when. Our discussions led us to ask whether a construction of the young child in this weakened position inadvertently leads to practice that is partial and not inclusive. Such practice may be built upon an understanding that there is a hierarchy of skill development and that language skill precedes curiosity, that children without language cannot engage in play that is driven by curiosity or enquiry; that these children need to be protected from over-exposure to ideas lest they cannot cope. We wondered whether a well-intentioned professional position, to ensure that children develop language skills, may mean that some children are restricted from access to play and pedagogy that might serve to support curiosity and conceptual thinking. This position, allied to a view, evident in our respondents, that children experience developmental delays because they are from families experiencing socio-economic deprivation, suggests a significant issue where practice cannot be inclusive. Our discussions about this issue led us to writing this chapter, and below we explore the nature of the threshold concept generally and make a case for the need for recognition of the capable child as a pre-requisite to inclusive practice (Artiles et al. 2010; Parekh 2017; Olszewski-Kubilius and Clarenbach 2012). We make this case, respectful of the challenges faced by ECEC professionals in their work with diverse communities, in order that the construction of the child acquires and retains its place as fundamental to inclusive provision.

We go on now to explore the notion of a threshold concept in order to articulate more clearly the power of this notion, and the implications of our thinking in this regard.

Threshold concepts

In order for us to consider this issue in a way that helps us consider professional learning, we use Meyer and Land's work on threshold concepts, and associated ideas of troublesome knowledge, and liminality. We also consider how discipline-specific conceptualisations, here in relation to the child, can be implicitly privileged in professional learning in a way that blinds us to the barriers we are seeking to overcome.

Meyer and Land (2003) introduced the idea of threshold concepts in their exploration of Higher Education Institute (HEI) curricula and higher education student learning. They offer the following description:

> A threshold concept can be considered as akin to a portal, opening up a new and previously inaccessible way of thinking about something. It represents a transformed way of understanding, or interpreting, or viewing something without which the learner cannot progress. As a consequence of

comprehending a threshold concept there may thus be a transformed internal view of subject matter, subject landscape, or even world view ... Such a transformed view or landscape may represent how people 'think' in a particular discipline, or how they perceive, apprehend, or experience particular phenomena within that discipline (or more generally).

(Meyer and Land 2003, 1)

In 2005 the authors characterise a threshold concept as a conceptual gateway and explain that these gateways can be:

transformative (occasioning a significant shift in the perception of a subject), irreversible (unlikely to be forgotten, or unlearned only through considerable effort), and integrative (exposing the previously hidden interrelatedness of something).

(Meyer and Land 2005, 373/4)

Associated with the transformative nature of the threshold concept is the likelihood of the transformed perspective involving an affective component, that is, a shift in values, feeling or attitude (Meyer and Land 2003, 5). In addition, Meyer and Land conclude that a threshold concept 'can of itself inherently represent ... troublesome knowledge' (2003, 2). Troublesome knowledge can be counter-intuitive, or even appear absurd at face value. Think of the young child as capable and competent and active and strong–arguably an absurd idea if taken at face value!

A threshold concept is distinguished from what might be considered a core idea or a core concept in a body of knowledge and understanding. A core concept is seen as a conceptual 'building block' that 'progresses understanding of the subject; it has to be understood but it does not necessarily lead to a qualitatively different view of subject matter' (Mayer and Land 2003, 4), whereas the threshold concept leads to just that, a transformed view.

Cousin (2006a, 4) explains that the prevalence of a 'common sense' or intuitive understanding of a concept can inhibit grasping and mastering a threshold concept. 'Getting students to reverse their intuitive understandings is also troublesome because the reversal can involve an uncomfortable, emotional repositioning'. In her own work, Cousin (2006a, 5) explored some of the emotional issues that make learning troublesome; she makes the case that we should temper the implicit suggestion in the idea of a threshold concept that the difficulty of its mastery inheres in the concept itself. 'While this is very often the case, we need to be aware that this difficulty cannot be abstracted from the learner or the social context.' For the ECEC practitioner or student there is the common sense understanding that the young child *is* weak, innocent and in need of protection by mere fact of being a child and therefore physically immature and lacking strength and knowledge to stand alone in the world. That the field of early childhood studies demands the construction of the child as capable and strong *is* counter-intuitive, even absurd. The need to conceptualise differently the state of childhood therefore is troublesome; it requires deep exploration of the meanings of the words being used and the concepts being brought into play. It requires that as adults we reconsider how we view our childhood selves, that we reconsider our adult relationship with the children around us. As Cook (2009) explains, the cultural force, in the wealthy sectors of the Global North at least, of the child as innocent is such that overcoming this force requires significant effort.

Cousin (2006a) suggests that the idea of *liminal states* provides a useful metaphor to aid our understanding of the conceptual transformations that students undergo when grappling with a threshold concept, and the difficulties or anxieties that attend these transformations. Meyer and Land (2003, 13) explain that the difficulty in understanding threshold concepts may leave the learner in a state of 'liminality … a suspended state in which understanding approximates to a kind of mimicry or lack of authenticity'. We wondered whether the following responses were indicative of liminality with regard to the threshold concept of the capable child. There is an indication of new learning and reflective commentary on professional action and alongside this, a pull towards the construct of the child as either unready or needy.

> It has helped us to add commenting and questioning alongside activities to enhance children's learning when they are at a stage where they are ready.
> (Response 34502591)

> I allowed the children to problem solve more for themselves rather than me give them the answer or do it for them.
> (Response 33818289)

Learning involves the occupation of a liminal space during the process of mastery of a threshold concept (Meyer and Land 2005); this involves a process of to-ing and fro-ing between old and new understandings as learners integrate understandings and explore the reach of new conceptualisations across the field. Cousin (2006a, 5) suggests that the idea that learners enter into a liminal state as they attempt to grasp certain concepts presents 'a powerful way of remembering that learning is both affective and cognitive and that it involves identity shifts which can entail troublesome, unsafe journeys'. The following responses seem to indicate that participants experienced affective shifts in their perception of themselves as professionals.

> I feel that the training has enhanced my understanding and has made me reflect on my performance and interaction with the children.
> (Response 33546581)

> I am not afraid that I don't know the answer why something appears as it does. I am more curious to find out.
> (Response 34347527)

When we are considering work such as ECEC that involves the deeply emotional work of 'professional love' (e.g. Cousins 2017; Page 2018), it is essential to recognise the implications of challenging the construction of childhood that underpins beliefs and practices. These implications can rock the foundations upon which professional identity is based and therefore require us to attend to affective learning as well as the cognitive learning of ECEC staff and students, in all forms of PL programmes. Relatedly, those working in the health professions, e.g. Tanner (2011) and Clouder (2005), agree that health professional students need to be touched emotionally during practice placements as part of the grappling with the threshold concept of 'care', though they appear to disagree over the extent to which these affective experiences are significant for professional identity formation. We return to this notion below when we consider implications for professional learning.

Threshold knowledge in early childhood education and care

In a small scale and localised study, Ashworth (2016) followed a group of undergraduate students in an English HEI, exploring their engagement with the concept of childhood presented to them during a year-long childhood and youth studies module. She applied threshold concept theory to her work and her findings showed students' prior understandings were deeply embedded, causing barriers to their engagement with this fundamental concept in their chosen discipline. Ashworth concludes that in order to engage with discipline-specific understandings, or threshold concepts (in her study, the concept of childhood), students needed to 'unlearn' prior knowledge that was based on lived experience of the concept under question. The pedagogical implications of engagement with childhood as a threshold concept for the discipline included providing time and space in which students could unpack deeply held personal understandings, in order that they may see anew the transformed landscape of their area of study.

Taylor (2015) explored the idea of threshold concepts in the accounts of ECEC students of their practice placement experience in Ireland. He concluded that it was the 'narrative interconnectedness' (Taylor 2015, 55), of the elements of the threshold concept that was evident in the students' descriptions of learning during placement. The root of their transformation to professional behaviours while on placement was the successful execution of an intervention such as an activity with younger children, which consists of planning, implementation and review stages. The threshold concept at play appeared to be the students' construction of themselves as professionally competent. Both these studies indicate the need for professional learning that supports reflective and practical engagement, over time, with the theoretical threshold concept(s) under consideration.

In the study and discipline of early childhood, we argue here that the conceptualisation of the capable child is probably a threshold concept. Specifically, conceptualising the young child as active, capable and agentic offers a transformed understanding of infant and young childhood, and of early education and care policy and practices, compared to the constructions of the young child that are routinely associated with the wealthy Global North. These have been well described by Cook (2009) and Ashworth (2016) as routinely reflecting the notion of the innocent child in need of protection, vulnerable to the corruptions of the modern world. Associated with this deficit construction of the child is the dominance, in much early education policy and practice, of the *developmental* child, in which development is understood as staged and necessarily sequential. The notion of readiness is located within these constructions of the young child; a child is deemed *un*ready until considered *ready* by an adult, whose judgement is based upon an assumed authority about what comes next for this child and is implicitly justified by the construction of the caring, protective nature of the practitioner. This concept may also be entrenched through outcome-focussed curricula and accountability measures in place for ECEC, especially with regard to education. Where children are deemed unready, unless they can perform certain feats, usually associated with language production, it is not surprising that language delay forms the basis of the responses we saw from the minority of staff in our project indicating children were not ready for exploratory play and enquiring talk. Finucane (2021) explores the concept of readiness in her consideration of the provision of early science experiences for young children in Ireland. She helpfully reminds us that emotive discussions about school readiness may be 'masking the need for critical debate about early childhood curriculum content and the types of pedagogies that contemporary literature suggests are most effective to support science learning' (Finucane 2021, 158). Our experience in this study would support her argument.

This brings us back to the 'issue'; as providers of professional learning for ECEC practitioners we are deeply situated within the discipline-specific understandings of the child, specifically the child as competent and capable. We read aspects of the data set, as presented above, as significantly problematic therefore, and understood this as a *deficit of understanding* in a minority of the practitioner group. Our understanding was similarly reflected by the local authority advisors (Flying Start leads) working with us, who described this small group of practitioners as 'not getting it' in their interview responses. By way of explanation of this latter point, during the interview with the Flying Start leads they commented on the receptiveness of the Flying Start staff to professional learning. Some staff were described as 'getting it', contrasted to those who were unable to 'get it' with the same level of conviction. In exploring these ideas, the interviewees appeared to equate the disposition to enact a responsive pedagogy with 'getting it':

> when a practitioner just got it, it [responsive pedagogy] would be applied really naturally throughout their day … and the conversation was, in the best case, phenomenal, but then there would be those forced conversations that had been put together with an activity that had been planned … and the activity became about trying to force those questions … whereas in other settings it was a really natural conversation.

What the Flying Start leads describe here as 'forced conversations' might be understood as 'mimicry', a performative behaviour that is undertaken to ensure that a perceived required action is completed, but is without underpinning understanding for the rationale behind the behaviour. Cousin (2006b) describes mimicry as a position during the liminal stages of grappling with a threshold concept. In this liminal position learners can feel, or be, 'stuck' and require further engagement with the concept to become unstuck. So, we might listen to the practitioners' comments with what Land et al. (2006) describe as a 'third ear' by which they mean 'listen[ing] not for what a student knows ... but for the terms that shape a student's knowledge' (Land et al. 2006, 200). When we use this third ear and read the terms 'delayed', 'not ready' and 'young', we understand that the practitioners' responses detailed above are shaped by understandings of the unready, developmental child, rather than the active and capable child. These terms then appear as barriers to adopting the threshold concept of a child as competent and capable. At times, it seemed that whilst individuals agreed with the concept of the capable child in principle, it is as though they then added, for clarification, 'but not for our children'. It is this clarification that is at the heart of what troubles us in terms of the non-inclusive approach to practice it embraces. In this liminal position, the capable child is constructed for other children but not for our 'special' children, who need more, greater, better... in order to succeed. This liminal position threatens inclusive practice, for example, where pedagogies that support critical thinking are held back from certain children, due to their perceived deficiencies, but offered to others, who are perceived as not having such deficiencies.

Construction of the child and inclusion–examples

As indicated in the previous section we are concerned that inclusive practices are restricted by certain deficient constructions of the young child. In this section, we work through some practice examples to exemplify the point. Having considered the nature of threshold concepts we want to work through the argument presented that, in order to offer an inclusive practice, practitioners need to have grasped the threshold concept that is the construction of the capable child.

Once we understand the child as active, capable and competent and apply this to *all* children, then our practice is based upon a foundation of equity, and inclusion.

Example 1. Toddler: risk/exploration

Aled is 2 years 3 months old, his language skills are developing well and he is relaxed in his setting, especially when playing within the vicinity of his key worker. He has been attending the setting since he was 2, when dad, who was the main carer at home, went back to work. The staff have noticed that Aled can be a little unbalanced when playing outside, he tends to fall easily and can become upset quickly when this happens.

Scenario 1: These staff hold a construction of the child as capable

The staff discuss Aled and air their concerns about his physical development, related to him falling over, and to his being upset when this happens. They agree that he is a generally happy and capable child and they have no immediate concerns that require action straight away. They decide to watch Aled closely, especially when playing outside, to understand better what happens when he falls. Aled's key worker and one other staff member observe and watch Aled over the coming week. They notice that Aled's instability is associated with him being absorbed in attending to other things while moving around, for example watching other children, calling to his friends, and carrying objects from place to place while playing with or exploring the object. They notice that Aled is so interested in what is going on around him that he doesn't pay any attention to what's underfoot.

On an icy day there is an increased risk of slipping outside, despite the grit that has been placed on the pathways; this applies to all the children but especially to Aled. The staff make a great game of showing all the children how ice is slippery and invite them all to feel the ice on a frozen puddle in the outdoor area, touch it, and–with the hand of an adult if they wished–to have a go walking on it, very slowly, to feel how their feet can slip. The staff vocalise their thinking all the time, using words to describe the experience of cold, ice, smooth, shiny, slippery, sliding, wobbly.

They also show the children what happens if they put grit on the ice, they notice together how the ice changes into water, doesn't look smooth or shiny any more, but looks rough and gritty. The children are invited to walk on the gritted areas and notice how they feel more stable.

When Aled goes outside to play with a few other children and their key worker, he is very attentive to the ground. He looks at it closely and burbles to himself while placing each foot slowly and carefully on different parts of the outdoor area to test how slippery it is. Aled's key worker is nearby and unobtrusively watching closely, though, on this occasion Aled does not fall and enjoys exploring the cold ground.

Scenario 2: These staff hold a construction of the child as developmentally vulnerable and in need of protection

The staff discuss Aled and air their concerns about him falling and being upset. They agree that he is a happy and capable child, but that they are worried about his falling and want to protect him from hurting himself. They decide to ensure that Aled is carefully supported when playing outside to understand better what happens when he falls, and prevent some of the mishaps. Aled's key worker makes sure she is always quite close by when Aled goes outside in the coming week. She notices that Aled likes her being close by and he starts asking for her hand while moving about on the uneven surfaces outside. Aled becomes a bit clingy when outside and appears fearful when he wobbles.

On an icy day there is an increased risk of slipping outside, despite the grit that has been placed on the pathways; this applies to all the children but especially to Aled. The staff decide that Aled should only go out when his key worker is able to hold his hand while he is moving about on the uneven surfaces. The frozen puddle is cordoned off to make sure no one slips on it, and the children are told to keep away from it. The staff vocalise their thinking, using words to describe the experience of cold, ice, dangerous, slippery, risk of falling over, risk of being hurt.

When Aled goes outside to play with a few other children and their key worker, he is very wary. He wants to hold the key worker's hand most of the time. When he does let go, she says 'be very careful now Aled!' as he takes a few steps away from her. Aled asks to go inside very soon afterwards.

Example 2. Pre-school: concept development

Meg is 2 years and 6 months old; she is settled and established within her setting; she has a slight delay in her language development. Meg's language development is supported within the setting through one-to-one targeted language activities with her key worker.

Scenario 1: These staff hold a construction of the child as capable

Meg is playing outside with her peers and key workers. Staff have set up an inspiration to play with loose parts such as drainpipes, tubes, boxes and balls. A group of four children including Meg have been working together balancing the pipes and tubes on boxes at different heights with the support of the adult. The children spend time balancing the tubes and exploring the resources with the support of the adults. The adults prompt children's thinking and action using open-ended questions.

Meg picks up some of the balls and rolls them down the tubes letting out excited squeals as the balls go shooting down the tubes. The other children and staff notice this and excitedly join in with Meg. The staff point out that some balls seem to travel faster down some tubes than others and invite the children to test it out, noticing which tubes are slower or faster and comment using phrases such as 'I wonder why this one is slower' and asking 'what do you think?' to Meg and the other children. Meg responds to this by lifting one end of the tube making the ball travel faster. The staff and children respond to Meg with excitement providing a narrative for Meg's actions such as 'Oh look Meg, you made the ball roll faster', 'I wonder if all the balls will go faster if we lift up the tubes', 'we have heavy and light balls, do they all do the same?' This prompts Meg to go and collect some of the heavier balls to test out the theory. The children spend the rest of the time outside exploring these ideas with Meg taking the lead in the activity.

During that week's staff planning meeting, the staff note that during the activity Meg demonstrated understanding of the concepts of fast/slow, heavy/

light and was able to respond to problem solving queries and open-ended questioning through her actions.

Scenario 2: These staff hold a construction of the child as developmentally vulnerable and in need of protection

Meg is playing outside with her peers and key workers. Staff have set up an inspiration to play with loose parts such as drainpipes, tubes, boxes, and balls. A group of four children including Meg have been working together balancing the pipes and tubes on boxes at different heights with the support of the adult. The children spend time balancing the tubes and exploring the resources with the support of the adults. The adults prompt children's thinking and action using open-ended questions.

Meg picks up some of the balls and rolls them down the tubes letting out excited squeals as the balls go shooting down the tubes. The other children and staff notice this and excitedly join in with Meg. The staff point out the colours of the balls to Meg, naming them and asking her to repeat the colour of the ball 'Red'. Meg stops playing, the staff allow time for Meg to respond, and she then attempts to form the word saying 'ed'. The staff respond by modelling the correct word back to Meg and providing praise for her attempt 'red, well done Meg, the ball is red'. While this has been happening, the other children have continued to play with the tubes and balls. Meg re-joins the others, though is now no longer leading the exploration; she continues to engage in the play with the pipes, rolling different colour and weight balls down the pipes. She is interested in the slope of the pipe and the speed of the ball, and experiments with this. The staff also engage excitedly in the play using opportunities to reinforce expressive language by naming colours and items with Meg. The children spend the rest of the time outside exploring the resources.

During that week's staff planning meeting, the staff note that during the activity Meg was able to begin to verbalise and label some of the objects and colours. The staff decide to build on this by introducing some further colour activities into the planning and to reinforce naming colours within Meg's one-to-one sessions next week.

Conclusion: implications and recommendations

The above illustrations are intended to provide a point of reflection for the reader. All the practice described is professionally appropriate; we want to highlight the way in which the (usually unspoken) construction of the child shapes the pedagogical offer made from the adults to the children in ECEC. The examples align to the competence of staff to observe, and to discuss their observations of children in planning for next steps. The differences in the responses to the scenarios are intended to demonstrate the restricted pedagogical offer we can make, if we hold a deficit view of a child, or a group of children. Whilst the deficit view is not poor practice necessarily, and both scenarios in each example represent what the staff involved consider to be in the best interests of the child, we hope that in reading them one recognises that there is a richness and affirming intention associated with the pedagogical offer made to the capable child.

In addition, we know from the work of Ladwig and McPherson (2017), de Araujou (2017) and others, summarised in Parekh's (2017) editorial, how perceptions of delay and deficit can lead to lowered expectations for children's outcomes, and how these can then become self-fulfilling prophesies. Parekh (2017) uses the example of children with English as an Additional Language (EAL), demonstrating how a delay in using English was conflated by education practitioners with a delay in all areas of children's development, and this led to lowered expectations of these children. This shows how a deficit construction of the child can lead to generalisation of reduced capability and potential, and subsequently this shapes the levels of expectation of attainment of certain children. Furthermore, lower expectations lead to a limited pedagogical offer, and a lack of opportunity for challenge. This scenario then limits children's opportunity for development and reinforces the deficit view of the child; hence the self-fulfilment of lowered expectations.

It seems inherent upon us, as providers of professional learning to support our students and practitioners, firstly, to recognise the foundational idea that practice is shaped by one's construction of the child. This is a philosophical idea, tied to notions of the social-political context and the shaping forces of our implicit understandings within it. Once this idea is grasped, then the threshold concept of the active, capable child can be readily met, considered, refuted, debated, enacted and tested. The developmental child and the capable child are not binary opposites; we must, through our practice, come to know how to support development through engagement with young children who we construct as capable. As providers of professional learning we need to learn to recognise when learners are operating in a liminal state, and support them through this. As Tanner (2015), Clouder (2011) and Taylor (2015) found in their work, described above, it is the practical enactment of, and reflection upon conceptual knowledge that supports learners in caring professions to cross a threshold and see differently the world in which they act. As Cousin (2006b) argues, we need to ensure that our curriculum design centres around the threshold concept of the capable child, which we argue here is essential for genuine inclusive practice in ECEC. Also, we argue that this concept should be robustly visible in our PL programmes, pro-actively explicit and a point of action and reflection in order that the pedagogical offer resulting from professional learning is inclusive and celebratory of children's capability as well as supportive of development across all its domains.

The drive for upskilling and professionalisation of the early years workforce is accelerating, for example, in Wales the ECEC agenda is moving swiftly with the development of a quality framework, a new suite of qualifications and a new curriculum in development. The status of the early years profession is, at last, increasing with changes to the Standard Occupational Classifications (Office for National Statistics 2020) reclassifying occupations in the early years sector into an associate professional's grade. These are significant steps towards the recognition of early years as a professional occupation and boosts the status of the sector and sector-relevant early years PL programmes. Therefore, we argue, this is a key point in time for ensuring that PL and associated qualifications develop our early years workforce to understand the child, *all children*, as primarily competent and capable.

In our reflections on the project we have discussed in this chapter, we are encouraged by the fact that the number of practitioners who maintained persistent deficit views was small and the majority of practitioners reported the children in their care as competent and capable. We hope that this reflects, in part at least, the socio-constructivist design of the PL delivery where practitioners had time to practice and reflect on the PL content, including the construction of the child underpinning the pedagogical offer, alongside the opportunity to unpack their reflections and learning in a supported professional space (see Gealy et al. 2020). Undergraduate programmes in early years have developed exponentially in recent years reflecting recognition of the need for both in-depth theoretical knowledge and practical competence to effectively work in the early years sector. This arena provides the opportunity to promote the threshold concept of the competent and capable child thus enabling opportunities for exploration and enactment of the concept from both an academic and practical perspective. We argue that the holy grail of inclusive practice is well served if those working in the ECEC sector adopt, for *all* the children they work with, the threshold concept of the capable child.

Key points

- Barriers to inclusive working may lie deeply within even the most practised and experienced staff working in the early childhood education and care (ECEC) sector.
- The construction of the capable, agential child may be a privileged conceptualisation, and a default construction of the dependent, deficit child may be in evidence across many ECEC practice contexts.
- The notion of the *threshold concept* (Meyer and Land 2003) may be useful, where a threshold concept can be considered as akin to a portal, opening up a new and previously inaccessible way of thinking about something.
- We propose that the conceptual construction of the capable child is a threshold concept in the study and practice of early childhood education and care.
- We argue that inclusive practice requires that the practitioner constructs *every* child as capable, and consider how this threshold concept may form the basis of inclusive praxis.

Further reading

Meyer, J.H.F. and Land, R. (Eds.) (2012) *Overcoming Barriers to Student Understanding: Threshold Concepts and Troublesome Knowledge*, London and New York: Routledge.

Parekh, G. (2017) The tyranny of 'ability', *Curriculum Inquiry*, 47(4): 337–343, doi:10.1080/03626784.2017.1383755

Waters, J. and Macdonald, N. (2020) Exploring the use of a rating scale to support professional learning in early years pre-school staff: the experience of one local authority in Wales, *Early Years*. doi:10.1080/09575146.2020.1742666.

References

Andersson, K., and Gulberg, A. (2014) What is science in preschool and what do teachers have to know to empower children? *Cultural Studies of Science Education*, 9 (2): 275–296.

de Araujo, Z. (2017) Connections between secondary mathematics teachers' beliefs and their selection of tasks for English language learners, *Curriculum Inquiry*, 47 (4): 363–389.

Artiles, A., Kozleski, E., Trent, S., Osher, D. and Ortiz, A. (2010) Justifying and explaining disproportionality, 1968–2008: a critique of underlying views of culture. *Exceptional Children*, 76 (3): 279–299.

Ashworth, H. (2016) Students' acquisition of a threshold concept in childhood and youth studies, *Innovations in Education and Teaching International*, 53 (1): 94–103.

Clouder, L. (2005) Caring as a 'threshold concept': transforming students in higher education into health(care) professionals, *Teaching in Higher Education*, 10 (4): 505–517.

Cook, D.T. (2009) Editorial. When a child is not a child, and other conceptual hazards of childhood studies, *Childhood*, 16 (1): 5–10.

Cousin, G. (2006a) An introduction to threshold concepts, *Planet*, 17 (1): 4–5.

Cousin, G. (2006b) Threshold concepts, troublesome knowledge and emotional capital: an exploration into learning about others. In: Meyer, J.H.F. and Land, R. (Eds.) *Overcoming Barriers to Student Understanding: Threshold Concepts and Troublesome Knowledge*, pp. 134–148. London and New York: Routledge.

Cousins, S.B. (2017) Practitioners' constructions of love in early childhood education and care, *International Journal of Early Years Education*, 25 (1): 16–29.

Cremin, T., Glauert, E., Craft, A., Compton, A. and Styliandou, F. (2015) Creative little scientists: exploring pedagogical synergies between inquiry-based and creative approaches in early years science, *Education 3–13*, 43 (4): 404–419.

Finucane, N. (2021) Factors influencing the provision of science learning experiences in early childhood education in Ireland: a case study of educators' perceptions and practices. Unpublished doctoral thesis. University of Sheffield.

Gealy, A., Tinney, G., Macdonald, N. and Waters, J. (2020) A socio-constructivist approach to developing a professional learning intervention for early childhood education and care practitioners in Wales, *Professional Development in Education*. doi:10.1080/19415257.2020.1742187.

Howard, S., Siraj, I., Melhuish, E., Kingston, K., Neilsen-Hewett, C., de Rosnay, M., Duursma, E. and Luu, B. (2020) Measuring interactional quality in pre-school settings: introduction and validation of the Sustained Shared Thinking and Emotional Wellbeing (SSTEW) scale, *Early Child Development and Care*, 190 (7): 1017–1030. DOI: doi:10.1080/03004430.2018.1511549.

Joseph Rowntree Foundation (JRF) (2018) *Poverty in Wales 2018*. Available at: https://www.jrf.org.uk/report/povertywales-2018 [accessed 16 August 2018].

Ladwig J.G. and McPherson, A. (2017) The anatomy of ability, *Curriculum Inquiry*, 47 (4): 344–362.

Land, R., Cousin, G., Meyer, J.H.F. and Davies, P. (2006) Threshold concepts and troublesome knowledge. 3. Implications for course design and evaluation. In: Rust, C. (Ed.) *Improving Student Learning–Equality and Diversity*, pp. 53–64. Oxford: OxfordCentre for Staff and Learning Development.

Meyer, J. H. F. and Land, R. (2003) Threshold concepts and troublesome knowledge. 1. Linkages to ways of thinking and practising. In: Rust, C. (Ed.) *Improving Student Learning–Ten Years On*, pp. 412–424. Oxford Brookes University: Oxford Centre for Staff and Learning Development.

Meyer, J. H. F. and Land, R. (2005) Threshold concepts and troublesome knowledge. 2. Epistemological considerations and a conceptual framework for teaching and learning, *Higher Education* 49: 373–388.

Office for National Statistics (2020) *SOC 2020*. Available at: https://www.ons.gov.uk/m ethodology/classificationsandstandards/standardoccupationalclassificationsoc/soc2020 [accessed 13 July 2021].

Olszewski-Kubilius, P. and Clarenbach, J (2012) *Unlocking Emergent Talent: Supporting High Achievement of Low-Income, High-Ability Student*. Washington, DC: National Association for Gifted Children. Available at: https://files.eric.ed.gov/fulltext/ED537321.pdf [accessed 13 July 2021].

Page, J. (2018) Characterising the principles of Professional Love in early childhood care and education, *International Journal of Early Years Education*, 26 (2): 125–141.

Parekh, G. (2017) The tyranny of 'ability', *Curriculum Inquiry*, 47 (4): 337–343.

Prout, A. and James, A. (1997) *Constructing and Reconstructing Childhood: Contemporary Issues in the Sociological Study of Childhood*. London: Routledge/Falmer.

Siraj, I., Kingston D. and Melhuish E. (2015) *Assessing Quality in Early Childhood Education and Care: Sustained Shared Thinking and Emotional Wellbeing (SSTEW) Scale for 2–5-year-olds Provision*. London: UCL IOE Press.

Sylva, K., Melhuish, E. C., Sammons, P., Siraj, I., Taggart, B., Smees, R., Toth, K. and Welcomme, W. (2014) *Effective Pre-school, Primary and Secondary Education 3–16 Project (EPPSE 3–16) Students' Educational and Developmental Outcomes at Age 16*. Department for Education Research Report RR354.

Tanner, B. (2011) Threshold concepts in practice education: perceptions of practice educators, *British Journal of Occupational Therapy*, 74 (9): 427–434.

Taylor, M. (2015) Threshold concepts in Irish early childhood education and care practice placements, *International Journal of Practice-based Learning in Health and Social Care*, 3 (1): 46–57.

Waters, J. and Macdonald, N. (2020) Exploring the use of a rating scale to support professional learning in early years pre-school staff: the experience of one local authority in Wales, *Early Years*. doi:10.1080/09575146.2020.1742666.

Welsh Government (2014) *Flying Start Strategic Guidance*. Cardiff: Welsh Government. Available at: http://gov.wales/docs/dhss/publications/120913fsguidanceen.pdf [accessed 16 January 2017].

Welsh Government (2019) *Welsh Index of Multiple Deprivation (WIMD) 2019 Results Report*. Cardiff: Welsh Government.

Index

children: and ability grouping 7, 148–163; autistic 5, 43, 44, 48–50, 51–54, 55; and barriers to participation 3, 7, 25, 61, 117, 125–127, 130, 169, 172, 174, 179 *see also children's participation*; as capable 2, 7, 18, 59, 60, 89, 90, 100, 131, 140, 152, 164–181; and complex embodiment 43; and conflict 81, 85, 114, 135–137, 140–143, 145; and dispositions in learning 117, 119–121; and labelling 64, 151–152, 157, 159; and learning subjectivities 3, 4, 5, 39, 43–58; with profound and multiple learning difficulties (PMLD) 6, 94–110; refugee 6, 79–93; and social embodiment 94–110
children's participation 1, 6–7, 13–28, 62, 64, 70, 81, 86–87, 90, 98, 107, 108, 111–134, 136–138, 148–163
children's play 6, 17, 43, 45, 46, 48, 53, 59, 84, 86–87, 89, 90, 100–106, 108, 119, 121–124, 129, 137, 141–143, 153, 154, 165, 167, 169, 173–177 *see also play-based pedagogy*
children's rights 5, 14, 19–25, 80, 111–113, 116, 130–131, 153 *see also rights approach to education*
co-construction 60, 65–66, 71, 84, 100, 114, 128, 129, 157–159
conversation analysis 6, 84–85, 93

enabling environments 44, 59–75
enactivism 6, 95, 96, 97–99
England 21, 65, 114, 128, 152
environmental affordance perspective 7, 135–147
ethics: and leadership 31, 35, 39, 40; of responsibility and care 1, 4, 43, 51
ethnomethodology 84

Forest School 135, 137, 139–141

inclusion: agenda of 1; and complexity/diversity increase 3–4; and complexity/diversity reduction 3; and constructions of the child 7, 38, 113, 115, 129, 167–179
inclusive education 1–3, 14, 24, 25, 32, 43, 44, 47, 48, 61, 94, 106; children's perspectives on 5, 115, 129, 154
inclusive pedagogy 2, 5, 6, 29, 31, 33–37, 39, 40, 43, 48, 54, 61–65, 149, 159; as enhanced provision 6, 61, 66–69, 119, 124; research methodologies for 4

leadership 5, 22, 23, 29–42, 143, 152

pedagogy: of care 84, 86, 88, 90; relational 5, 19, 44, 46, 98, 108, 139
play-based pedagogy 16–19, 25, 61–68, 71, 72, 112, 115 *see also children's play*
posthumanism 43–44, 46–47
post-structuralism 6, 63–65, 71, 72
professional learning 7, 19, 24, 30, 33–34, 65, 131, 164, 169, 172–173, 178 *see also teacher education*

rights approach to education 5, 13–28, 137 *see also children's rights*

Scotland 13

teacher education 3, 6, 23, 25, 94 *see also professional learning*
threshold concepts 7, 168–174, 178–179
Tuff spots 59, 61, 67–72

United Nations Convention on the Rights of the Child 5, 14–16, 20–23, 62, 82, 89, 111
United Nations Convention on the Rights of Persons with Disabilities 94

Wales: additional learning needs 3, 15, 25, 126, 130; Children's Commissioner 5, 14, 15, 19, 20–21, 116; Curriculum for Wales 2022 16, 18–19, 24, 65, 116; Foundation Phase 6, 7, 16–19, 24, 65–68, 111–113, 115–116, 119, 128, 129, 141, 152, 156

For Product Safety Concerns and Information please contact our EU
representative GPSR@taylorandfrancis.com
Taylor & Francis Verlag GmbH, Kaufingerstraße 24, 80331 München, Germany

www.ingramcontent.com/pod-product-compliance
Lightning Source LLC
Chambersburg PA
CBHW052022290426
44112CB00014B/2338